SELF-TALK AND GROW RICH

A New Millennium guide for individuals tired of living from paycheck to paycheck who would rather live the good life of wealth and riches.

JAMES L. MOSLEY

Foreword by

Bishop George D. McKinney, Jr., PH.D., D.D.

SELF-TALK AND GROW RICH

ISBN 0-939241-83-8

Printed in the United States of America

International Scene Publishing Company
1220 Rosecrans St., Suite 411
San Diego, CA 92106-2674
Fax: 858-453-7335
Web site: http://www.confessaholic.com
E-Mail: testimonies@confessaholic.com

TABLE OF CONTENTS

ACKNOWLEDGMENTS v

FOREWORD vi

PREFACE vii

INTRODUCTION xii

MISSION STATEMENT xxi

AUTHOR'S NOTES xxii

CHAPTER 1 .... **1**
Why God Wants You To Be Rich
Part 1 Six Reasons Why God Wants You To Be Rich - Reason No. 1
Part 2 Six Reasons Why God Wants You To Be Rich - Reason No. 2
Part 3 Six Reasons Why God Wants You To Be Rich - Reason No. 3
Part 4 Six Reasons Why God Wants You To Be Rich - Reason No. 4
Part 5 Six Reasons Why God Wants You To Be Rich - Reason No. 5
Part 6 Six Reasons Why God Wants You To Be Rich - Reason No. 6

CHAPTER 2 .... **35**
Part 1 – Why Is 90% Of The Body Of Christ Broke In This Great Land Of Opportunity?
Part 2 – Lack Of Knowledge In Natural Things Can Be Detrimental And Destructive
Part 3 – Lack Of Knowledge In Spiritual things Can Be Detrimental And Destructive

CHAPTER 3 .... **49**
Part 1 – Your Words Have Awesome Power – They Can Create And They Can Destroy
Part 2 – What Is Self-Talk? How Uncontrolled Self-Talk Works In Children. How Uncontrolled Self-Talk Works In Adults

CHAPTER 4 .... **69**
Part 1 – What Is Controlled Self-Talk?
Part 2 – Benefits Of God's Living Word. It Is The Same Yesterday, Today, And Forever

CHAPTER 5 .... **79**
Three Kinds Of Faith
Part 1 – What Is Sense-Knowledge Faith?
Part 2 – What Is Natural-Human Faith?
Part 3 – What Is Revelation Faith?

CHAPTER 6 .... **105**
Why Do People Put Great Trust In Man And Little Trust In God?

CHAPTER 7 .... **113**
Part 1 – What Is AFaith-Building Confession?
Part 2 – Author Reveals $500 Billion Scripture, That Defines The Word "Confession," That Builds Strong Faith

CHAPTER 8 .... **123**
Founding Fathers Had It Right

CHAPTER 9 .... **131**
4 Keys To Receiving Your Covenant Inheritance Of Wealth And Riches In This New Millennium
Part 1 – How To Use Self-Talk Faith-Building Confessions To Build AStrong Godly Foundation
Part 2 – How To Use The Cornerstone Scripture To Build AStrong Godly Foundation
Part 3 – Relationship Required To Qualify For An Inheritance
Part 4 – Fellowship Required To Qualify For An Inheritance
Part 5 – The Secret To Receiving Your Covenant Inheritance Of Wealth And Riches Revealed

CHAPTER 10 .... **163**
8 Keys To Keeping And Increasing Your Covenant Inheritance Of Wealth And Riches

CHAPTER 11 .... **211**
Part 1 – Seven Reasons Why Self-Talk Faith-Building Confessions Work
Part 2 – Testimonials
Part 3 – How To Write Your Own Self-Talk Faith-Building Confession

CONCLUSION **260**

CHAPTER 12 .... **265**
How To Use Faith-Building Confessions To Become Victorious In Other Areas Of Life

APPENDIX **284**

RESOURCES **292**

FAITH-BUILDING PRODUCTS & MATERIALS **294**

ABOUT THE AUTHOR .... **.296**

ACKNOWLEDGMENTS

First, I pay thanks to the Wonderful Counselor for divine favor, assistance, and impartation of revelation knowledge given me while preparing this book. The number of people who have encouraged and supported me in the preparation of this book have been numerous. I thank them all, and am especially grateful to the following:

My wife, Magdeline,

and daughters, Cristel and Abigail Amber;

Marion Bremner,

Valerie Brown,

Gloria Coty,

Ron Edmundson,

Christy Giangreco,

Teyon A. Johnson,

Lee Jones,

Mary Ann Paul,

Ron Perkins,

Troy Rooks,

and to all those saintly men and women from whom I have benefited by hearing them teach and preach the unadulterated Word of God.

FOREWORD

BY BISHOP GEORGE D. MCKINNEY, JR., PH.D., D.D.

James Mosley has rendered a great service to the Body of Christ by sharing his knowledge and wisdom in the area of finance.

Self-Talk And Grow Rich is both inspirational and informative. It deals with the biblical view of wealth; who owns it and how to obtain it.

Today, there is much talk and anticipation concerning the transfer of significant wealth to the hands of the "Community of Faith." This book is "must reading" for those who are preparing for this transfer of wealth. The author clearly establishes the truth that God owns everything (Psalm 24:1). Thus, the wealth belongs neither to the greedy rich nor the needy poor. The wealth belongs to God Who entrusts His wealth into the hands of men and women.

This book is filled with biblical illustrations and quotations. The illustrations and explanations are practical, and reveal that the author is a serious student of the Bible.

I strongly recommend that pastors and lay leaders in every congregation read and apply the principles taught in *Self-Talk And Grow Rich.* I also recommend that this book be required reading by couples in pre-marriage counseling.

Bishop George D. McKinney, Jr., PH.D., D.D.

George D. McKinney, Jr., Ph.D., D.D., is the Bishop of the Southern California Second Ecclesiastical Jurisdiction of the Churches of God in Christ, the largest Black Pentecostal denomination in the country. He presides over sixty churches. He is the pastor and founder of St. Stephen's Church of God in Christ in San Diego, California. He has been a featured speaker at Urbana Mission Conferences and Promise Keepers. His ministry includes conducting conferences on the "Recovery of Family Life" and "Urban Ministry." He was selected as Mr. San Diego, Man of the Year 1995-96.

He earned a B.A. in sociology from the University of Arkansas in Pine Bluff, an M.A. in systematic theology from the Oberlin College Graduate School of Theology, and a Ph.D. from the California Graduate School of Theology.

He has authored several books including *The Theology of Jehovah Witnesses* and *Christian Marriage*: *An Act of Faith and Commitment.* His literary contributions also include the best-selling book titled *Cross The Line: Reclaiming The Inner City For God*, which he co-authored with William Kritlow in 1998.

PREFACE

This preface is unorthodox in that it does not follow the general pattern set forth by literary scholars. Instead, the author has called an emergency New Millennium board meeting for all those who are reading this book and who have a burning desire to be blessed with wealth and riches, so that they can be a blessing to others.

The author has just called this board meeting to order. And he is now explaining that the purpose of the meeting is to clarify some items on the Agenda, so that each member (reader) is totally familiar with the ground rules, the intent and the terms used throughout the pages of this book.

Agenda

Item 1. The Holy Bible is God's book. It is written primarily to believers (Christians) and it is the undisputed (inspired) living Word of God. The principles and precepts outlined in *Self-Talk And Grow Rich* are based directly on the spiritual laws and precepts written in the Holy Bible.

The Bible is the World's Greatest Book! It is also the world's best-selling book. The Guinness Book of Records (1999 Issue) announced the following: "The World's best selling and most widely distributed book is the Bible, with an estimated 3.88 billion copies sold between 1815 and 1998."

Some Famous Men Had The Following Things To Say About God And His Bible

"It is impossible to rightly govern the world without God and the Bible."

George Washington (1732–1799)
First President of the United States

"I believe the Bible is the best gift God has ever given to man. All the good from the Savior of the world is communicated through this book. All things desirable to men are contained in the Bible."

Abraham Lincoln (1809–1865)
16th President of the United States

"It is impossible to mentally or socially enslave a Bible-reading people."

Horace Greeley (1811–1872)
Publisher and journalist

"A thorough knowledge of the Bible is worth more than a college education."

Theodore Roosevelt (1858–1919)
26th President of the United States

"Indeed, it is an indisputable fact that all the complex and horrendous questions confronting us at home and worldwide have their answer in that single book (the Bible)."

Ronald Reagan (1911 -)
40th President of the United States

Self-Talk And Grow Rich contains many biblical Scriptures and it is of the utmost importance that we grasp the following: *All Scripture is inspired by God and is useful to teach us what is true and to make us realize what is wrong in our lives. It straightens us out and teaches us to do what is right* (2 Timothy 3:16, NLT).

Item 2. This item has to do with gender. In some cases, when the word "man" is used in this book, it refers to mankind (the human race) which includes man, woman, boy and girl.

Item 3. When the Name "Jesus" is used throughout this book, it unequivocally means the Anointed One, Jesus Christ of Nazareth; and it is synonymous with God the Son, Savior, Messiah, Lord and Christ, among many others.

Item 4. When the Name "God" is used in this book, it means God, the Supreme Being, the Creator Who is written about in the Holy Bible. The Name "God" is also synonymous with Jehovah, God the Father, Heavenly Father, and Heavenly Parent, among others.

Item 5. When the name "Bible" is used, it refers to the Holy Bible, the sacred Scriptures of Christians.

Item 6. The intent of *Self-Talk And Grow Rich* is to reach out to unbelievers, inspire them to do an about-face and pray the prayer of salvation, receive Jesus Christ of Nazareth as their Lord and Savior, be saved (born again) and take on a spirit of being divinely blessed to be a blessing to others.

Item 7. *Self-Talk And Grow Rich* summons believers to take on a higher level of awareness of God's plan and purpose for His children, and begin this New Millennium with strong faith.

Item 8. Know that you can't compartmentalize God. Therefore, none of the inscriptions set forth in this book are absolutes, and the methods and procedures prescribed are not necessarily the only way to gain the God-kind of prosperity in health, in wealth, and in riches. However, the inscriptions shared in this book are the ones which God imparted to the author to reveal to others; to benefit believers as well as non-believers and heighten their revelation knowledge of God's promises and their legal rights to those promises.

Item 9. Repetition in literary writing such as books and other printed matter is the thing that copy editors strive to avoid. I personally experienced this when writing my first two books. But within the covers of this book, you will find a hefty blend of repetition designed to enlighten and to follow a spiritual law found in the Scriptures which says...*"Faith comes by hearing"* (Romans 10:17).

This Scripture does not say that faith comes by hearing it only one time. No! It says faith comes by hearing. In other words, the more you hear it, the stronger your faith becomes; and it is strong faith that pleases God and moves the mountains of sickness, poverty, trials, and tribulation in your life.

Item 10. This next item on the agenda may seem strange and out of place, but those adhering to it will have cracked the combination lock to a divine treasure. The author exhorts you to read this complete book word by word, page by page, **aloud**. By doing so, you are operating in two powerful spiritual laws. The first law is the spiritual law of sowing and reaping (Galatians 6:7), and the second is the spiritual law that governs faith. Thus, *"faith comes by hearing, and hearing by the Word of God"* (Romans 10:17, NKJV).

Item 11. Bible translators have been challenged when translating certain words of the Hebrew and Greek languages into modern English. Here are four such words: heart, soul, mind, and spirit. Because these words appear synonymous (at different points) throughout the Bible, they sometimes defy specific identification. Therefore, the author has elected to present these words in a combination which you will see written as: (mind and) heart, (heart and) spirit, (soul and) spirit, which serves to show inclusion but not at the risk of exclusion, and insures that a vital component is not left out.

Moreover, there are many things written in the Bible of which man has not yet received full revelation, and I firmly believe that these words remain a mystery to some as they are presented in certain settings within the Bible. However, we do know that man is a three-dimensional being. He is a **spirit**, he has a **soul**, and he lives in a **body** (1 Thessalonians 5:23). Man's body is the tent that houses his spirit and soul. We do know that spirit and soul are not the same thing. Hebrews 4:12 says that by the Word of God, soul and spirit can be divided. To help you understand the three dimensions of man, repeat **aloud** the following three statements:

A. With my "body," I contact the physical realm.
B. With my "spirit," I contact the spiritual realm.
C. With my "soul," I contact the intellectual realm.

Man is a spirit. God created man in His own image (Genesis 1:26-27), and the Bible says that God is a Spirit (John 4:23-24). The human spirit is the part of man that knows and communicates with God. With your spirit, you contact your Heavenly Father in the spiritual realm. Man possesses a soul, the intellect, the sensibilities (five senses), the will, and emotions. And man lives in a body.

We do know that the spirit and soul separate from the body at the time of physical death. This is revealed in the account of the rich man and Lazarus in Luke 16:19-31.

Item 12. *Self-Talk And Grow Rich* establishes a "Mission Statement" for its readers which outlines a spiritual creed, setting a standard which will produce (for those who adhere to it) life-transforming, destiny-changing experiences; financially, spiritually, physically, mentally, domestically, and socially in this New Millennium.

Item 13. Full understanding of the Scriptures and some of the terms used in this book may present a challenge to some, especially for those who are not Christians and those who are (new) babes in the faith. My advice is to always pray before reading this book and ask God to reveal to you the knowledge of His Word and He will reveal it to you. It is written in the book of 1 Corinthians:

But people who aren't Christians can't understand these truths from God's Spirit. It all sounds foolish to them because only those who have the Spirit can understand what the Spirit means. 1 Corinthians 2:14, NLT

Item 14. The key prerequisite for receiving your covenant inheritance of wealth and riches is, "**You must be born again.**" What if I asked you the most important question of your life, "What will happen to you when you die?" If you are unsure of the answer to this question, or if you are afraid you will not spend eternity in heaven with Jesus, relatives, friends, and other saints, then there is Good News for you!

You can settle the most important question of your life and begin to enjoy all the blessings that God the Father has for you! Asimple prayer of salvation is provided for you in Appendix A. Turn now and pray the prayer of salvation to receive Jesus as your Savior and be saved (born again).

Item 15. The message that is amplified throughout the pages of this book is that **you** must know and believe that you are already blessed by God to be a blessing to others. And you already have a heavenly bank account that contains your covenant inheritance of wealth and riches. All that is required for you to receive your inheritance is to be "born again," use your mouth to confess your inheritance, have strong "faith" and much "patience," and let your Heavenly Father fulfill His promises.

This concludes all the items on the agenda. My sincere desire is that these items presented will be beneficial to you as you read through *Self-Talk And Grow Rich.*

The motion to adjourn this meeting is accepted.

INTRODUCTION

Unknowingly to me at that time, the making of *Self-Talk And Grow Rich* actually began almost two decades ago. I worked for the then Ohio Bell Telephone Company; its new name is Ameritech. I held a position on the corporate staff's training, research, and development team. It was early spring of 1982, and as I sat in a company-sponsored, management-training seminar, I discovered that the training material and the instructor's teachings were being presented from a secular viewpoint, but the concepts and principles mirrored biblical precepts and principles. In fact, this training material had Holy Bible written all over it. I was elated once I fully grasped that this training seminar was different from the many others I had attended over the years.

This particular training seminar was designed to enhance staff management personnel's communications and personal development skills. Some of the concepts and principles, which were akin to the Holy Bible, have stuck with me like Super Glue.

Following are the core concepts that were the foundation of the training material.

Human beings act not in accordance with the truth, but in accordance with the truth as we perceive it (through the five senses) or believe it.

Human beings'behavior is controlled by beliefs, either negative or positive. Hence, we work, play, love and strive in life not according to the reality of what we can do, but in accordance with what we believe we can do.

The stated resolve for the above dilemmas was:

If we can change the way we believe, we can change the way we act. We build our beliefs through our thoughts, our self-talk, our speech, and by the words, statements, and conversations of others. As these thoughts, words and statements accumulate, they build patterns and beliefs in our (mind and) heart's memory file. Inevitably we become that which we allow our ear gates to receive from self-talk or from others, whether it be positive or negative.

This seminar taught that speaking affirmations **aloud**, along with imagery exercises performed regularly, would bring about desirable changes in beliefs, alter behavior, and cause outside things to change.

I applied the affirmation and imagery techniques to certain areas of my life that needed improvement, and it worked.

Soon I began to modify my daily affirmations to conform with biblical precepts, and instead of saying affirmations, I began to call my daily readings Faith-Building Confessions. I continued to see supernatural manifestations of things in my life resulting from my daily faith-building confessions.

I have kept almost all of my 3x5 inch faith-building index cards which show the date I started my faith-building confessing, the Bible Scripture that supports the confession, and the positive present-tense confession statement; also the date that God made the confession a reality.

It was during the latter part of 1982 that I rededicated my life to Jesus Christ of Nazareth; and at that time I began stockpiling Bible Scriptures, especially those that promised believers things in this life. Because of my research background, I was driven to search for the benefits that belong to believers, and what believers need to do to receive those benefits.

Over a period of time of studying the Bible and meditating on God's Word, I fully realized that faith-building confessions bring possessions. When I saw this principle of **confessing**, **believing** and **receiving** throughout the Bible, and I had experienced it working in my own life, I was fully persuaded that repetitive, faith-building confessions were the **hidden secret** to receiving things from God (supernaturally), and that it was a way to obtain the promises of God.

I was ordained as an Elder on February 10, 1989 at Christian Fellowship Center Ministries, Cleveland, Ohio, under the leadership of Bishop Bill McKinney. My calling was that of a teacher and I thoroughly enjoyed preparing for and teaching God's precepts. I also served as Vice President of Victory for Veterans, an outreach ministry that conducted Bible studies and other enrichment activities for hurting veterans at Veteran Medical Centers throughout Northeast Ohio.

In my mind, I thought that I would use the Bible Scriptures that I had been stockpiling to someday write a program and transfer them to a hand-held computer for my own personal use, and for quick reference when preparing Bible lessons. However, looking back now, I can clearly see that my thoughts were not God's thoughts.

I wrote my first book in 1990, entitled *Snore No More*, which is a popular health care book, but there was an unsatisfied feeling in my spirit of wanting to write about the Word of God. In 1997 I revised (updated) my book and reissued a second edition. But the tug on my spirit to write about the Word of God had become stronger. On June 11, 1997, in my hotel room while vacationing in San Diego, I wrote this confession:

"Dear Heavenly Father, I ask that You use me in service for You according to Your will. I am willing and I will be obedient. I confess this in the wonderful Name of Jesus Christ of Nazareth."

The Scripture that I wrote on the piece of paper to support this confession was John 14:13-14. I still have the slightly faded, light grey, Humphrey's Half Moon Inn Suites note pad sheet with my confession written on it.

I began reading this confession aloud three or four times daily, along with seventeen others. Lo and behold, during the month of October of the same year, at different times when I would be reading my confession aloud, a small still voice would say "inheritance." The same thing occurred in November and while reading my confessions aloud on Christmas Day, this same still voice said, "Inform My people, all of My people, of their inheritances. Make it clear and easy to read and understand."

Praise the Lord! This was the answer to my confession and it validated the words of Jesus Christ of Nazareth written in John 14:13-14, NKJV, which says, *"And whatever you ask in My Name, that I will do, that the Father may be glorified in the Son. If you ask anything in My Name, I will do it."*

I began immediately combing through my stockpile of Scriptures and notes in preparation for writing this book. Now it was clear that God's purpose in my gathering of these Scriptures and notes for so many years, was to transmit His Word to you in this setting.

As I was putting the final pieces together for this book, I received another impartation from God while reading my confessions. The voice of Father God told me specifically what to tell you to do in order to receive your covenant inheritance of wealth and riches. I will share His instructions later on in this book.

Some of my associates and family members knew I was writing a book, but up until then I had not felt released by God to share His specific instructions on how to receive your covenant inheritance of wealth and riches.

However, I was led by the Holy Spirit on Friday night, June 4, 1999 to share God's instructions with our Family Life Fellowship Group, a bi-monthly gathering of church members who live in the same area. I not only told the group what God's instructions were for them to receive their covenant inheritance of wealth and riches, but I also passed around a handout which showed exactly what needed to be done and how to do it.

Well, if you have been operating in the things of God, you know that when you get a Word from God, Satan will come along and try to trick and deceive you the same way he did Eve and the same way he tried to deceive Jesus Christ of Nazareth. From time to time, Satan would raise questions in my mind like, "Are you really sure that your God wants you to write about inheritance?" "What if people won't believe you and make a mockery of you and your book?" Every time these thoughts manifested I resisted them in the mighty Name of Jesus Christ of Nazareth, and these thoughts would leave.

As stated earlier, I had shared the information on how to receive God's covenant inheritance of wealth and riches with my Family Life Fellowship on Friday night, June 4, 1999. Coincidentally, Ayo Oritsejafor, the pastor of a 10,000 member church in Nigeria was to be a guest speaker at our church, Seedtime & Harvest on Sunday, June 6, 1999, and on Monday,

June 7, 1999. This was one day after I had publicly revealed God's instructions on inheritance to our Family Life Fellowship Group.

Can you guess what Pastor Ayo's topic was for those two days?

His message was "How to Enter Into Your Inheritance." Praise the Lord!!! Jesus Christ of Nazareth said, *"It is also written in your law, that the testimony of two men is true"* (John 8:17). He also said, *"...by the mouth of two or three witnesses every word may be established"* (Matthew 18:16).

As Pastor Ayo's powerful, anointed message unfolded on receiving your inheritance, I simply shook my head in awe, as did others who had attended our Family Life meeting. Occasionally during those two nights, tears of joy freely flowed from my eyes as I realized the awesomeness of God the Father, and how He confirms His Word. Praise the Lord!

The main focus of *Self-Talk And Grow Rich* is to share with you, God the Father's instructions on how to receive your covenant inheritance of wealth and riches.

Self-Talk And Grow Rich is a New Millennium guide for individuals tired of living from paycheck to paycheck, pension check to pension check, social security check to social security check, who would rather live the good life of wealth and riches.

What would it take for you to change the course of your life, beginning this New Millennium with a renewed attitude, a new self-talk, and a new self-worth?

What would it take for you to believe and not doubt in your (mind and) heart that God is a God of prosperity and not the God of poverty?

What would it take for you to be convinced that God rewards those who sincerely seek Him?

What would it take for you to really believe that God wants you to be rich and healthy?

What would it take for you to be fully persuaded that you are a member of a royal family? That you are a king or queen and should reign (rule/dominate) victoriously in every area of your life?

What would it take for you to be fully persuaded that you already have a covenant inheritance of wealth and riches (mega millions of dollars) in your heavenly bank account?

Well, according to the Holy Bible, everything stated so far already belongs to you. They are gifts to you from God the Father. His only Son, Jesus Christ of Nazareth, gave His life; He died for you, so that you could live an abundant, prosperous, and healthy life.

In God's mind, He already sees you in possession of everything He has promised in His Word. This includes good health, and material and financial riches, which are definitely in His promises to you.

Self-Talk And Grow Rich strongly emphasizes an urgent need for believers to become abundantly prosperous financially in this New Millennium, to help pay the cost of spreading the "Good News" of the gospel, to leave an inheritance to your children's children, and to share God's money with the poor and needy.

Additionally, *Self-Talk And Grow Rich* places strong emphasis on an urgent need for believers to become balanced: financially, spiritually, physically, mentally, domestically, and socially; thereby being well equipped to be victorious in every area of life. This is God's plan and purpose for every believer.

Many books and periodicals tell you what to do, but oftentimes the reader is short-changed because of a lack of how to do it. It is like someone telling you to have faith, but failing to effectively tell you how to have it. In other words, they should tell you what specific steps you need to take in order to have faith.

Well, *Self-Talk And Grow Rich* strives not only to inform and identify concepts and techniques that individuals can do to become prosperous in every area of their lives, but it clearly explains how to accomplish your dreams, needs, desires, and the promises of God.

The message that *Self-Talk And Grow Rich* delivers is likened to a guided missile, fired to search out and destroy negative self-talk. It transmits a forceful message that negative, life-defeating self-talk is a vicious enemy and that it is destructive. The Bible says *"Life and death is in the power of the tongue."*

Unconsciously, negative self-talk and negative voices from others has infiltrated our (minds and) hearts resulting in the negative words molding our beliefs and habits, and setting us on a course of poverty, sickness, and bondage in many areas of our lives.

For instance, financial prosperity has a negative connotation to most people (especially people of faith), because they have been taught against it. It does not matter who you are, you are a product of your teaching! I do not believe that regular people want to be poor. Therefore, I am convinced that many of those who have been taught against prosperity do believe, deep down in their (heart and) spirit, that God wants them to prosper, but because of erroneous teaching, their minds have not accepted this fact.

There is one way to prove this: Offer one of them $10,000; tell them God told you to give it to them, and see if they are willing to accept it. I think you already know the answer. Believe me, they will accept it in a heartbeat! Their minds might say no, but their (heart and) spirit and hands will say yes.

In his book, *Fit, Function and Flourish*, the Rev. Tom Peers writes,

"A number of evangelists and well-known pastors preach against prosperity teaching. But I am not convinced that they believe what they are saying either. The next time one of them preaches against prosperity and then makes a pitch for money, send him a letter stating that if it is not God's will for you to prosper, then it can't be God's will for him to prosper. His theology would change very quickly if enough listeners did this."

I agree 100% with Rev. Peers and I wonder, if you followed those ministers, pastors, and evangelists who preach against prosperity, would they be driving an old, beat-up, barely-running car? Would their house be an overcrowded, rundown, rodent and cockroach infested apartment in the ghetto?

Mother Teresa, a Nobel Peace Prize recipient, was a stellar example of carrying on the work of Jesus Christ, on the streets of Calcutta and around the world, caring for the poorest of the poor.

Throughout the years, my wife and I have been led and have counted it joy to contribute money (sow seeds) into her ministry, the Missionaries of Charity in Calcutta. Mother Teresa established this charity to operate on divine providence only. She forbid any form of fundraising or soliciting for money. Her ministry depended totally on God providing and meeting the needs of the ministry. This is as it should be; if God gave the vision, He supplies the provisions.

Those in ministry who preach against the prosperity message should fully and unequivocally follow Mother Teresa's example and embrace the doctrine of divine providence.

Based on my understanding of the Bible, I believe that the anti-prosperity message is inspired by Satan to keep people in bondage. The Bible clearly does not say that "Money is the root of all evil," instead it actually states that *"the love of money is at the root of all kinds of evil"* (1 Timothy 6:10, NLT). I also wonder if this anti-prosperity message is part of the reason why prayer requests made to local churches and major ministries are overwhelmingly people requesting prayer and assistance in the area of finances?

In his book, *Breaking the Financial Barriers*, Dennis Burke (a minister of the gospel for over two decades) wrote, "Satan erects barriers that are designed to stop you and keep you from advancing in life. One of the barriers the enemy erects is in the area of finances. We receive prayer requests from all over the world, and one of the most frequent requests we receive is in the area of finances.

"Financial pressure is one of the major causes of strain in marriage, distress in families, and frustration in many of God's people. God's Word instructs believers in how to overcome pressure and to break down the barriers of lack!"

Dr. E.W. Kenyon writes in his book, *Sign Posts on the Road to Success*, "Modern preaching has produced the modern spiritual failure that we see in the church. Failures are not ready-made; they are the product of the teaching that we have had or the absence of the right teaching.

"I am convinced that most people will come to the level of the Father's purpose if they know how. The spiritual failure I am talking about is one which is born of God, but has never developed, one which has remained in an infant state through many years because of malnutrition. They feed upon theories of men rather than upon the Word of God."

Strong messages that literally scream from page to page throughout this book are "You will never really be free until you are financially free." "The rich rule over the poor and the borrower is servant to the lender." "Jesus Christ's substitutional sacrificial death for you was so that you should reign victoriously as king or queen in this life, and not as a servant."

Far too many people are led to believe that some are born with and some without. People are led to believe that some have inherited or were blessed with more abilities than others. This is not true unless you choose to believe it.

The principles and techniques prescribed throughout *Self-Talk And Grow Rich* are intended to erase these kinds of beliefs. This book will inspire you to believe that God loves you very much, that He is not a respecter of persons, and that His desire is for you to be abundantly prosperous.

Self-Talk And Grow Rich reveals the essential keys needed to unlock your personal heavenly bank account which contains your covenant inheritance of wealth and riches. It uncovers other hidden treasures that belong to you, so that you can reign victorious in every area of this life.

This book unveils how a revolutionary new application of biblical principles, combined with positive managed speech, can be used to improve every aspect of your life. It is demonstrated through easy-to-read-and-understand self-talk techniques and exercises. Also provided are examples of how these biblically-based principles worked in the lives of men and women who made the Hall of Faith in the Bible. Highlighted are examples of how the prescribed principles and techniques worked in the lives of some of the rich and famous.

My testimony is "I have been shoestring poor and I have been rich; and rich is much, much better! You cannot help someone else when you are living on a shoestring yourself."

My favorite (invented) quote is "You get what you say sooner or later." I also share the results of my own personal experiences, of nearly two decades, using managed "self-talk (faith-building) confession" techniques to achieve success supernaturally. And how I amassed close to 3/4 million dollars in liquid worth in 1989, and how I have personally had thousands of dollars in supernatural debt cancellation. Moreover, the examples of how these principles and techniques have positively affected the lives of others are also presented for your perusal.

Self-Talk And Grow Rich is laden with rich biblical precepts that concur 100% with the prescribed antidotes to eliminate the living from paycheck-to-paycheck syndrome within the Body of Christ.

Self-Talk And Grow Rich is a forerunner in fully explaining negative self-talk and how to correct it. The awesome power of words is looked at for a clearer understanding of how words can build and how they can destroy. The word "faith" is dissected carefully so that the reader has full knowledge of right and wrong faith. *Self-Talk And Grow Rich* also shows the way to activate strong faith in God's Word and His promises to you.

The essence of *Self-Talk And Grow Rich* is to raise the bar and heighten the awareness level of believers to kingship and queenship status. Its aim is to deliver informative procedures and useful techniques that will activate meaningful and lasting changes in the lives of people. Its intent is that the reader will adopt eagle-like traits of high self-esteem and high self-worth. Its mission is to inspire the reader to examine his/her self-talk and then to make the necessary changes as prescribed in this book to produce their dreams, desires, and destiny early in this New Millennium.

Remember this...

The greater danger for most of us is not that our aim is too high and we miss it, but that it is too low and we reach it.

One of my favorite songs is an upbeat gospel tune, "*Expect Your Miracle.*" I have adopted this song as the theme song for *Self-Talk And Grow Rich* which is played at all of my appearances. This song was recorded many, many years ago by the Clark Sisters, but the words are very timely for today. They transmit powerful inspiration for those who desire to be abundantly prosperous in this New Millennium.

The inspirational words from this song permeate throughout the pages of this book.

"I'm looking for a miracle, I expect the impossible, I feel the intangible, I see the invisible...I'm looking for a miracle, I expect the impossible, I feel the intangible, I see the invisible...The sky is the limit to what I can have, oh yeah! The sky is the limit to what I can have. Just believe and receive it, God will uphold it today, hey! hey! Just believe and receive it, God will uphold it today!!!!!!"

As you read *Self-Talk And Grow Rich*, keep the words from this inspirational song playing softly in your (mind and) heart's memory file. Know that the sky is the limit to what you can have! You get what you say sooner or later! You are already richly blessed by God to be a blessing to others, and all your needs and desires (consistent with God's Word) are available to you today!

MISSION STATEMENT

To inspire, excite and challenge everyone who reads *Self-Talk And Grow Rich* to rise to a higher spiritual level in this New Millennium, and to take on an unwavering desire to be richly blessed by God to be a blessing to others. To motivate each person reading this book to go out daily to seek and save lost souls.

To exhort everyone who reads this book to take on a bountiful spirit of love, and make the symbolic meaning of the cross their number one priority in life in this New Millennium. The vertical part of the cross represents God; it commands you to *"love the Lord your God with **all** your heart, **all** your soul, and **all** your mind"* (Matthew 22:37). The horizontal part of the cross represents your neighbor (your fellowman); it commands you to *"love your neighbor as yourself"* (Matthew 22:39).

To inform you that the motives and desires for gaining your covenant inheritance of wealth and riches must be for the sole purposes of leaving an inheritance to your children and your children's children, supporting God's storehouse (the local church), sharing with the poor and needy, and to support the work of ministries that seek to save the lost.

To notify you that you already have a heavenly bank account which contains your covenant inheritance of wealth, riches and good health.

To encourage you to take on a spirit of knowing and fully believing that it is impossible to please God without faith. Anyone who wants to come to Him must believe that there is a God and that He **rewards** those who sincerely seek Him! (Hebrews 11:6)

To assure everyone that with God all things are possible.

To beseech you to know, to confess, and to believe that you are already richly blessed by God to be a blessing to others!

To challenge you to become a faith-building confessaholic. A confessaholic is a person who persistently and relentlessly confesses God's Word concerning his/her challenging situations, to develop faith and victory in all areas of his/her life.

To exhort you to give God the glory, praise, honor, and thanks in all things.

AUTHOR'S NOTES

The definition of a ghostwriter is somebody who writes something for or with another person on the understanding that the other person will receive sole credit as the author.

I did not have a ghostwriter collaborate with me on this book, nor on my other books. But I must admit that I did have the Holy Ghost's assistance and guidance in preparing this book. Most of the material in this book was given to me by direct prompting of the Holy Spirit. Much of this revelation knowledge was given to me while praying, fasting, and studying the Bible or while reading aloud my faith-building confessions.

I pay all the honor, glory, praise and thanks to my Heavenly Father for His guidance and assistance. All the credit for this book goes to Him, and His Son. For in all that I do, Jesus Christ of Nazareth must increase and I must decrease.

Self-Analysis

At this point, I am going to ask you to stop reading now. Stand in front of a mirror and look directly into your eyes. Ask yourself the following questions:

1. Am I totally satisfied with my present life spiritually? Financially? Mentally? Physically? Domestically? Socially?
   A. If your answer to this question is no, mentally step ahead into the future five years, then read and answer questions number two, three and four!
   B. If your answer to this question is yes, then read item number 5.
2. Where do I want to be five years from now spiritually? Financially? Mentally? Physically? Domestically? Socially?
3. Do I need to improve spiritually? Financially? Mentally? Physically? Domestically? Socially?
4. If you answered yes to any of the areas mentioned in question number three, I encourage you to get pencil and paper. Write down the areas where you feel you need to improve. Don't wait; it is important that you write them down and put the date on the paper. Hold on to this paper because you will use it later when we discuss how to write your own self-talk (faith-building) confessions.
5. Your reading this book is not an accident, it is by divine direction of the Holy Spirit. With your application, this book will be a tremendous blessing to you. I encourage you to continue reading this book aloud and be richly blessed by God so that you can be a blessing to others!

CHAPTER 1

REASONS WHY GOD WANTS YOU TO BE RICH

Throughout my study of the Bible, the Holy Spirit has revealed to me six key reasons why God wants His children to be rich, and prosper in every area of life. But before we examine these six reasons, there is a weighty question that needs to be asked and resolved in your mind before we move into deeper waters.

Is God A God Of Poverty Or Prosperity?

The word poverty means a state of being poor, lacking money or material possessions. The word prosperity means a state of financial, material or spiritual bountifulness. At this point, we are focusing in on the financial and material aspects of prosperity; this means a state of good fortune, especially of financial success and economic well-being.

Do you believe that it is God's desire that you be poor, down and out, living on a shoestring, broke, busted and disgusted?

Contrary to some who think poverty with humility is spiritual, I submit to you that it is the will of God for you to be abundantly rich financially. In fact, the Holy Bible says that God actually gets pleasure when you prosper...*"Let the Lord be magnified, Who takes pleasure in the prosperity of His servant"* (Psalm 35:27, Amp.).

God is pleased when you prosper financially and materially as long as you don't forget that it is God Who gives you the power to get wealth and riches. The word "pleasure" means enjoyment, delight and gladden. We could paraphrase the preceding Scripture this way: Let the Lord be magnified, Who takes enjoyment, delight and is glad in the prosperity (economic well-being) of His servant (His born-again believers).

Be mindful of this, not only is it God's will for you to prosper materially and financially, but He also gives us the formula. He tells us how to achieve and maintain prosperity and success.

It is written in the book of Joshua:

> *This book of the law shall not depart out of your mouth, but you shall meditate on it day and night, that you may observe and do according to all that is written in it; for then you shall make your*

> *way prosperous and then you shall deal wisely and have good success (Joshua 1:8, Amp.).*

According to Vine's Expository Dictionary of Biblical Words, the word "meditate" is common to both ancient and modern Hebrew, and it means to moan, growl, utter or **speak**. God is clearly telling us that if we read, study, believe, pray, self-talk (speak) and obey His Word, then we will succeed and make our way prosperous (have economic well-being).

This is truly refreshing and Good News to see in the Bible that God wants you to live an abundant, wise, prosperous and successful life.

Conditional Terms

Notice closely that the preceding Scripture is conditional; this means that you are responsible for not letting the Word of God depart from your mouth. You have a responsibility to meditate on (consider, study, examine attentively and speak) God's Word day and night. You are responsible for making your mind, heart and body obey and do God's Word.

The flip side of this Scripture would say: If your mouth is void of God's Word, if you spend no time studying and meditating on the Word of God, if you disobey His Word, and if you follow the ways of the world, then you will make your way into poverty.

It seems very strange to me, but there are actually people who do not want economic well-being; people who do not want to succeed in life. How can you be a blessing to others if you are barely getting by yourself?

Here is another parallel Scripture that provides the formula and gives further enlightenment on how to obtain and maintain financial and material prosperity.

> *Blessed (happy, fortunate, prosperous, and enviable) is the man who walks and lives not in the counsel of the ungodly (following their advice, their plans and purposes), nor stands (submissive and inactive) in the path where sinners walk, nor sits down (to relax and rest) where the scornful (and the mockers) gather. But his delight and desire are in the law of the Lord, and on His law (the precepts, the instructions, the teachings of God) he* ***habitually meditates (ponders, and studies)*** *by day and by night. And he shall be like a tree firmly planted (and tended) by the streams of water, ready to bring forth its fruit in its season; its leaf also shall not fade or wither, and* ***everything he does shall prosper*** *(and come to maturity)* (Psalm 1:1-3, Amp.).

Another compelling Scripture that serves to further reveal God's plan and purpose is unveiled in the book of Ecclesiastes:

> *Even so, I have noticed one thing, at least, that is good. It is good for people to eat well, drink a good glass of wine, and enjoy their work, whatever they do under the sun, for however long God lets them live.* ***And it is a good thing to receive wealth from God and the good health to enjoy it****. To enjoy your work and accept your lot in life, that is indeed a gift from God. People who do this rarely look with sorrow on the past, for God has given them reasons for joy* (Ecclesiastes 5:18-20, NLT).

Notice with me for a moment the language used in these inspiring Scriptures:

It is a good thing to receive wealth from God (not a bad thing) and the good health to enjoy that wealth (not bad health). Praise the Lord!

A profound Scripture in the book of 3 John seals the fact that God is a God of prosperity, and that it is not His desire that you live from paycheck to paycheck, broke, busted, disgusted and in debt bondage.

The Holy Spirit inspired the apostle John to inform us thusly:

> *Beloved, I pray that you may* ***prosper in all things*** *and be in* ***health****, just as your* ***soul*** *prospers* (3 John 2, NKJV).

This Scripture clearly does not say that "I pray that you may prosper in every way (or in all things) except financial and material things. No! All things means all things financially and materially.

The Scriptures presented thus far definitely reveal that divine prosperity is not a momentary or passing phenomenon, but rather that it is an ongoing, progressing state of success and economic well-being; it is a part of God's plan and purpose for His children to prosper.

It gives me great pleasure to inform those who were not fully persuaded, that it is God's desire and will for them to be abundantly prosperous financially and materially. Moreover, God has a definite plan why He wants you to be financially prosperous. His reasons are unveiled in the upcoming pages of this chapter.

Now, let's go back to the beginning of this topic and discuss the six reasons why God wants you to be rich.

Part 1
Six Reasons Why God Wants You To Be Rich

Reason No. 1

God wants you to be rich so He can fulfill the covenant (promises) He made with your ancestors (Abraham, Isaac and Jacob).

It is written in the book of Deuteronomy,

> *Always remember that it is the Lord your God who gives you power to become rich, and he does it to fulfill the covenant he made with your ancestors* (Deuteronomy 8:18, NLT).

God's Covenant With Abraham

Abram, whose name was changed to Abraham, received God's call directly from God and He established His covenant with him in this way.

> *Then the Lord told Abram, "Leave your country, your relatives, and your father's house, and go to the land that I will show you. I will cause you to become the father of a great nation. I will bless you and make you famous, and I will make you a blessing to others.* ***I will bless those who bless you and curse those who curse you. All the families of the earth will be blessed through you.*** *" So Abram departed as the Lord had instructed him, and Lot went with him. Abram was seventy-five years old when he left Haran. He took his wife, Sarai, his nephew Lot, and all his wealth, his livestock, and all the people who joined his household at Haran, and finally arrived in Canaan* (Genesis 12:1-5, NLT).

Know this, God keeps His promises, and it is impossible for Him to lie. *For example, there was God's promise to Abraham. Since there was no one greater to swear by, God took an oath in His own Name, saying:*

> *"I will certainly bless you richly, and I will multiply your descendants into countless millions." Then Abraham waited patiently, and he received what God had promised. When people take an oath, they call on someone greater than themselves to hold them to it. And without any question that oath is binding. God also bound himself with an oath, so that those who received the promise could be perfectly sure that he would never change his mind. So God has given us both his promise and his oath. These two things are unchangeable because* ***it is impossible for God to lie.*** *Therefore, we who have fled to him for refuge can take new courage, for we can hold on to his promise with confidence.*
> Hebrews 6:13-18, NLT

God Confirms His Covenant To Isaac

Isaac, Abraham's son, was the heir of the covenant that God had made with his father. When Abraham was ninety-nine years old, the Lord appeared to him and said, *"Sarah, your wife will bear you a son. You will name him Isaac, and I will confirm my everlasting covenant with him and his descendants"* (Genesis 17:19, NLT).

God's Covenant Blessings Given To Isaac

> *Now a severe famine struck the land, as had happened before in Abraham's time. So Isaac moved to Gerar, where Abimelech, King of the Philistines, lived. The Lord appeared to him there and said, "Do not go to Egypt. Do as I say, and stay here in this land. If you do, I will be with you and bless you. I will give all this land to you and your descendants, just as I solemnly promised Abraham, your father. I will cause your descendants to become as numerous as the stars, and I will give them all these lands.* ***And through your descendants all the nations of the earth will be blessed.*** *I will do this because Abraham listened to me and obeyed all my requirements, commands, regulations, and laws." So Isaac stayed in Gerar (*Genesis 26:1-6, NLT).

Jacob also obeyed God, and God blessed him with the same covenant He had made with his father and his grandfather (see Genesis 35:1-12).

Promise Of Material And Financial Blessings

The first promise that God made to Abraham is applicable for the family of believers today. Let's take a closer look at what God promised Abraham and what He has promised the family of believers.

> *Then the Lord told Abram, "Leave your country, your relatives, and your father's house, and go to the land that I will show you. I will cause you to become the father of a great nation.* ***I will bless you and make you famous, and I will make you a blessing to others. I will bless those who bless you and curse those who curse you. All the families of the earth will be blessed through you***" (Genesis 12:1-3, NLT).

Notice keenly the last sentence in the above Scripture; it says "all" the families of the earth will be blessed through you (Abraham). I submit to you that the blessings mentioned here hold true for "all" the families of believers of the earth. God's promise that all the families of the earth will be blessed refers to material and financial blessings, and through Jesus Christ of Nazareth those same blessings belong to you.

God Almighty is still on the throne fulfilling His promise to our ancestors to bless us (believers) in the same way He greatly blessed Abraham. Abraham was extremely rich in livestock and in silver and gold (Genesis 13:2).

Remember, God wants you to be rich so He can fulfill the covenant (promises) He made with your ancestors (Abraham, Isaac and Jacob).

Part 2
Six Reasons Why God Wants You To Be Rich

Reason No. 2

God wants you to be rich so that you will be obedient to His Word and leave an inheritance to your children's children.

We read in the Bible from the days of Abraham, Isaac and Jacob, that it was God's plan and purpose for righteous men to leave an inheritance to their children and their children's children. This same tradition is witnessed throughout the Bible, of fathers blessing their children with hefty inheritances. The Bible says, *"Abraham left everything he owned to his son Isaac"* (Genesis 25:5, NLT).

God's Financial Plan Unveiled

If you closely examine the Word of God concerning inheritance you will find a foolproof financial plan that assures offsprings' financial and material stability.

I have four candid questions to ask you:

1. Do you know whether your grandparents set aside an inheritance of house and riches for you?
2. If you are married, do you know whether your spouse's grandparents set aside an inheritance of house and riches for him/her?
3. Have you set aside an inheritance of house and riches for your children?
4. Have you set aside an inheritance of house and riches for your children's children?

Thinking back now to when I was just starting out in my marriage, if my grandparents had left me an inheritance of house and riches, and if my wife's grandparents had left her an inheritance of house and riches, this would have given us a huge jump start when we needed it the most.

In my case, my grandparents had gone on to be with the Lord before I got married. Instead of starting out with a house (fully paid for) and riches, we started out paying monthly rent. Our household furniture and appliances were purchased on credit, as was the car we drove and even the clothes we wore. Other things, too, were purchased on what was called a revolving credit account at Sears, Western Auto and other retailers. What a terrible way to start married life! If God's financial plan of leaving an inheritance to your children's children had been operating in my life, I could have avoided all the credit and high interest, and with house and riches, I guarantee life would have been much, much better!

God's financial plan is revealed in the book of Proverbs thusly:

> *A good man leaves an inheritance to his children's children. Houses and riches are an inheritance from fathers.*
> Proverbs 13:22; 19:14, NKJV

God's financial plan would have certainly helped me years ago, and the absence of His financial plan being in place in the lives of believers and nonbelievers is the major cause of woes for many families.

Are You Or Were You In These Statistics

- Today it is not unusual for a young couple to be over $100,000 in debt within the first two years of marriage.
- Approximately 50% of all marriages fail and finances are listed as the leading cause of divorce by a factor of 4 to 1.
- Nearly 80% of divorced couples between the ages of 20 and 30 state that financial problems were the primary cause of divorce.
- Another 80% of couples divorce again within three years of remarrying because of debt.
- More than 60% of all first-time home loans require two salaries to make the payments.

Obedience, on the part of parents and grandparents, to God's Word concerning leaving an inheritance to your children's children could have averted most of the failing statistics listed above.

I guarantee you that neither Isaac or Jacob, nor any of Abraham's covenant descendants had to borrow money or purchase things on a credit account. Let's look at how Abraham blessed his son Isaac. The Bible reveals this account through the mouth of Abraham's head servant this way...

> *I am Abraham's servant he explained; and the Lord has blessed my master richly; he has become a great man. The Lord has given him flocks of sheep and herds of cattle, a fortune in silver and gold, and many servants and camels and donkeys. When Sarah, my master's wife was very old, she gave birth to my master's son, and my master has given him everything he owns.*
> Genesis 24:34-36, NLT

The servant didn't say that Abraham had given his son a few valuable things and an insurance policy. No, he said, "my master has given him everything he owns." This is the profile of Abraham's leaving an inheritance to his son Isaac, and it is a lofty example for believers to follow today.

Now let's look at a profound, in-your-face Scripture that puts closure to this topic. God wants you to be rich so that you will be obedient to His Word and leave an inheritance to your children's children.

The following Scripture was written by the apostle Paul when he wrote to Timothy, and to you.

> *But those who won't care for their own relatives, especially those living in the same household, have denied what we believe. Such people are worse than unbelievers* (1 Timothy 5:8, NLT).

The bottom line is, God's Word commands you to take care of your relatives while you are alive, to leave an inheritance to your children and to your children's children, so that they can reign as kings or queens and not as a servant in bondage to creditors and lenders. The Bible clearly tells us that, *"The rich ruleth over the poor, and the borrower is servant to the lender"* (Proverbs 22:7).

Set Your House In Order

My wife and I have maintained an updated family will for the past twelve years and we rely solely upon the Holy Spirit and sound financial and legal counseling. I exhort all born-again believers to set their house in order (first thing in this New Millennium) by preparing a family will or by insuring that an existing one is up to date. Seek the wise counsel of a recommended Christian-based financial management service and an attorney, in setting up an inheritance for your children and your children's children.

Remember, God wants you to be rich so that you will be obedient to His Word and leave an inheritance to your children, and to your children's children.

Part 3
Six Reasons Why God Wants You To Be Rich

Reason No. 3

God wants you to be rich so that you can be willing and obedient to support the work of the ministry by paying your tithes (a tenth of your substance/income/inheritance) and offerings into God's storehouse (the local church).

Abraham gave Melchizedek tithes long before the law was established. The Bible says,

> *As Abram returned from his victory over Kedorlaomer and his allies, the king of Sodom came out to meet him in the valley of Shaveh (that is, the King's Valley). Then Melchizedek, the king of*

Salem and a priest of God Most High, brought him bread and wine. Melchizedek blessed Abram with this blessing:

> *"Blessed be Abram by God Most High, Creator of heaven and earth. And blessed be God Most High who has helped you conquer your enemies."*

Then Abram gave Melchizedek a ***tenth*** *of all the goods he had recovered* (Genesis 14:17-20, NLT).

Satan Is A Deceiver

Tithing is the one subject with which many people have major challenges and struggles. It is also an area in which Satan has clouded the minds of people with negative connotations regarding giving into God's Kingdom. The age-old, doubt-peddling question that Satan cleverly plants in the minds of people is this: Is tithing under the Old Testament or the New Testament? Limited space will not permit full justice to this important subject of paying tithes and sharing offerings.

I was delivered from all challenges about tithing when I came across what Jesus Christ of Nazareth had to say about tithing. In the book of Matthew, Jesus says the following:

> *"How terrible it will be for you teachers of religious law and you Pharisees, Hypocrites! For you are careful to tithe even the tiniest part of your income, but you ignore the important things of the law – justice, mercy, and faith.* **You should tithe, yes**, *but you should not leave undone the more important things."* Matthew 23:23, NLT

Look closely at four very important words which Jesus Christ of Nazareth speaks. "You should tithe, yes." He didn't say that believers should not tithe. No! Our Lord and Savior tells us that we should tithe. Neither did He differentiate between Old and New Testament believers.

Another one of Satan's clever tricks is to get people to focus on man (the pastor/minister/reverend) when paying tithes, rather than focusing on paying their tithes and offerings to God. It is the same as what happened to the apostle Peter, while walking on the water: Once you take your eyes off the Lord, you get into real deep trouble. When your eyes are off the Lord, it allows Satan to begin influencing your thoughts with fear and doubts. When doubts and fear come on the scene, faith leaves.

Satan will plant thoughts such as: The minister/pastor is using the money to buy fine clothes, drive a big car or live in a large home. My immediate response to these thoughts would be...SO WHAT! Drug dealers and pimps wear fine clothes, drive big luxury cars and live in large luxury penthouses and mansions, and they are the scum of the community.

Men of God who are set aside to do God's work should reign as kings in life and not as bums. They should not be considered the less fortunate or someone who takes a vow of poverty. No! They should set high standards (examples) in every area of life.

I came across two Scriptures in my treasure of stockpiled Scriptures that have forever settled (in my spirit) the questions of paying tithes and sharing offerings into God's storehouse (the local church). The first Scripture is found in the book of 1 Corinthians and it says,

> *So then, whether you eat or drink, or whatever you may do, do all for the honor and glory of God (*1 Corinthians 10:31, Amp.).

The second Scripture is found in the book of Colossians and it says...

> *And whatever you do (no matter what it is) in word or deed, do everything in the name of the Lord Jesus and in (dependence upon) His Person, giving praise to God the Father through Him.* Colossians 3:17, Amp.

Plant Your Tithes In Good Soil

Concerning the local church, I first do my homework with the help of the Holy Spirit to insure that the storehouse (the church) is good, fertile ground for paying my tithes and sowing my offerings. When I pay tithes and sow offerings, I look beyond man and I look to God, for He is my source and resource. I see myself honoring God when I pay tithes and sow offerings, as it should be.

It is written in the Book of Proverbs:

> *Honor the Lord with your capital and sufficiency (from righteous labors), and with the first fruits of all your income. So shall your storage places be filled with plenty, and your vats be overflowing with new wine* (Proverbs 3: 9-10, Amp.).

The Word of God indisputably commands you to honor the Lord with your capital. It does not say honor the reverend or the pastor. It says honor the Lord with the first fruits of all your income/wealth.

Honor God And Not Man With Your Tithes And Offerings

Think about this: Reverend or Pastor Doe could leave your church for a number of valid or invalid reasons. If you were giving the first fruits of your income/wealth to honor, satisfy and please him, what happens to your giving if he leaves? Do you stop giving? No! Because you are commanded by the Word of God to honor the **Lord** with the first fruits of your income/wealth and not man.

The reality is that when you bring God your tithes and offerings, you are only giving back to God what was already His. He is the One Who blessed you with the income/wealth for you to be a good steward by supporting the works of His Kingdom and sharing with the poor and needy.

Let's face it, man can and sometimes does change vocations in life, but God Almighty never changes. He is always the same; yesterday, today, and forever. And the Bible says, *"He will never leave you nor forsake you."* (Hebrews 13:5) Praise the Lord!

Let's take another look at Proverbs 3:9-10, NLT. The Word of God says...

> *Honor the Lord with your wealth and with the best part of everything your land produces. Then He will fill your barns with grain, and your vats will overflow with the finest wine.*

Unless you are a farmer or a winemaker, this overflowing prosperity could mean that your bank account is full and you own an abundance of property and things.

Conditional Terms

Please notice with keen eyes and spiritual ears that this Scripture is "conditional." In other words, the material and financial prosperity mentioned in the latter part of the Scripture is dependent totally upon you doing the first part.

Those who disobey the first part of this Scripture please Satan because two things happen:

1. The works of the ministry and God's Kingdom are limited in their effectiveness.
2. You lose out because you shut the windows of heaven and stop the blessings and benefits of God from coming to you.

Huge Benefits Promised To Tithers

Another Scripture that is laden with promises of awesome, divine benefits of blessings and protection is found in the book of Malachi. But before we look at the Scripture in Malachi, I would like to pause for a couple of brief spiritual commercials.

Spiritual Commercial No. 1

> *Every Scripture is God-breathed (given by His inspiration) and profitable for instruction, for reproof and conviction of sin, for correction of error and discipline in obedience, (and) for training*

in righteousness (in Holy living, in conformity to God's will in thought, purpose, and action). So that the man of God may be complete and proficient, well-fitted and thoroughly equipped for every good work (2 Timothy 3:16-17, Amp.).

Spiritual Commercial No. 2

Give, and (gifts) will be given you, good measure, pressed down, shaken together and running over, will they pour into (the pouch formed by) the bosom (of your robe and used as a bag). For with the measure you deal out, (with the measure you use when you confer benefits on others), it will be measured back to you (Luke 6:38, Amp.).

I really favor the King James Version of this Scripture because it identifies who gives you your return gifts. It says, "shall men give into your bosom!" Let's read aloud the King James Version.

Give, and it shall be given unto you; good measure, pressed down, and shaken together, and running over, shall **men** *give into your bosom. For with the same measure that you mete withal it shall be measured to you again* (Luke 6:38, KJV).

This Scripture clearly reveals that your wealth and riches do not fall out of the sky. The Word of God says, *"shall men give into your bosom."*

We know that divine returns are supernatural and God uses unlimited and unnatural ways to get His work accomplished. He may choose to have an angel of the Lord give into your bosom, or your return on your giving could be hidden in the mouth of a fish. God could give you ideas, concepts, and insight on how to invest wisely which would produce your return.

Know this, that the law of sowing and reaping works and when you give in love, selflessly, you are guaranteed a divine return.

Tap Into The Law Of Divine Return

The principle of sowing and reaping is the law of divine return.

When a farmer sows seed, he expects a harvest. When a person puts money in a bank, he expects interest in return. The same is true with God; give to Him and He gives in return.

It's the law of sowing and reaping; since giving is an act of obedient faith in God and in His Word, one may be disappointed at the little blessing he receives when he has not actively invested or sown seed in the Kingdom of God. This thinking may be evident in the many people who come to church, enjoy and gain from the preaching and use the facilities, but give little or no thought to meeting the expenses.

Nature teaches us, does it not, that it is foolish to expect a harvest when you have not planted any seed? Moreover, you wouldn't walk up to a bank teller and expect to get money out, unless you have first put money in. Then how can you expect God to honor your desire for financial return, when you have not honored His command to give?

You should remember the words of Jesus Christ of Nazareth, *"It is more blessed to give than to receive."*

Now, let's push play, and pick up on our discussion of tithes and offerings.

Benefits From Paying Tithes And Sowing/Sharing Offerings

Another exciting Scripture that is full of the benefits of material and financial blessings and divine protection is found in the book of Malachi. Hold on to your seat belts; these Scriptures are powerful, inspiring and super beneficial to you! Make sure that you read these Scriptures aloud.

> *"For I am the Lord, I do not change; Therefore, you are not consumed, O sons of Jacob. Yet from the days of your fathers, You have gone away from My ordinances and have not kept them. Return to Me, and I will return to you," Says the Lord of hosts, But you said, "In what way shall we return?" "Will a man rob God? Yet you have robbed Me!" But you say, "In what way have we robbed You?"* ***"In tithes and offerings****. You are cursed with a curse, for you have robbed Me. Even this whole nation.* ***Bring all the tithes into the storehouse, that there may be food in My house, and prove Me now in this," says the Lord of hosts, "if I will not open for you the windows of heaven, and pour out for you such blessing that there will not be room enough to receive it. And I will rebuke the devourer for your sakes****, So that he will not destroy the fruit of your ground, Nor shall the vine fail to bear fruit for you in the field," says the Lord of hosts; "and all nations shall call you blessed, For you will be a delightful land," says the Lord of hosts* (Malachi 3:6-12, NKJV).

Conditional Terms

Notice closely that this Scripture is "conditional." If you bring all your tithes into the storehouse (the local church), then these are the things that God says will happen.

1. Your tithes and offerings will help to meet the needs of the church and help spread the Good News of Jesus Christ of Nazareth.
2. God will open the windows of heaven for you and pour out

for you a blessing (material and financial) that there shall not be room enough to receive it.

3. Other people will see the prosperity in your life and they will call you happy and blessed.
4. God says that He will personally rebuke the devourer (Satan) for your sake and will not allow him (Satan) to destroy any of your property, material or financial possessions.

One Area Where God Says "Test Me"

Brothers, sisters, and friends, these are promises of great blessing and protection that God guarantees you when you tithe.

The words "*prove Me now*" are strong, bold and confident words. God's Word in these Scriptures challenges you to put His Word to the test (over a period of time). He says "*and try Me now in this*." In other words, God is saying to you that when you are willing and obedient to His Word concerning tithing, He will open up the windows of heaven for you and pour out a blessing for you that there will not be room enough to receive. Praise God!

As these Scriptures indicate, God will richly bless you when you tithe. However, keep in mind that all of these divine blessings are conditional. Actually, when you bring your tithes and offerings into God's storehouse (your local church) you are only paying back to Him what is already His.

There is a saying that goes like this:

If you don't give according to your means, God will see that your means are according to your giving.

The World's System Requires Much More Than God

Think about this: Have you ever had a Sears charge card? Or a Ward's charge card? Or have you ever had a personal (finance) loan account? Or have you ever had a secured credit card? If your answer to any one of these questions is yes, then you know that the interest rate on these kinds of accounts range from 20 to 27% or more, with hidden charges. The way this works is, let's say you purchased a product that cost $1,000. You could pay 21% interest on the balance (in this case, the interest cost to you would be $210) and your total pay-back amount would be $1,210 which is very much bloated. Most people will pay these extremely high interest rates without giving it too much thought. Brothers, sisters, and friends, I speak and write this from personal experience. Early on, when I was starting out, I had a Sears charge card, and I have had to take out personal loans. These things can keep you in bondage.

God's System Is Best

I discovered that God wants us to be rich, wealthy, healthy, and not in bondage to payments and debts. I began to change my attitude about who I was in Christ Jesus. I realized that I am the lender and not the borrower. I began to change my confession to, *"My Lord is my shepherd, I shall not want" (Psalm 23:1) and "My God supplies all my needs according to His riches in glory by Christ Jesus"* (Philippians 4:19).

At the same time, I began to tithe on a regular basis and I started to see supernatural financial increases in my life. There is a saying that holds true to form...

Many people give the tenth – the tenth of what they ought to give.

It is strange that most people freely give fifteen percent or more gratuity to waitresses, waiters, bellhops, taxi drivers, and pizza delivery men to mention a few. They give these tips effortlessly, almost automatically, sometimes even when the service rendered was not pleasing. But for some strange reason, when it comes to giving to God a mere ten percent, it becomes a challenge and a struggle for many believers.

Know this, that your return on your giving to God will far outweigh any other form of giving; there is just no comparison.

Now let's take a closer look at tithing. God commands a dime (10%) out of every dollar. Surely you don't want 10 cents to keep you out of God's blessings of spiritual, physical, material, financial prosperity, and divine protection. Moreover, think about this. If you can't live on 90% of your income, chances are, you are not likely to make it on 100% either.

The bottom line is, I strongly exhort you to be willing and obedient to God's commands for you to tithe. In doing so, you will reap the enormous benefits that God has already guaranteed to you, and He stakes His Word on it.

Tiny Steps First

When I stopped smoking cigarettes back in 1982, I did it gradually. I was smoking a high-rated tar and nicotine type of cigarette (17.0 mg). So, I changed to a brand that was a little lower in nicotine and tar. The first two or three days of adjusting to the lower nicotine and tar was not pleasurable, but I stuck with my game plan and it worked. Eventually, I was down to a (1.0 mg) cigarette. All during this time, I was reading aloud my faith-building confession at least three times a day. It read like this...

I believe in my heart and spirit that I am a non-smoker. I no longer have a craving or desire for cigarettes because they are poison to my body. And my body is the temple of God; the Holy Spirit lives within my body, and I am now maintaining it properly. I confess this in the mighty Name of Jesus Christ of Nazareth! (1 Corinthians 6:19)

After about a week of smoking the tasteless (1.0 mg) cigarettes, I purposed in my heart and in my spirit that I would not smoke another cigarette ever. Ever since, I have not smoked a cigarette.

The transition to becoming a non-smoker was made easier for me by a number of reasons. The key to my success in quitting smoking was threefold!

1. My sincere desire to quit smoking.
2. My gradual withdrawal to lower nicotine and tar cigarettes.
3. I took control over my mind and body by using my self-talk (faith- building) confession to bring non-smoking into reality for me. In other words, I had to re-program (renew) my (mind and) heart memory file by speaking the thing that was not, as though it was. I took a similar approach when I started to tithe.

Babies crawl first, then they take tiny, wobbly steps before walking. When I first started to tithe, I didn't pay 10% of my income. Instead, similar to my approach to stop smoking, I started out gradually paying 2% while confessing daily my goal of being a 12% tither. My goal was to increase 2% bi-monthly until I reached my 12% objective, which I accomplished with ease. My current objective is to be a 25% tither.

This gradual approach worked for me, and it may work for others. Although, the approach of tithing 10% from the start may work for some. The essential thing is that you start tithing because there are huge spiritual and material blessings (from God) linked to your tithing.

Resist The Spirit Of Condemnation

I appeal to you, don't get under condemnation concerning tithing. Start with what you can. Don't wait until you can pay 10%. Start paying, even if it is only 2% (Praise the Lord!) but keep a firm goal and a set date to reach 10% or more. The tenth verse in Malachi, chapter 3, NKJV says: *"Bring all the tithes into the storehouse, that there may be food in My house, and try Me now in this."*

God's Word in this Scripture challenges you to put His Word to the test. God says *"And try me now in this."* I am firmly convinced that the test is really meant for the believer also. God certainly does not need our money, but He knows that we need to give it as an act of faith and obedience.

Self-centeredness, stinginess, and hoarding of money short circuit the blessings God wants to open up to us.

Tithe, Time, Talent And Income

Although money is the overwhelming force that causes things to happen in today's world system, I firmly believe that God is also pleased when you tithe with things other than money. In addition to tithing on your income, you may consider tithing 10% of your weekly hours to work in God's Kingdom.

When we fail to give to God our tithes (10% of what we earn) and offerings, we rob both Him and ourselves. Why did I say that the believer is also being tested concerning God's command to tithe? First, the Bible says that God looks at the heart:

It is so written in the book of 1 Samuel...

> *When they arrived, Samuel took one look at Eliab and thought, "Surely this is the Lord's anointed!" But the Lord said to Samuel, "Don't judge by his appearance or height, for I have rejected him. The Lord doesn't make decisions the way you do! People judge by outward appearance, but the Lord looks at a person's thoughts and intentions"* (1 Samuel 16: 6-7, NLT).

Clearly, we can see that God looks at the heart and at faith; the willingness and obedience to His Word is what counts. He looks directly at man's heart and gauges his thoughts and intentions.

Do You Really Love The Lord?

I firmly believe that it is hard to find a person who really loves the Lord Jesus Christ, but does not give to support the Kingdom of God and the work of the ministry. If you love, you will give freely and unselfishly.

Our Heavenly Father is the supreme example of love, for it is written, *"for God so loved the world that He gave His only Son, so that everyone who believes in Him will not perish but have eternal life"* (John 3:16).

In the book of Matthew, the following words of wisdom are revealed...

> *"Wherever your treasure is, there your heart and thoughts will also be* (Matthew 6:21, NLT).

If you truly love your spouse, you will give to him/her freely; if you love your children, you will give and give more. If you truly love the Lord Jesus Christ, your Lord and Savior, you will give freely. Praise the Lord!

Blessings Or Curses

My sincere desire is that these past Scriptures have inspired everyone to get in on the divine blessings that result from tithing into God's Kingdom. And it is my wish for those who are already tithers, that these inscriptions have sparked them to consider tithing above the 10% level. Remember, everything in God's way of doing things is based on **faith**.

Perhaps you might prayerfully consider tithing on the salary or income that you would desire to make. In doing so, God will be pleased with you, and you will reap a harvest of blessings. So great a harvest, you won't have enough room to take it in. Praise the Lord!

In closing this topic on tithing, there are two highly important activities I must share with you.

1. I exhort tithers to add to their daily faith (building) confessions menu, a confession of divine return on their giving. Faith-building confessions for divine return on giving are provided in Appendix B.
2. After you have prayed and asked God to reveal to you the amount of your covenant inheritance of wealth and riches, and once it is revealed to you, take the following steps:
    A. Sit down with a calculator, pencil and paper, and figure out how much of your inheritance goes to tithes, how much goes to offerings, and how much goes to the poor and needy.
    B. Write a faith-building confession that says, "I believe I am cheerfully paying (whatever the amount is) tithes on my covenant inheritance. I see myself writing out the check to my church (the name of your local church). And I am believing for divine return on my giving."
    C. Write a similar confession for your offerings and for your contributions to the poor and needy. Chapter 11 provides instructions on How To Write A Faith-Building Confession.
    D. Add these self-talk faith-building confessions to your daily menu of confessions.

To finalize this topic, know that God the Father wants you to be rich so that you can be a good steward over your income and your covenant inheritance of wealth and riches; so you can pay your tithes into His storehouse (your local church) to help support the work of the ministry and help spread the Good News of Jesus Christ of Nazareth.

Think about these things:

It is more blessed to give than to receive, but the average man is willing to let the other fellow have the blessing!

Remember, our Heavenly Father doesn't depend on nor does He rely upon pagans to support the work of His Kingdom, but He does depend on and rely upon believers to support the work of His Kingdom.

If you would be rich and wealthy; first, think on, and self-talk your faith-building confession for divine return on your tithe, and set your sincere desire to be a cheerful tither. Possess a spirit of giving to the poor and needy, then shall wealth and riches be in your house.

Remember, God wants you to be rich so that you can be willing and obedient to support the work of the ministry by paying your tithes (a tenth of your substance/income/inheritance) and offerings into God's storehouse (the local church).

Part 4
Six Reasons Why God Wants You To Be Rich

Reason No. 4

God wants you to be rich so that you can give/share a portion of your income and a portion of your covenant inheritance of wealth and riches as an offering to God's storehouse (your local church). So you can help support the work of the ministry, meet the needs of the poor and needy within the local church body and in the community, with a key focus on reaching the lost of the world with the Good News of Jesus Christ of Nazareth.

The Bible says that the Early Church believers shared their possessions with others. This account is revealed in the book of Acts thusly...

> *All the believers were of one heart and mind, and they felt that what they owned was not their own;* ***they shared everything they had****. And the apostles gave powerful witness to the resurrection of the Lord Jesus, and God's great favor was upon them all.* ***There was no poverty among them****, because people who owned land or houses sold them and brought the money to the apostles to give to others in need* (Acts 4:32-35, NLT).

Let The Holy Spirit Be Your Guide

I urge believers to be prayerful and seek the guidance of the Holy Spirit when sowing/giving offerings, especially to projects, programs, and causes outside the local church. Rest assured that the Holy Spirit will assist you in your decision to give and in the amount to give.

There are many voices beseeching you for your offering for various religious causes, especially via television and radio, and now also the internet. Keep in mind that God demands that you be a good steward over that which He has blessed you with. No one but you is responsible to insure that your offerings are being sown into good ground.

Financial giving is compared to a seed that a farmer uses to plant a crop. Can you imagine a farmer planting seeds in stony or bad ground? No! Then the same should hold true for believers; their offerings should go into good ground which will produce a bountiful harvest.

Offering, as it is used in this topic is a gift of money, or its equivalent (time, talent, goods) to a godly cause, charity, or humanitarian or public institutional cause.

The Bible clearly tells us to support missionaries and ministries. Here's what it has to say...

> *For these (traveling missionaries) have gone out for the Name's sake (for His sake) and are accepting nothing from the Gentiles (the heathen, the non-Israelites).*
>
> *So we ourselves ought to support such people (to welcome and provide for them), in order that we may be fellow workers in the Truth (the whole Gospel) and cooperate with its teachers.*
> 3 John 7-8, Amp.

As mentioned previously, you should tithe to God's storehouse, your local church. But offerings are above your tithes, and offerings should be given to other men and women who are preaching the Gospel, especially to missionaries, evangelists, prophets, and teachers.

When you give to support missionaries and ministries, you get double credit because the law of sowing and reaping kicks in for you in this life. In addition, you get part of the credit for things they do, because you had a part in it. Everyone who gets saved, everyone who rededicates his/her life to God, every healing, and every miracle gets credited to your heavenly account, because you helped support the missionaries or the ministries.

Offerings And Tithing Are Not The Same

Tithing and offering were discussed earlier, so you should have a general knowledge of what they are; but to illuminate the difference between tithing and offerings, let's push "stop" and rewind to some Scriptures we discussed earlier which are found in the book of Malachi.

> *Should people cheat God? Yet you have cheated me! "But you ask,'What do you mean? When did we ever cheat you?' "You have cheated me of the tithes and offerings due to me. You are under a curse, for your whole nation has been cheating me."*
> Malachi 3:8-9, NLT.

This passage clearly reveals that sowing offerings and paying tithes are separate. The word "and" is a conjunction that joins the words "tithes" and "offerings" together. Grammatically this points out a difference; "and" is used to join two separate and distinct things. Furthermore, because the first tenth of what God blesses you with already belongs to Him, when you bring God your tithe you are only paying back to Him what was already His.

Know this, that sowing an offering is over and above the amount that you pay in tithes. Tithing and offerings can be likened to your putting $500 into your bank money market account and $250 into your bank savings account. They are two totally different accounts, but both are interest bearing accounts which pay you earned interest.

Notice closely the strong words that God uses toward those who withhold tithes and offerings. He says, "You have cheated/robbed me of the tithes and offerings due to me. You are under a curse, for your whole nation, people of similar characteristics, have been cheating/robbing me."

When you sow an offering, you give honor to God which is grandly stated in the book of Psalms.

> *Give to the Lord the glory He deserves! Bring your offering and come to worship Him* (Psalm 96:8, NLT).

The law of sowing and reaping is activated when you sow offerings into God's storehouse (the local church) and into other ministries and godly causes. Here's what the law states...

> *Do not be deceived, God is not mocked; for whatever a man sows, that he will also reap* (Galatians 6:7, NKJV).

The spiritual and natural law of sowing and reaping is seen in this revelation-knowledge Scripture. Also, the law of divine return is revealed in this Scripture.

As it was stated earlier, when a farmer sows/plants seeds, he expects a harvest. When a person puts money into a bank account, he expects to accrue earned interest in return. And when you pay tithes and share offerings, you should confess and believe for divine return.

God's Interest Rate Is Thirty, Sixty, One Hundred, And A Thousand Percent

The same principle that governs interest rates also holds true with God; give to Him and He gives in return. However, the huge difference between the bank and God is that God doesn't return just four or five percent interest. Under His system He returns thirty, sixty, one hundred, and even a thousand times as much as you have sown. It's the spiritual law of sowing and reaping and it works all the time.

In the Kingdom of God, the law of sowing and reaping reaches into all aspects of life. You must sow whatever seeds you have available to you. In other words, anything you have can be a seed – your time, your talent, your love, your money, your work – anything can be sown into the field of God's Kingdom.

Whatever seeds you sow, when sown in faith, will set your increase in motion. Moreover, I strongly suggest that when you sow seeds into God's Kingdom that you should continuously read aloud your faith-building confessions, believing for a divine return on your seed and giving thanks to God in advance for the return.

Believers Miss Their Blessings By Not Confessing For Divine Return On Their Giving

Confession and believing in faith for return on seeds sown is a vital step in reaping (receiving) a harvest from God, and this is where many well-meaning spirit-filled believers miss it. They either lack faith for divine return on their giving because they do not systematically use faith-building confessions for return on their giving, or they give up and stop saying their faith-building confession for a return on their giving.

When you give into God's Kingdom, you don't just plunk the money in the container and that's it. No! That's just the beginning. You have got to mix **faith** with your giving. The adversary (Satan) will hinder your return on your giving if you don't persistently confess faith for the return on your giving.

Read Daniel 10:12-14 and you will gain insight as to why it is vitally important to exercise your faith for a divine return on your giving.

Think about this: When a farmer plants (sows) a seed in the ground, his work doesn't end with the planting. In fact, his work really just begins; he has to continuously cultivate the soil, fertilize, eliminate weeds, water, and protect the plants from insects, worms, birds, and animals. So it is, with the offerings that you sow into God's Kingdom. You must continuously cultivate, fertilize, and protect your seed/offerings (from the devourer, Satan) with your daily faith-building confession for divine return on your giving/sharing.

Someone might ask, "Are you saying that I should say a faith-building confession every time I give/sow an offering into God's Kingdom?" My reply is yes! Your confession for divine return on your giving/sharing should be a part of your daily menu of faith-building confessions.

Someone else might ask, "What do I need to say when making a confession for a divine return on my (giving/sowing) offerings?" The answer to this question is, that faith-building confessions for divine return on tithing, offerings, and sharing with the poor and needy are prescribed for your use in Appendix B.

Remember, God wants you to be rich so that you can give/share a portion of your income and a portion of your covenant inheritance of wealth and riches as an offering to God's storehouse (your local church).

So you can help support the work of the ministry, meet the needs of the poor and needy within the local church body and in the community, with a key focus on reaching the lost of the world with the Good News of Jesus Christ of Nazareth.

Part 5
Six Reasons Why God Wants You To Be Rich

Reason No. 5

God wants you to be rich so that you can be a blessing to the poor and needy. The apostle Paul had a meeting with the Ephesian elders, and he told them...

> *I have never coveted anyone's money or fine clothing. You know that these hands of mine have worked to pay my own way, and I have even supplied the needs of those who were with me. And I have been a constant example of how you can help the poor by working hard. You should remember the words of the Lord Jesus: "**It is more blessed to give than to receive**"* (Acts 20:33-35, NLT).

The Bible has much to say about the poor. In fact, there are 235 verses in the King James Version of the Bible that mention the word poor in one way or another.

The words poor and poverty are basically synonymous, and in Scripture they can mean socially or spiritually poor. However, in this topic, socially poor is under the microscope.

The Bible makes three things very clear about the poor:

1. You will always have the poor with you (Matthew 26:11).
2. Those who give to the poor are abundantly blessed by God. (Psalm 41:1-2; Proverbs 28:27)
3. And those who close their eyes to the poor will have many a curse (Proverbs 28:27).

As it was mentioned in the introductory section of this book, my wife and I have (over the years) counted it all joy to sow seeds of offerings (money) into Mother Teresa's ministry, the Missionaries of Charity, in Calcutta, India. Mother Teresa's ministry focuses solely on caring for the poorest of the poor, which is what the Bible commands. The results of our being obedient to the leading of the Holy Spirit to give into the Missionaries of Charity Ministry and other ministries has (over the years) produced windfalls of blessings both spiritually and materially within our family.

Divine Benefits That Result From Giving And Sharing With The Poor And Needy

When you give generously to the poor and needy, either from your daily income or from your covenant inheritance of wealth and riches, it will cause a number of positive things to occur:

1. You will be glorifying God through your generous gifts, for your generosity to the poor and needy will prove that you are obedient to the Good News of Jesus Christ of Nazareth.
2. The needs of Christians and others will be met.
3. Those that are helped will joyfully express thanksgiving to God.
4. They will pray for you with deep affection because of the wonderful grace of God shown through you.

The Bible reveals the benefits to those who give to the poor and needy in many Scriptures throughout the Bible. The following is an abbreviated list of Scriptures that highlight some of the benefits that result from giving to the poor and needy:

> *Whoever gives to the poor will lack nothing, but a curse will come upon those who close their eyes to poverty.* Proverbs 28:27, NLT
>
> *Oh, the joys of those who are kind to the poor. The Lord rescues them in times of trouble. The Lord protects them and keeps them alive. He gives them prosperity and rescues them from their enemies* (Psalm 41:1-2, NLT).
>
> *If you help the poor, you are lending to the Lord and He will repay you!* (Proverbs 19:17, NLT)
>
> *Remember this, a farmer who plants only a few seeds will get a small crop. But the one who plants generously will get a generous crop. You must each make up your own mind as to how much you should give. Don't give reluctantly or in response to pressure. For* ***God loves the person who gives cheerfully****. And God will generously provide all you need.*
>
> *Then you will always have everything you need and plenty left over to share with others. As the Scriptures say, Godly people give generously to the poor. Their good deeds will never be forgotten. For God is the one who gives seed to the farmer and then bread to eat. In the same way, he will give you many opportunities to do good, and he will produce a great harvest of generosity in you* (2 Corinthians 9:6-10, NLT).

I encourage you to always confess divine returns on your giving. Faith-building confessions for divine return on tithing, offerings and sharing with the poor and needy are prescribed for your use in Appendix B.

Remember this: You can give without loving, but you can't love without giving. Charity gives itself rich; covetousness hoards itself poor.

Remember, God wants you to be rich so that you can be a blessing to the poor and needy.

Part 6
Six Reasons Why God Wants You to Be Rich

Reason No. 6

God wants you to be rich; therefore He fulfills His inspired Word throughout the Bible, blessing you so that you can be a blessing to others.

My testimony is, I have been shoestring poor and I have been rich, and rich is much, much better! You can't help others when you are living on a shoestring yourself.

God told Abraham (Abram) and He is telling you the same thing today, *"I will bless you and make you famous, and I will make you a blessing to others"* (Genesis 12:2, NLT).

Now remember, it is written in the book of Galatians,

> *And now that you belong to Christ, you are the true children of Abraham. You are his* ***heirs****, and now all the promises God gave to him belong to you* (Galatians 3:29).

You own whatever God promised Abraham. The Bible clearly reveals that from the beginning of time, God's plan and purpose for those who put their trust in Him would be to bless them with great wealth and riches and good health.

We see this truth unfold when God tells Abraham (Abram), *"I will bless you and make you famous, and I will make you a blessing to others. I will bless those who bless you and curse those who curse you. All the families of the earth will be blessed through you"* (Genesis 12:2-3, NLT).

Abraham Was Blessed Financially And Materially

The Bible superbly reveals how God blessed Abraham. This account given in the Bible cannot be confused with being blessed spiritually. Look what Abraham's servant had to say,

> *I am Abraham's servant, he explained. And the Lord has blessed my master richly; he has become a great man. The Lord has given him flocks of sheep and herds of cattle,* ***a fortune in silver and gold****, and many servants and camels and donkeys* (Genesis 24:34, NLT).

A close study of Abraham clearly unveils that his blessings from God were due solely to his unwavering faith in God and in God's Word.

Abraham Was Blessed With Good Health And So Are You

The account given in the Bible says that Abraham lived for 175 years and he died at a ripe old age, joining his ancestors in death. Think about this, the Bible does not make any mention of Abraham ever being sick or with disease during the 175 years that he lived. God's plan and purpose was to bless Abraham with wealth and riches, to make his name great, to make him a blessing to others, and then to bless him with good health. However, this plan was all contingent upon Abraham's faith in God and His Word, and his obedience to God's Word.

In other words, God's plan and purpose for those who put their trust in Him is that His blessings of wealth and riches will overtake them so that they can be a blessing to others and enjoy good health. God's purpose and plan has not changed. It is still very much in effect today for those who are willing and obedient to step up to the plate lionheartedly and say, "I am a believer, and no matter what the cost, I hold fast to my confession of faith in God and in His Word."

The Bible says...

> *Because of Abraham's faith in God, he was unequivocally willing to offer up his son, Isaac, (whom he loved very much), as a sacrifice, a burnt offering to God* (see Genesis 22:1-14).

Abraham Was Blessed Spiritually

Abraham's spiritual blessing of eternal life came as a gift from God because of Abraham's strong faith in God. It is written in the book of Genesis:

> *And behold, the word of the Lord came to him saying, This man shall not be your heir, but he who shall come from your own body shall be your heir. And He brought him outside his tent into the starlight and said, Look now toward the heavens and count the stars, if you are able to number them. Then He said to him, so shall your descendants be. And he (Abram) believed in (trusted in, relied on, remained steadfast to) the Lord, and* ***He counted it to him as righteousness (right standing with God)*** (Genesis 15:4-6, Amp.).

God's Promises To Abraham Belong To You Also

Let's pick up on what the angel of the Lord told Abraham, and what the angel of the Lord is telling you today.

The Amplified Bible expands this Scripture thusly:

> *The Angel of the Lord called to Abraham from heaven a second time. And said, I have sworn by Myself, says the Lord, that since you have done this and have not withheld (from Me) or begrudged (giving Me) your son, your only son. In blessing I will bless you and in multiplying I will multiply descendants like the stars of the heavens and like the sand on the seashore.* ***And your Seed (Heir) will possess the gate of His enemies. And in your Seed (Christ) shall all the nations of the earth be blessed and (by Him) bless themselves, because you have heard and obeyed My voice.*** Genesis 22:15-18, Amp.

I believe that if you are to be counted honest, you must agree that these Scriptures clearly reveal that God's plan and purpose is to bless you the same as He blessed Abraham, with wealth and riches and the good health to enjoy it!

Now let's fast forward to the New Testament and see how the Holy Spirit illuminates revelation knowledge to strengthen your faith toward the things that God has already promised you. Through Jesus Christ, the promises already belong to you now!

The apostle Paul reveals divine truths in the book of Galatians that should set your mind totally free concerning your covenant rights and (blood bought) covenant inheritance through Jesus Christ of Nazareth. The apostle Paul says...

> *God promised this Good News to Abraham long ago when he said, "All nations will be blessed through you." And so it is:* ***All who put their faith in Christ share the "same blessing" Abraham received because of his faith*** (Galatians 3:8-9, NLT).

The apostle Paul's next rendering of divine truths is glorious revelation knowledge for believers.

> *Let me put it another way. The law was our guardian and teacher to lead us until Christ came. So now, through faith in Christ, we are made right with God. But now that faith in Christ has come, we no longer need the law as our guardian. So you are all children of God through faith in Christ Jesus. And all who have been united with Christ in baptism have been made like him. There is no longer Jew or Gentile, slave or free, male or female. For you are all Christians – you are one in Christ Jesus.* ***And now that you belong to Christ, you are the true children of Abraham, you are his "heirs," and now "all" the promises God gave to him belong to you*** (Galatians 3:24-29, NLT).

God's Promises Of Wealth And Riches And Good Health Belong To You Now

Notice closely the last sentence in the previous Scripture. The Word of God says "and now," it does not say tomorrow; nor does it say in heaven, or someday in the by and by. But it says "and now" (this very moment), "all" (not a few or some, but all) the promises God gave to him (Abraham) belong to you.

This truth is vital to the believer today and it must be believed. It must settle deep down in your spirit that everything Abraham had financially and materially belongs to you today!

The question someone might ask is, "How do I get the same things that God gave Abraham?" Well, my response to that question would be to do the same thing Abraham did. He had strong faith in God and in God's Word.

The primary focus of *Self-Talk And Grow Rich* is to prescribe the specific steps to help you receive the same blessings God gave Abraham.

Abraham Was A Billionaire

Bible scholars indicate that by today's money standards, Abraham, Lot, Isaac, Jacob, and Job were billionaires. David was so rich that he gave more than a billion dollars (in today's currency) toward the building of the temple alone. However, Solomon was a super billionaire. The Bible says he was richer than all who had gone before him.

> *So I became great and increased more than all who were before me in Jerusalem. Also, my wisdom remained with me and stood by me* (Ecclesiastes 2:9, Amp.).

Notice that not only did God give Solomon super wealth, but He also gave him wisdom to manage his affairs. Remember this, wealth and wisdom are co-partners and wealth without wisdom beckons poverty and ruins.

Let's revisit a Scripture we discussed earlier...

> *Now that you belong to Christ, you are the true children of Abraham. You are his* ***heirs****, and now all the promises God gave to him belong to you* (Galatians 3:29, NLT).

Focus closely (for a moment) on the word "all" in the above verse. The word "all" is our red flag word which alerts you to ascertain what the "all" is all about. It is a pregnant word which means everything that one has, the whole of, entire, total, and nothing left out.

Renew Your Mind

The Word of God says that the same blessings God gave Abraham belong to you. Therefore, I exhort you to begin to think big now! Start now to change your self-talk to reflect how God sees you. He sees those who are born again as heirs to His promises to Abraham. God sees you with abundant blessings of wealth and riches and good health. He sees you being blessed in the same way that Abraham was greatly blessed. Even more than Abraham, because believers (today, right now) have a better covenant (than Abraham had) based on better promises through Jesus Christ of Nazareth (see Hebrews 8:6).

Strong Faith And Action Unlock The Windows Of Blessing From Heaven

How do you think a father would feel if the son in the following narrative was his son? Abiological father left his son an inheritance, and the son was notified by the attorney as to what steps he needed to take to receive his inheritance. But for some unknown reason, the son didn't go forth boldly and receive what rightfully belonged to him. Let's say that the father who is now in heaven, became aware of his son's inaction. How do you think the father would feel?

The first thing that comes to my mind is that the father would be disappointed and displeased, because the son didn't have the insight and wisdom to receive what had been bequeathed to him. Secondly, I feel that it would show a lack of respect (a slap in the face, so to speak); in fact, it would be total disobedience to the desires of the father.

Well, this same situation arises when believers do not mix faith with action which is required to receive their covenant inheritance of wealth and riches and good health. As it is with the biological father, I firmly believe that our Heavenly Parent is very much displeased when believers are not operating in faith in the fullness of His promises.

Believing Precedes Blessings

Aclose study of Abraham reveals that all of his blessings (material and economic well-being) followed his believing in God and acting on God's Word. The same holds true for you today; your blessings will follow your believing and acting on God's Word.

God's agenda hasn't changed.

God's plan and purpose to bless His covenant people with wealth and riches and good health is revealed from the very beginning. It is recorded in the book of Psalms this way...

> *But he brought his people safely out of Egypt, loaded with silver and gold; there were no sick or feeble people among them.* (Psalm 105:37, NLT)

We also see the Word of God amplifying His plan and purpose for His chosen people in the book of Ecclesiastes. It unfolds in this way...

> *Even so, I have noticed one thing, at least, that is good. It is good for people to eat well, drink a good glass of wine, and enjoy their work, whatever they do under the sun for however long God lets them live. And* ***it is a good thing to receive wealth from God and the good health to enjoy it****. To enjoy your work and accept your lot in life, that is indeed a gift from God. People who do this rarely look with sorrow on the past, for God has given them reasons for joy (Ecclesiastes 5:18-20, NLT).*

In the New Testament, we see that God's Word is the same yesterday, today, and tomorrow. The apostle John writes the following in a letter to Gaius.

> *Beloved, I pray that you may prosper in every way and (that your body) may keep well, even as (I know) your soul keeps well and prospers* (3 John 2, Amp.).

I submit to you that in the apostle John's statement, *"I pray that you may prosper in every way,"* he is writing about financial and material prosperity. His statement that reads *"and that your body may keep well,"* he is referring to Gaius's physical prosperity. Spiritual prosperity kicks in when the apostle writes *"even as (I know) your soul keeps well and prospers."*

Again we see embedded in the Word of God, an unwavering pattern of God's plan and purpose to bless you with wealth and riches and good health. Notice that the apostle John knew in his own spirit that Gaius's soul was keeping well and prospering (spiritual prosperity). But the apostle says that, *"I pray that you may prosper in every way* (material and financial prosperity) *and that your body may keep well"* (physical prosperity). There are three things that the apostle John is focusing on in this revelation knowledge Scripture, all of which we have been redeemed from: Believers have been redeemed from poverty, sickness and spiritual death (Galatians 3:13-14, 29).

Like Gaius, we get the salvation and spiritual prosperity right, but it's the poverty and sickness areas that present the greatest challenges.

Let's look at it this way, the Word of God says that we have been redeemed from the curse of the law; poverty, sickness and spiritual death were part of the curse outlined in the law (Deuteronomy 28:15-22, 27-29, 35, 58-60).

Since we are redeemed "from" poverty and sickness, through Jesus Christ's death and resurrection, He would have had to redeem us "to" wealth and riches. Also, to good health, which has been God's plan and purpose for His covenant children from the beginning.

This next Scripture should seal forevermore God's Word in your spirit concerning His plan and purpose for you to be abundantly prosperous financially. The apostle Paul writes the following revelation knowledge for you today...

> *You know how full of love and kindness our Lord Jesus Christ was. Though he was very rich, yet for your sakes he became poor,* ***so that by his poverty he could make you rich.*** 2 Corinthians 8:9, NLT

Now, I am aware that some of the anti-prosperity folks will try to make this Scripture out to be referring to spiritual prosperity, but if they would just take the time to read all of 2 Corinthians, chapter 8, they will find that the whole chapter is about money and giving, and nothing is mentioned about spiritual prosperity.

Let's dissect this New Testament revelation Scripture a little closer. Question, do you think that Jesus Christ of Nazareth became poor spiritually? The verse says, *"Though he was very rich, yet for your sakes he became poor."*

I don't believe anyone could honestly say that Jesus was poor spiritually.

Question: How many spiritually-poor people do you see walking around without sin, healing the sick, casting out demons, raising the dead, and setting people free from all kinds of satanic bondage? My answer to this question is, NONE! Jesus definitely didn't become poor spiritually, but He became poor by leaving the abundant wealth of heaven.

The Great Wealth In Heaven

Let's take a mental and spiritual tour of heaven...

> *The angel who talked to me held in his hand a gold measuring stick to measure the city, its gates and its wall. When he measured it, he found it was a square, as wide as it was long. In fact, it was in the form of a cube, for its length and width and height were each 1,400 miles. Then he measured the walls and found them to be 216 feet thick (the angel used a standard human measure).*
> *The wall was made of jasper, and the city was pure gold, as clear as glass. The wall of the city was built on foundation stones inlaid with twelve gems; the first was jasper, the second sapphire, the third agate, the fourth emerald, the fifth onyx, the sixth carnelian, the seventh chrysolite, the eight beryl, the ninth topaz, the tenth chrysoprase, the eleventh jacinth, the twelfth amethyst. The twelve gates were made of pearls, each gate from*

*a single pearl. And the main street was pure gold as clear as glass (*Revelation 21:15-21, NLT).

The Bible says that the main street in heaven was pure gold; not gold plated, but pure gold. The entire city, which measured 1,400 miles long, 1,400 miles wide, and 1,400 miles high was solid gold. I am not aware of any place on earth that has that kind of wealth and riches.

Clearly, we can see that Jesus Christ of Nazareth left behind great wealth and riches when He came to the earth. And as He walked the rough and dusty roads of Palestine, it was no comparison to the streets of gold in heaven.

This clearly substantiates the Bible when it says, "*Though He was very rich, yet for your sakes He became poor, so that by His poverty He could make you rich.*" Praise the Lord!

Jesus Christ Of Nazareth Bore Your Poverty — Redeemed You From Poverty To Wealth, Riches And Good Health

Your covenant inheritance of wealth, riches and good health already belongs to you. It resides temporarily in the spirit realm. The way to receive it is by reading (aloud) daily the faith-building confessions which are prescribed in this book.

Jesus Christ of Nazareth redeemed you from spiritual death, which was one-third of your redemption. As people of faith, we hear much about our redemption from spiritual death through the shed blood of Jesus. Now, don't get me wrong, redemption from spiritual death is the most important thing because without it, one will never see the Kingdom of God. And I eagerly look forward to seeing Jesus Christ and visiting with relatives and friends who have gone on to live eternally in heaven.

One-Third Of Your Redemption

Spiritual death is the one-third of your redemption that has to do with what happens to you when you leave this earth realm and move to your new address in the heavenly city.

The Last Two-Thirds Of Your Redemption

Two-thirds of your redemption has to do with the kind of lifestyle that you are living while you are still here on planet earth. In other words, it has to do with the quality of your life. Think about this: At the same time that Jesus Christ of Nazareth redeemed you from spiritual death, He also shed His precious blood to redeem you from poverty and sickness. The Good News is, you received a threefold redemption. He redeemed us from the threefold curse of the law, which is spiritual death, poverty and sickness. A clear understanding and revelation of the latter two-thirds of your redemption will set you free from a poverty mentality, poverty confession and a broke, busted, and disgusted syndrome; and your confession about sickness will change.

Think about this, do you believe that God redeemed you from spiritual death to put you back to spiritual death? Do you think that He shed His precious blood for your redemption from sickness to put sickness back on you? Do you think that Jesus Christ of Nazareth suffered, died, and rose again for your redemption from poverty, to put you back into poverty? Would you want to put your son or daughter in poverty? Well, the obvious answers to those questions are No, No, No, and No!

The apostle Paul informs us that as born-again believers, we have been redeemed from the curse of the law. The key words in this discussion are "redeemed from." If you are redeemed from something, then you must be redeemed to something. The opposite of "from poverty" is "to wealth and riches," and the opposite of "from sickness" is "to good health." Praise the Lord!

> *Christ has redeemed us from the curse of the law, having become a curse for us (for it is written "cursed is everyone who hangs on a tree")* (Galatians 3:13, NKJV).

God's Word doesn't say "We are going to be redeemed," No! It says we are already redeemed. If a Savior leaves you where and as you are, from what has He saved you?

The Bible says,

> *Always remember that it is the Lord your God who gives you power to become rich, and he does it to fulfill the covenant he made with your ancestors* (Deuteronomy 8:18).

God wants you to be rich so that He fulfills His covenant (promises) to Abraham made a long time ago when He said:

> *All nations will be blessed through you. And so it is, all who put their faith in Christ share the same blessings that Abraham received because of his faith* (Galatians 3:8-9).

Unquestionably, God wants you to be rich, wealthy and healthy. My sincere desire is that the unveiling of these inspired words of God has served to illuminate and seal these truths in your spirit forever. Remember, it is God's plan and purpose to bless you with wealth and riches and make you a blessing to others.

Now that we are fully basking and rejoicing in the enlightened Word of God, let's pause for a humor break!

What kind of a giver are you? Are you like a cow or a pig?
One day the farmer observed a serious discussion between the cow and the pig. It seems that the pig was upset because the cow got all the praise and attention.
The pig said, "Everyone praises you because you give milk every day; they make butter from your milk, and they rave about the other things, the other products they get from your milk."
The pig continued on by saying, "I give bacon, ham, pork chops, and they even pickle my feet and ears; they barbecue my ribs, and I still don't get any respect."
The cow replied, "Well, Mr. Pig, the big difference is I give while I am alive, you only give after you are dead!"

Remember, God wants you to be rich; therefore He fulfills His inspired Word throughout the Bible, blessing you so that you can be a blessing to others.

CHAPTER 2

WHY IS 90% OF THE BODY OF CHRIST BROKE IN THIS GREAT LAND OF OPPORTUNITY?

PART 1

We live in a golden age in America and this New Millennium finds us in the richest land ever on the face of the earth. Aland of abundant opportunities for those who are determined to succeed in life, in business, the arts, medicine, education, investment, religion, industry, or whatever you choose to do. Indeed, if you have a burning desire to succeed, you can become successful in this great country.

We witness boatloads of people risking (losing) their lives to cross our shores and truckloads of people attempting to cross our borders to enter this great land of freedom and opportunity.

Recently, the American Broadcasting Company (ABC) aired a special program titled, *Is America Number One?* with John Stossel as host. This program clearly highlighted the vast advances in technology, medicine, and other fields, and the ease of pursuing entrepreneurship in America, compared to other countries around the globe. This program featured individuals from other countries who had ideas for business and a burning desire to succeed; but because of bureaucracy and red tape in their country, they couldn't get to first base.

These individuals had to leave their countries and come to America, the land of opportunity. They set up businesses and became successful entrepreneurs in this great land of opportunity for all. Mr. Dinesh D'Souza with the American Enterprise Institute said the following during a segment of this ABC special. "The secret is now out; people know if you want to be the pilot of your own life, if you want to make your destiny, there is only one place to do it, and that is in America."

At the close of the twentieth century, we witnessed a booming and robust economy in America; the stock markets soared, breaking records, especially those stocks in high tech and internet ventures. We witnessed many, many entrepreneurs becoming millionaires, and some billionaires, overnight when their companies went public with stock offerings, stock splits, and buyouts.

When the sun set on the twentieth century, it could be truly said that America is Number One. It is the land of opportunity for all who dare to get busy and put their hands to the plow.

Real Facts About People And Their Income

Let's take a brief look at 100 men who start out even, at the age of 25. Do you have any idea what will happen to these men by the time they are 65?

Each one of these 100 men who started out even, had high goals and expectations to be successful in life. But something caused their dreams to be shattered by the time they reached 65 years old. According to the Social Security Administration, Office of Research and Statistics Reports, issue date of January 1996:

...by age 65, 16 of the men will have died.
...66 of the men will have an annual income under $30,000.
...13 of the men will have incomes greater than $30,000.
...And only 5 will have annual incomes over $60,000.

Source: Social Security Administration, Office of Research and Statistics, January 1996 – Income of the Population 55 or Older, 1994 U.S. Bureau of the Census, April 1996

What we can deduce from the above statistics is:

...Only 1 of the 100 men will be rich at age 65.
...4 of the 100 men will be financially independent at age 65.
...5 of the 100 men will still be working at age 65.
...8 of the 100 men will be barely getting by with not enough income to really enjoy their leisure days.
...66 of the 100 men will end up broke, busted, and disgusted at age 65.
...13.8% of them will live below the poverty threshold which is $15,569 for a family of four.

Source: U.S. Census Bureau, 1995 Report.

Of all people age 25 today, 16% will not live to the age 65. For those who do, inflation will change the amounts required for a comfortable retirement income. Very few people are fortunate enough to reach retirement and have enough income to enjoy their leisure days, or even comfortably afford necessities. There are plenty of reasons why people don't plan, but these are the results of procrastination, poor planning, no follow-through, and especially a lack of knowledge. Imagine the pain of reaching your golden years only to find yourself partially or fully financially dependent on others.

A Major Problem Is A Lack Of Knowledge

Indeed, these failing results of people being financially broke at age 65 show the inevitable results of not planning for retirement. With some, the problem may be the inability to save on a systematic basis; with others, it is often a case of good intentions and poor follow-through. With many, it is the poor selection of savings and investment products. However, I firmly believe that the overwhelming reason why people don't prosper financially is due to a lack of knowledge. A person will never develop, grow, progress, succeed, or rise beyond his or her level of knowledge.

Christians: Income And Financial Prosperity

The Body of Christ would receive an F on their report card if they were graded today on their income and financial prosperity.

> ...We do know that a survey conducted by the T.D. Jakes Ministries revealed that 51% of Christian marriages end in divorce, and this figure mirrors or surpasses that of heathen marriages. We do know that in the general public, money woes (financial problems) are the leading cause of separations and divorces.
>
> As it was stated before, we do know that nearly 80% of divorced couples between the ages of 20 and 30 state that financial problems were the primary cause of divorce.
>
> ...We do know that approximately 50% of all first marriages fail and finances are listed as the leading cause of divorce by a factor of 4 to 1.
>
> ...We do know that another 80% divorce again within three years of remarrying because of debt.
>
> Resource: *Things You Didn't Know*. Pamphlet by John Avanzini.

We can clearly see that the by-product of believers and non-believers being broke adversely affects the family and destroys God's plan and purpose for mankind.

> ...We do know that a special issue of Forbes Magazine listed America's 400 Richest People of 1999. Only one lone believer was obvious among the group, and that was Thomas Monaghan, founder of Domino's Pizza. His net worth was listed at $950 million. (The front runner was William (Bill) Gates, III, the world's richest man and computer software icon, founder and chairman of Microsoft. Bill's net worth was listed at $85 billion and growing).

The Bible says, *"Meditate upon these things; give thyself wholly to them, that thy profiting may appear to all"* (1 Timothy 4:15, KJV). The Bible tells us that *"Godliness is profitable"* (1 Timothy 4:8). If your profiting is to appear to all, then it is to show.

> ...We do know that most Christian ministries, including local churches, list finances as one of the leading problem areas confronting their members and their communities.

...We do know that in his book, *Breaking Financial Barriers,* Dennis Burke writes: "One of the barriers the enemy erects is in the area of finances. We receive prayer requests from all over the world, and one of the most frequent requests we receive is in the area of finances. Financial pressure is one of the major causes of strain in marriage, distress in families and frustration in many of God's people. God's Word instructs believers on how to overcome pressure and break down the barriers of lack."

....We do know that Dr. Ed Dufresne, an anointed minister of God, spoke at the ten-year anniversary conference at Seedtime and Harvest Church in San Diego, California (my home church) on September 16, 1999, and he said "90% of the Body of Christ is broke." He also prophesied that an earthquake would hit Southern California soon, but no one would be injured or killed. Exactly thirty days later a 7.1 magnitude earthquake hit Southern California. The earthquake occurred at 2:46 AM local time on October 16, 1999. The earthquake was located in a remote, sparsely populated part of the Mojave desert, approximately 47 miles east-southeast of Barstow and 32 miles north of Joshua Tree.

If an earthquake of this magnitude had occurred in an urban area, such as Los Angeles or San Diego, the destruction and loss of lives could have been catastrophic. This earthquake has been dubbed"The Hector Mine Earthquake." Dr. Dufresne prophesied on September 16, 1999 that no one would be injured or killed in the coming earthquake. Can you guess what actually happened? The reports from the Hector Mine Earthquake were that nobody was injured, killed, and little damage was reported. Praise the Lord!

...We do know that Dr. Dufresne dropped a bombshell when he revealed at this conference that while he was in Peru, God spoke to him saying that "90% of the Body of Christ is broke." God also told him that His will is that we "cast all our cares upon Him, for He cares for us." 1 Peter 5:7

I unequivocally choose to believe Dr. Dufresne 100% and with 35 years in the ministry, I believe that his word is more reliable than secular polls, ABC, CBS, NBC or CNN. When Dr. Dufresne gets a word from God, you can take it to the bank, because it will be timely and beneficial to the hearer.

90% Of The Body Of Christ Is Broke – This Must Be Reversed Now!

Indeed, I should be writing that 90% of the Body of Christ is rich and wealthy and 10% is broke. It would have to be utterly embarrassing for a wealthy biological father to see his children living from paycheck to paycheck, pension check to pension check, and social security check to social security check. It would have to grieve the father, knowing that he had set aside enough money to meet all their needs and desires, but for some reason, his children decided to ignore it and do things on their own.

Our Heavenly Father, Who cares much more for us than our biological father could ever care, must be terribly grieved that 90% of His children are broke. Especially since, through the death and resurrection of His Son, Jesus Christ of Nazareth, God has provided His children with an inheritance of wealth and riches (Galatians 3:29).

The believer's inheritance is much, much better than any in the natural.

Upon Jesus' death and resurrection, your covenant inheritance of wealth and riches was activated. Jesus is now seated in the heavens waiting on you to activate your faith, so that He can officially transfer your inheritance of wealth and riches from your heavenly bank account to you. Praise the Lord!

The Body of Christ must reverse the ugly 90% trend of being broke, and become the 90% group with wealth and riches, early in this New Millennium.

God is our source and He is our resource. In other words, He is our point of origin. He told His prophet Dr. Ed Dufresne, that His will is that we cast all our cares upon Him for He cares for us. What this means is, the ball is in our court. As long as we carry poverty mentality, poverty living, poverty thinking, and poverty confessions on our own shoulders, we actually handcuff God. You must throw your hook into the water before you can expect to catch a fish. Likewise, you must cast your cares (financial woes, broke, busted, and disgusted) upon Him, for He cares for us.

The Bible says...

> *You parents, If your children ask for a loaf of bread, do you give them a stone instead? Or if they ask for a fish, do you give them a* snake? *Of course not! If you sinful people know how to give good gifts to your children, how much more will your Heavenly Father give good gifts to those who ask Him.* Matthew 7:9-10, NLT

The Bible also tells us...

> *Always remember that it is the Lord your God who gives you power to become rich...* (Deuteronomy 8:18, NLT).

God further reveals His instructions and His bona fide promises to us...

> *Keep on asking, and you will be given what you ask for. Keep on looking, and you will find. Keep on knocking, and the door will*

> *be opened. For everyone who asks, receives. Everyone who seeks, finds. And the door is opened to everyone who knocks.*
> Matthew 7-8, NLT

The apostle Paul sets the record straight concerning God's plan and purpose for believers. He writes:

> *You know how full of love and kindness our Lord Jesus Christ was. Though he was very rich, yet for your sakes he became poor,* ***so that by his poverty he could make you rich.***
> 2 Corinthians 8:9, NLT

Clearly, we can see that it is God's will and His plan and purpose for His children to live above the circumstances, have good gifts, and possess riches in this life.

At this point, I must ask four candid questions.

1. How can you consistently and substantially support God's storehouse (the local church) if you are broke and living from paycheck to paycheck, in bondage to monthly payments?
2. How can you leave an inheritance of house and riches to your children if you are broke?
3. How can you leave an inheritance to your children's children if you are broke?
4. How can you help feed, clothe, and meet the needs of the poor and needy if you are broke?

Well, I know that you figured out the answers to these questions, but what you may not know is that God's will and His plan and purpose is for you to do the things mentioned above. *Self-Talk And Grow Rich*'s objective is to point you in the direction whereby you can fully operate in God's plan and purpose for your life and, at the same time, have God meet all your needs and all your desires in life.

Now, let's go back to our main topic which asked the question, "Why is 90% of the Body of Christ broke in this great land of opportunity?"

I'm fully aware that some people are plain lazy and they have no ambition, no desire, and no destiny in life. Others are lackadaisical procrastinators who are forever putting things off until a later date, which never seems to come. But my experience with people and my research and study of human behavior has convinced me that most people want to prosper in every area of their lives. They want to have a balanced life; they want to do right by their children and their children's children. They want to help support God's storehouse (the local church), and they sincerely want to help the poor and needy in their church, community and elsewhere. But they are unable to do these things since they are barely getting by, paycheck to paycheck, broke, and living on the corner of Busted and Disgusted Avenue.

I expressed my view early that the major reason why people wander in the wilderness of financial bondage for a lifetime is because of a lack of knowledge.

God told His prophet Hosea, *"My people are destroyed for lack of knowledge"* (Hosea 4:6).

Observe closely with me, what God didn't say. He didn't say that "My people are destroyed because they are disobedient;" He didn't say that "My people are destroyed because 90% of them are broke." No! He said, "My people are destroyed for lack of knowledge."

PART 2

LACK OF KNOWLEDGE IN NATURAL THINGS CAN BE DETRIMENTAL AND DESTRUCTIVE

The following letter appeared on the internet. It is from the New York State Comptroller Office.

> Message from State Comptroller, H. Carl McCall
> Dear Friend,
>
> The State of New York is currently holding billions of dollars in unclaimed funds. Some of this money may belong to you!
>
> For your protection, banks, insurance companies, utilities, investment companies and many other businesses are required by State law to surrender inactive accounts to the State.
>
> As State Comptroller, I serve as custodian of this money until you claim it. The State of New York never takes ownership of this money. If you can prove you are entitled to the money, I will gladly return it to you, at any time, without charge.
>
> This homepage will tell you how to avoid having your money turned over to the State and how to get it back if it is abandoned.
>
> **It's your money – don't leave it unclaimed!**
>
> Sincerely,
> H. Carl McCall
> New York State Comptroller

This letter that Comptroller McCall has written, highlights the classic example of people who have not claimed billions of dollars due mainly to lack of knowledge.

Unclaimed Property/Funds

Eighty million Americans are owed a share of $300 billion (and they don't even know it) in uncashed checks and non-refunded deposits, forgotten bank accounts and safe deposit boxes, abandoned stocks and bonds, unpaid insurance and retirement benefits, and a host of other financial assets.

Assets become abandoned in the eyes of the law after the owner (or rightful heir) fails to make a deposit or withdrawal on a bank account; forgets to apply for a benefit, insurance policy payout, credit or refund due; or when institutions hold uncashed checks, money orders, or gift certificates after a statement is returned as undeliverable by the post office. Those left holding the assets: banks, insurance companies, employers, unions, brokerages, and utilities; even landlords, retail stores and restaurants are required to turn them over to the "protective custody" of the government in a process called "escheat." Here they await your claim!

Think it couldn't possibly be you? Think again!

Did you forget about an old bank account, unredeemed savings bond or gift certificate, uncashed check, nonrefunded deposit, or unused benefit? Were records lost due to theft, fire or flood? Maybe you never even knew you were named an heir or beneficiary in a relative or friend's will or life insurance policy, or that you were entitled to a settlement from a class action lawsuit!

If you've moved, changed your name after marriage or divorce, or switched jobs over the years, it can be difficult to find you. Often, being declared missing results simply from computer or clerical errors, or the expiration of a post office forwarding order!

Money that belongs to you might be sitting in a state property office just waiting for you to claim it. Every state has a department that oversees unclaimed property/funds within the comptroller's office.

Let's read what the State of California Comptroller's Office has to say about unclaimed property:

> **Unclaimed Property Program Description**
>
> You may be one of the millions of Californians owed money by the State!
>
> The State of California is currently holding more than \$2.6 billion in Unclaimed Property value, belonging to approximately 5.2 million individuals and organizations. This property is mostly money left inactive or dormant by the owner for more than three years.

This is what the State of Florida has to say about its unclaimed property program:

> Currently, the Comptroller's Office holds more than \$500 million in unclaimed property, mostly from dormant accounts in financial institutions, insurance and utility companies, safe deposit boxes and trust holdings. In addition to money and

securities, the state's holdings include tangible property such as watches, jewelry, coins, currency, stamps, historical items and other miscellaneous articles. Unclaimed money is deposited into a state school fund, and is used exclusively for public education. There is, however, no statute of limitations. Citizens have the right to claim property, at no cost to them, at any time, regardless of the amount.

New York is holding $4.2 billion for over 15 million citizens. Add $2.6 billion from California and consider that Florida, Massachusetts, and Texas contribute $2 billion more...Well, pretty soon it starts to add up to real money!

But this isn't just a big state phenomenon. It's happening everywhere. Tiny Rhode Island owes 60,000 residents $60 million! And many accounts involve sizeable sums. Recently, a Louisiana citizen received a check for $1,026,738 and one lucky Texas resident collected $4,251,987.

A conservative estimate is $300 billion waiting to be reclaimed by 80 million owners. The total is growing by more than $8 million per day nearly $3 billion per year – thanks to recent changes in the law. But that's just what states are holding!

What About Federal Agencies?

No one knows exactly how many hundreds of billions of dollars federal agencies are safeguarding, but a government report said that return of the money owed would negatively affect the deficit.

Government agencies holding funds have a strong incentive not to contact owners or heirs – they get to spend the cash that goes unclaimed. There are time limits on many types of claims, despite what you may have heard. There is no national database of unclaimed funds. Legal notices in newspapers and missing owner databases online contain only a small fraction of accounts actually available for claim.

Assets may be held just about anywhere, regardless of where you now live. Federally generated assets (unredeemed savings bonds, uncashed IRS refunds, unpaid Social Security and VA benefits, etc.) are not included in state databases. Foreign nationals may need to follow special procedures to locate and claim lost assets.

Indeed you can see that it is very possible to have hundreds, thousands, and even millions of dollars and not even know it (due to a lack of knowledge).

The sad part is that many of those 80 million people who are owed money are living in poverty, or living from paycheck to paycheck, barely getting by.

You can find out if you have unclaimed property/funds on the internet. Most state comptrollers' offices have a web page that has a link for unclaimed property. You can access these web pages by initiating an "unclaimed property" search on the internet.

The following are some tips on how to keep property from becoming unclaimed!

- Keep an accurate record of all financial matters
- Notify all banks and companies of a new address when moving
- At least once a year, make a deposit or withdrawal on all bank accounts
- Promptly cash all checks received
- Contact the company immediately if stock dividends are no longer received
- Inform a family member, attorney, or trusted friend, of the whereabouts of all financial records

I'm profoundly impressed with seven words that New York State Comptroller H. Carl McCall made in the letter shared earlier. He said, **"It's your money – don't leave it unclaimed."**

Unclaimed funds and property are a clear cut example of how a lack of knowledge in natural things can be detrimental. You can be certain that many of the eighty million Americans who are owed money are living in poverty, but due to a lack of knowledge, their money or property will go unclaimed.

I ask you to keep Comptroller McCall's words in your mind, because they will loom big in our next discussion about lack of knowledge in spiritual things can be detrimental and destructive.

PART 3

LACK OF KNOWLEDGE IN SPIRITUAL THINGS CAN BE DETRIMENTAL AND DESTRUCTIVE

God told His prophet Hosea, *"My people are destroyed for a lack of knowledge"* (Hosea 4:6). Notice very closely that God didn't say that the ungodly are destroyed for a lack of knowledge. No! He said, "My people (godly people) are destroyed for a lack of knowledge." One translation says, *"My people are being destroyed because they don't know Me"* (Hosea 4:6, NLT). This verse could be paraphrased thusly, "My people are destroyed because they don't know Me, they don't know My ways, they don't know My Word, and they don't know My instructions for them."

As it was pointed out in the previous section, a lack of knowledge in natural things can cause people to live in bondage in many areas of their lives. And a lack of knowledge can be detrimental to one's progress and it can result in death. We see this all the time in the judicial system. A lack of knowledge of existing laws on the part of an attorney can result in a defendant being sentenced to a long stay in prison or even sentenced to the electric chair or lethal injection. This can occur even in cases where the person is innocent. However, many of these cases are overturned on appeals. Likewise, a lack of revelation knowledge in spiritual things can result in godly people living in bondage in many areas of their lives, and it can most certainly be detrimental to one's spiritual growth and development. It can also result in physical death.

When God's people are ignorant of the Word of God and the principles that are contained in it, then they are going to experience destruction. In addition, if God's people do not have the wisdom to live life according to God's Word, they will go under.

Now let's look at a classic example of two believers who died because they didn't know the Word of God.

This Narrative Is The Ananias And Sapphira Story

> *There was also a man named Ananias who with his wife, Sapphira sold some property. He brought part of the money to the apostles, but he claimed it was the full amount. His wife had agreed to this deception.*
>
> *Then Peter said, "Ananias, why has Satan filled your heart? You lied to the Holy Spirit, and you kept some of the money for yourself. The property was yours to sell or not sell, as you wished. And after selling it, the money was yours to give away. How could you do a thing like this. You weren't lying to us, but to God."*
>
> *As soon as Ananias heard these words, he fell to the floor and died. Everyone who heard about it was terrified. Then some young men wrapped him in a sheet and took him out and buried him.*
>
> *About three hours later, his wife came in, not knowing what had happened. Peter asked her, "Was this the price you and your husband received for your land?" "Yes," she replied, "that was the price."*
>
> *And Peter said, "How could the two of you even think of doing a thing like this – conspiring together to test the Spirit of the Lord? Just outside that door are the young men who buried your husband, and they will carry you out, too."*
>
> *Instantly, she fell to the floor and died. When the young men came in, and saw that she was dead, they carried her out and buried her beside her husband. Great fear gripped the entire church and all others who heard what had happened* (Acts 5:1-11, NLT).

I have no choice but to believe that Ananias and Sapphira didn't know what the Word of God had to say about lying. This resulted in their operating in a lack of knowledge which caused them to expire.

God's Word has the following things to say about lying...

There are six things the Lord hates – no, seven things he detests:

> *Haughty eyes,* ***a lying tongue****, hands that kill the innocent, a heart that plots evil, feet that race to do wrong,* ***a false witness who pours out lies****, Aperson who sows discord among brothers. Proverbs 6:16-19, NLT*
>
> *Even strong young lions sometimes go hungry, but those who trust in the Lord will never lack any good thing. Come my children and listen to me, and I will teach you to fear the Lord. Do any of you want to live a life that is long and good?* ***Then watch your tongue. Keep your lips from telling lies!*** *(Psalm 34:10-13, NLT).*
>
> *The Lord hates those who don't keep their word, but he delights in those who do (Proverbs 12:22, NLT).*
>
> *So when you make a promise to God, don't delay in following through, for God takes no pleasure in fools. Keep all the promises you make to him. It is better to say nothing than to promise something that you don't follow through on. In such cases,* ***your mouth is making you sin****. And don't defend yourself by telling the Temple messenger that the promise you made was a mistake. That would make God angry, and he might wipe out everything you have achieved (Ecclesiastes 5:4-6, NLT).*
>
> *A false witness will not go unpunished, and a liar will be* ***destroyed*** *(Proverbs 19:9, NLT).*

I wish I could have shared these Scriptures with Ananias and Sapphira before they told Peter the lie. I am sure their outcome would have been different.

When there is no knowledge of God's Word or His principles in a society, there is social chaos and destruction. In our day, there is a real lack of knowledge of God in most countries around the world. The result is violence, crime, corruption, and evil in the land.

A favorite quote of mine is "You will never rise above the level of your knowledge." In other words, if you don't know that something valuable or beneficial is available to you, you won't be moved to receive it.

Covenant Inheritance Of Wealth And Riches Left Unclaimed

I firmly believe that a lack of knowledge concerning God's promises is the main reason why 90% of believers are broke.

Let's read some of God's Word and His promises.

> *There is no longer Jew or Gentile, slave or free, male or female. For you are all Christians – you are one in Christ Jesus. And now that you belong to Christ, you are the true children of Abraham.* ***You are his heirs, and now all the promises God gave to him belong to you*** *(Galatians 3:28-29, NLT).*

The word "heirs" in the above Scripture means one who inherits or is entitled to inherit a gift by will, especially of money or personal property. The apostle Paul continues by informing us of the blessing we have in Jesus Christ of Nazareth.

> *What's more, the Scriptures looked forward to this time when God would accept the Gentiles, too, on the basis of their faith. God promised this good news to Abraham long ago when he said, "All nations will be blessed through you." And so it is.* ***All who put their faith in Christ share the same blessing Abraham received because of his faith*** (Galatians 3:8-9, NLT).

The central question that leaps from the above Scripture is "how was Abraham blessed?" If we find the answer to this question, we then know how we are blessed by God, and what we are heirs to.

The answer is found in the book of Genesis,

> *I am Abraham's servant, he explained.* ***"And the Lord has blessed my master richly; he has become a great man. The Lord has given him flocks of sheep and herds of cattle, a fortune in silver and gold, and many servants and camels and donkeys."*** Genesis 24:34-35, NLT.

<u>There it is</u>! It's the answer to what the blessings are that belong to you now because you put your faith in Jesus Christ of Nazareth. It's your covenant inheritance. Bible scholars say that by today's money standards, Abraham was a billionaire. I believe that we can safely say that your heavenly bank account has a fortune in silver and gold in it, more than enough to make you wealthy and rich.

What Triggered Your Covenant Inheritance Of Wealth And Riches?

God promised Abraham long ago that all nations would be blessed through him and so it is. All who put their faith in Christ share the same blessing Abraham received because of his faith (Galatians 3:8-9, NLT).

Jesus Christ of Nazareth triggered the fulfillment of God's promise. His death and resurrection consummated and probated your covenant inheritance of wealth, riches, good health, and eternal life.

The Holy Spirit inspired the apostle Paul to reveal to you that you are rich now (in the sight of God).

> *You know how full of love and kindness our Lord Jesus Christ was. Though he was very rich, yet for your sakes he became poor, so that by his poverty he could make you rich.* 2 Corinthians 8:9, NLT

Jesus Christ of Nazareth is now seated in heaven on the right side of God the Father. He is waiting on you to use your self-talk (faith-building) confessions to receive your covenant inheritance of wealth and riches. Your strong faith pleases God and Jesus Christ, Who officially probated your inheritance to your heavenly bank account, **making it available to you based on your faith**. Praise the Lord!

In the previous section, we read a letter from New York's Comptroller, H. Carl McCall, concerning unclaimed property/funds in the State of New York. I'm reminded of the last seven words in his letter. He wrote, "It's your money. Don't leave it unclaimed."

I believe that Jesus Christ of Nazareth is saying to you, "**It's your covenant inheritance of wealth, riches, and good health; don't leave it unclaimed**."

He who expects nothing will never be disappointed.

God's hands are tied, He cannot provide you the promises until you know them, confess them, and believe them.

CHAPTER 3

YOUR WORDS HAVE AWESOME POWER – THEY CAN CREATE AND THEY CAN DESTROY

PART 1

Words are the most powerful things in the universe. Words make us or break us. Words heal us or make us sick. Words destroy us or make us full of life. They can make us happy, healthy, joyous, rich and wealthy.

What we spoke yesterday or yesteryear makes life what it is today. Words are containers that deliver life or death, riches or poverty.

Words can be likened to a precision-guided cruise missile, ejected and aimed to kill, steal, and destroy the listener. Words can be likened to an American Red Cross helicopter, fully loaded with food, medicine, clothing, and caretakers delivering goods and services to provide life, and life more abundantly.

Untold numbers of people have been whipped and defeated in life financially, spiritually, physically, mentally, domestically, and socially, all because they believed and self-talked the wrong things. They either knowingly or unknowingly, allowed their own words to hold them in poverty, or bondage, or in sickness and disease. The bottom line is, they allowed their words to rob them of a productive and victorious life.

Think And Self-Talk The Solution And Not The Problem

Unfortunately, most people's self-talk and their speech to others focuses on the problem and not the solution. They are what I call problem-minded people. Beware that problem-minded self-talk is a vicious enemy to your personal growth and development and to a prosperous life.

You have probably been around individuals who consistently dwell on the problems of life and never offer any viable answers or solutions. In most cases, these problem-minded individuals generally have a stinking thinking, negative attitude about life in general. The reason this is so, is because they are reaping what they sow. As they self-talk the problem, they will also reap that same problem and all its negative attributes in their everyday conscious life.

Spiritual Law Of Sowing And Reaping

This law says:

> *...For whatever a man sows, that and that only is what he will reap (*Galatians 6:7, Amp.).

This law is plain and simple, if you speak negatively, you are unconditionally guaranteed to reap the same in reality.

I was born in Marietta, GA, and my Uncle Strick, who was a master farmer, lived about 25 miles away in Smyrna, GA. At that time, Smyrna was largely a farming area, but now it is a thriving suburb of Atlanta. I can remember visiting with my uncle, my Aunt Mattie, and my cousin Claude, each summer. Boy, how my brother and I looked forward to those visits. I was around eight or nine years old and my brother William was three years younger than I. Claude was my age. One of our daily chores was to go out to the garden and bring back things that my aunt had told us to get for dinner. I can remember how neat all the rows in the garden were and how large the vegetables grew. Row after row of huge cabbages, tomatoes, watermelons, corn, squash, beets, etc. I definitely remember the mouth-watering meals my aunt would prepare from scratch in a very short time, nothing frozen, nothing pre-cooked. She would kill the chicken, boil the water, scald the chicken, pull the feathers off, cut the chicken up, fry it, and cook the vegetables and bread all within about 45 minutes.

My uncle raised most of the food we ate, the pigs, cows, chickens and all the vegetables. The food we ate was fresh, untreated, unprocessed, and simply scrumptious down to the last crumb.

My Uncle Strick planted (sowed) his best corn seeds in the ground in the spring, and in mid-summer when he walked out to the garden area where he had planted the corn, he wouldn't find tomatoes or potatoes growing instead of corn. No! When corn is planted, it produces after its own kind. It produces corn. When a tomato seed is planted, it produces after its own kind. So it is with your thoughts, your self-talk, and your speech to others, it reproduces after its own kind. By the way, my uncle's name was Will Strickland, so we called him, Uncle Strick. I got my passion for gardening from him.

Spiritual Law Governing Reproduction

Let us see and read what the Creator Himself has to say concerning His law.

> *And God said, "Let the earth put forth (tender) vegetation; plants yielding seed and fruit trees yielding fruit whose seed is in itself, each according to its kind, upon the earth." And it*

> *was so. The earth brought forth vegetation: plants yielding seed according to their own kinds and trees bearing fruit in which was their seed. Each according to its kind. And God saw that it was good (suitable, admirable) and He approved it. And God said, "Let the earth bring forth living creatures according to their own kinds; livestock, creeping things, and (wild) beasts of the earth according to their kinds." And it was so. And God made the (wild) beasts of the earth according to their kinds, and domestic animals according to their kinds, and everything that creeps upon the earth according to its kind. And God saw that it was good (fitting, pleasant) and He approved it (*Genesis 1:11-12, 24-25, Amp.).

First, we see God using words to create things, and then we see the things producing according to their own kind. I will pause here for a brief sidebar.

Things written thus far have been on a serious note, and rightly so, kind of on the taking care of business side; but I thought we ought to get a chuckle in now and then, so here is that opportunity.

The question was asked, "Why did God create the water, the earth, plants, trees, day, night, sea monsters, animals, birds and everything else before he created man?"

The answer was, "He saved man for last because He wanted to fix it so that no man could try to take credit for what God had done!"

Words Can Affect Your Immune System And Your Body

The Holy Spirit inspired the writer James to tell you that if you never say the wrong thing, you're able to control your body and curb your entire nature. One of the meanings of the word "nature" is...the basic quality of something. Thus, the words that you speak can control the quality of your human spirit, your mental faculties, and your physical body.

These are the words of the writer, look and read this Scripture aloud. It contains powerful revelation knowledge that will help you better understand the power of words.

> *For we all often stumble and fall and offend in many things. And if anyone does not offend in speech (never says the wrong things), he is a fully developed character and a perfect man, able to control his whole body and to curb his entire nature.*
> James 3:2, Amp.

Medical science tells us that every cell in the body is renewed or changed every seven to eleven years. But, as we just read in the book of James, the words that you self-talk and speak to others are able to control your whole body and curb your entire nature. WOW!

Let's look at some other Scriptures that provide further insight into the power that words have on our health, our minds, and on our entire beings.

> *The wise in heart are called prudent, understanding, and knowing, and winsome speech increases learning (in both speaker and listener)* (Proverbs 16:21, Amp.).

This Scripture shows the effects of words on the soul of both the speaker and the listener.

The mind of the wise instructs his mouth, and adds learning and persuasiveness to his lips (Proverbs 16:23, Amp.). This Scripture reveals the impact words have on the mental faculties.

A gentle tongue (with its healing power) is a tree of life, but willful contrariness in it breaks down the spirit (Proverbs 15:4, Amp.). This Scripture amplifies how gentle words produce healing power for the physical body, but the opposite breaks down the spirit.

There are those who speak rashly, like the piercing of a sword, but the tongue of the wise brings healing (Proverbs 12:18, Amp.). This Scripture shows how words can bring healing to the human spirit, soul and physical body.

He who guards his mouth keeps his life, but he who opens wide his lips comes to ruin (Proverbs 13:3, Amp.). This Scripture unveils how words can impact longevity.

A (self-confident) fool's mouth is his ruin, and his lips are a snare to himself (Proverbs 18:7, Amp.). This Proverb uncovers how words can cause destruction and entrapment.

Death and life are in the power of the tongue, and they who indulge in it shall eat the fruit of it (for death or life) (Proverbs 18:21, Amp.). This Proverb shows the awesome power of words. They can cause death and they can cause life.

Kind words are like honey, sweet to the soul and healthy for the body (Proverbs 16:24, NLT). This Scripture is one of my favorites on this subject. It illuminated my awareness of the power of words on man's overall being. I have shared this Scripture with countless others in this manner: I would ask this question, "Did you know that when you speak kind words to someone you are transmitting sweet, pleasurable impulses to that person's (mind and) heart?"

Then I would ask, "Did you know the kind words you speak to others actually minister a more potent supernatural medicine than any doctor could prescribe?" The kind words you speak are more effective than antibiotics or any of man's other wonder drugs?

Lastly, I would ask, "Did you know that when you speak kind words to others, you are hearing what you said, and that you receive the same mental, spiritual, and physical benefits that the listener received?"

When I am finished with this discussion, I generally sense that the person or persons with whom I shared this, fully understand the power of words.

The wisdom revealed in these proverbs (inspired by God) are utterly awesome! They showcase the power that your words have, and how they can affect your entire life. These Scriptures are just a few that speak on this subject. There are many, many more throughout the book of Proverbs and throughout the Bible.

I exhort you to read aloud and study other Scriptures relative to the mouth; lips, tongue, speech and words, to further increase your knowledge and wisdom on this vital subject.

Real-Life Proof Of The Power Of Words On The Whole Body

One clear-cut example that bears these Scriptures true is a situation which I am sure you may have experienced.

If you have ever had someone say harsh, degrading, insulting, negative words to you, then you know that your heart beats faster, blood pressure rises, you may perspire, your facial expression changes (you get ugly), anger builds up, and your attitude and body language drastically change.

All this occurs because harsh, insulting words were spoken to you. The person did not physically touch you, they spoke words.

Think about this, the person who spoke the harsh words does not have to be face to face with you. The words could be said during a telephone conversation. It could have been something supposedly said by someone a month ago, and now it was being restated to you by a different person. It does not matter, your mental and physical demeanor will be the same as if it was spoken to you face to face. The power is in the words!

What Would A Replay Of Your Old Self-Talk Reveal?

What if a video or audio tape from your (mind and) heart memory file of your every thought, all of your self-talk, and your words spoken to others for the past 24 months was to be flashed on a drive-in movie screen located near your home. This showing would take place in four days for all your family, neighbors, friends, acquaintances, church friends, your minister or pastor or priest, and co-workers to see. Many individuals would probably want to leave town before the video or audio tape was shown or played.

We can and do hide our thoughts and self-talk from others, especially the bad things. In fact, most of our self-talk is done when we think no one else is around, kept in the closet. However, be forewarned that your thoughts and your self-talk done in secret is recorded in your (mind and) heart memory file.

There is an old saying that goes like this, "Things that are done in the dark will come to the light."

It is a wise decision to give serious attention to controlling your thoughts and self-talk, starting the first thing each morning until your head hits the pillow at night. It is a full-time job to effectively manage your thoughts and self-talk, but you will come to learn and enjoy the huge benefits of doing so.

Some Folks Let It All Hang Out

You have probably heard someone say, "I speak my mind." In other words, they say whatever their thoughts are, good or bad, positive or negative, productive or destructive, or whether it hurts or heals. There are great dangers in this raucous and reckless kind of mind-set. Especially when the thoughts and words spoken are negative in nature. It can and will adversely affect the individual, as well as those who heard the negative speech.

For those individuals who eagerly desire a life-changing experience in their finances (and in other areas of their life) as they move into this New Millennium, they must rid themselves of negative, life-defeating thoughts and self-talk. It is extra baggage that must be discarded to make room for new, bold self-talk (faith-building) confessions that are beneficial and profitable.

Negative Words From Kosovo

This story is a fallout from the conflicts arising from Kosovo and the Balkan.

There was a thirty-year-old Albanian activist named John in Kosovo, where ethnic cleansing was being violently forced upon his people. He was married and had two young children whom he loved dearly. He felt strongly that he had to take a stand against injustice, in hopes that it would pave the way for justice in the future for his people and his children. His wife was passive and felt that her husband should not speak out publicly against the Serbs. Often at his work place he had spoken out in opposition to the persecutions and genocide. This resulted in him being told that there was no longer work for him. After two or three weeks went by, tension started to build up in his home. This was fueled by the uncertainty of what the future would hold for his family without his job. There was also high tension in his community; people fearful for their lives, jobs, and homes.

One day the pot boiled over and a ferocious family quarrel erupted between John and his wife. For the first time during their six-year marriage, she cursed him with very bad words and blamed all of their woes on him for speaking out. This fight only compounded the pressures he was already going through and left him feeling down and out.

A few days later he was walking home after searching for a job, when four hooded men jumped him. He resisted, and they slugged him. Repeatedly, he tried to escape. Finally, they beat him to the ground and began to hit him violently. When he began to plead with them to stop, one of the attackers pulled his gun out and shot John three times, once in the chest and twice in the stomach. The attackers left a note that identified them as a right wing group in favor of the government's drive to rid Kosovo of Albanians.

John recovered from the beating and gun shot wounds after spending three months in the hospital. He soon fled to his native home to stay with family in Albania. There, he was being interviewed by a writer for a local newspaper, and he was asked to recap the events of the past year in Kosovo that stood out the most in his mind.

One might think that John's recap of his past 12 months would definitely include the widespread persecution and genocide that he had personally seen. And surely, he would mention that he was beaten, shot three times, and had spent three months in the hospital recovering. But No, John told the news writer that the foremost thing in his mind was the terrible words his wife had spoken to him during their family quarrel. He said that he still felt the pain in his heart from her words.

As you can clearly see in this narrative, words are powerful. They can do untold damage to the listener when they are uncontrolled, negative, life-defeating words.

Words That Are Enemies To Faith, Growth, Development, And Prosperity

Top 6 Hit List of Words to avoid when making self-talk (faith-building) confessions:

Hope - "Hope that I will have money to pay my bills"
Try - "I am trying..."
Can - "I can..."
Claim - "I claim the promises"
Like - "I'd like to change..."
Expect - "I expect to..."

Top 8 Best List of Words that are beneficial enhancers to faith, growth, development, and prosperity:

The Word of God commands you to speak on the following eight key words which are taken from Philippians 4:8:

"Whatsoever things" are....

True -	***Lovely***
Honest -	***Good Report***
Just -	***Virtue***
Pure -	***Praise***

"Think on and self-talk these things."

Detailed information explaining why you must avoid certain words, and why certain words are beneficial is outlined in the section on How To Write Your Own Self-Talk (Faith-Building) Confession.

> ***Always remember, that death and life are in the power of the tongue, and he who is wise chooses to speak life, because by doing so, he also adds life to himself.***

PART 2

WHAT IS SELF-TALK?

There are two kinds of self-talk, uncontrolled and controlled self-talk. In this section we will unveil the effects of uncontrolled self-talk.

Uncontrolled Self-Talk

Uncontrolled self-talk can range from the everyday natural kind of self-talk such as, "I wonder where in the world I put my keys," to much more destructive words. Words which can steal from, destroy, and kill the hearer. They are negative words that are filled with hatred, scandal, bitterness, jealousy, and deadly venom. Whether they are spoken to one's self or others, they can cause pain, distress, and destruction.

How Uncontrolled Self-Talk Works In Children

If you have ever been around a youngster playing alone, you probably witnessed the truest form of self-talk. My five-year-old daughter, Abigail, is the younger of our two children, and she loves to play with her dolls, coloring books and her other toys. Her sister, Cristel, is seventeen, and after school she is busy with homework. My wife and I will set aside time to play and color with Abigail; and when you tell her, "I will play or color with you after dinner," she will not let you forget. As soon as dinner is over, she will remind you of your promise.

Even though she attends a notable daycare center with additional activities, such as ballet and gymnastics training, she still has lots of play left in her when she gets home. This special attention that she requires is understandable since she has no sibling (her age) at home to play with her.

I have observed her up close, playing with her dolls and other toys, and she will be talking to herself and talking to her dolls. She will speak in a girl's voice to mimic the girl doll or she will speak in a boy's voice to mimic the boy character. She role-plays the mommy's and daddy's part, even mimicking their voices, also. Some of the things she says are hilarious, and I am in wonder as to how she comes up with some of the things she says. Not only does she mimic the doll's voices; she also puts the action into it. She gets the dolls to interact by moving their arms and legs to have them walk or sit while mimicking their voices according to what's going on. This is a classic form of self-talk because it is pure. Children will say what's on their minds (all based on what they have heard) and sometimes their self-talk can even be amazing.

Abigail has a red play telephone that her uncle in Singapore gave her, and she loves to play with it. The telephone conversations that she holds when playing alone are spectacular. The words she uses, the phrases, the facial and hand gestures, and her body language are all fit for a Hollywood script.

A child's self-talk is almost 100% influenced by mom, dad, and other family members' speech. The speech from their peers at daycare or school, television, and the internet highly influence all children's self-talk. Children are flooded with negative and positive information, which forms their patterns of beliefs and habits. It forms their habits for playing, and their habits and beliefs in real life.

Protect Your Children From Verbal Contamination! Place A Guard Around Their Ear Gates!

Don't neglect the children! We should have at least the same concern for the kind of information that our children are hearing as we do in making sure that they eat and sleep properly. There are some cartoons on TV that I do not allow my daughter to watch.

Children must rely on their parents to filter out all of the world's negative life-defeating talk, so that their minds and hearts are not contaminated by all the worldly voices being thrown at them.

Children are not alone when it comes to self-talk. Therefore this should come as no surprise to you; adults are masters at self-talk...some a lot more than others.

Self-Talk Defined

A noun is a word that is the name of a person, place or thing. My Merriam-Webster Computer Dictionary says that the word "self" is a noun, and it means, one's own person or one's own self. And the word "talk" means to speak words, to express one's thoughts in speech. My paraphrase for the meaning of self-talk is, "What one says when one talks to one's self."

How Uncontrolled Self-Talk Works In Adults

Adults tend to follow the same patterns of self-talk as children. However, with adults it is broadened, because the opportunities to use self-talk are much greater. The many events that occur in an adult's life each day give way to reactions that often manifest in positive or negative self-talk.

You may have said or heard someone else say, "The way things are going, I can tell this is going to be a bad day." At the end of the day, if the question was asked, "How was your day?" the majority of the time the answer would be, "I had a bad day, nothing seemed to work right."

Another statement that I am sure you have heard is, "I am sneezing, so I must be catching a cold." Chances are, if you check back with that person in the next day or so, guess what? They will have what they said; they will have a cold. Why is this so? Well, it is so because it is based on a spiritual law of sowing and reaping. In other words, what you say is exactly what you reap.

Let's look at what this law says.

> *Don't be misled; remember that you can't ignore God and get away with it: a man will always reap just the kind of crop he sows!* (Galatians 6:7 TLB)

If you sow negative self-talk, you will reap negative results. It's a law that works concerning spiritual as well as natural things.

One of my strong passions is gardening. I really enjoy the whole aspect of gardening, especially the trip to the garden each morning expecting to see the plants coming out of the ground. Maintaining a garden takes some work, but it pays off at harvest time. I also enjoy sharing my harvest with others, such as family and neighbors. There is nothing like sitting in front of a plate of fresh cooked string beans and potatoes along with sliced, luscious tomatoes, all from your own garden. Yummy. Yummy! When I sowed bean seeds in my garden, I didn't get corn. The plant that came up was a bean plant. If you sow positive self-talk, you will reap positive results. It's a law that doesn't fail; it will work all the time, season after season.

This subject of sowing and reaping will be unfolded for a much clearer understanding a little later.

It Is OK To Talk To Yourself

I have found that I self-talk the most when I have misplaced something, especially keys. I will say something like, "Where could I have put those keys?" or "I can't believe the keys are not here." Or the classic one, "My wife must have moved the keys."

Some adults feel silly or embarrassed when talking to themselves, especially when someone else overhears them. We do not normally go around talking to ourselves openly in public. However, we have seen people on the streets that carry on exhaustive conversations with themselves. Their self-talk is sometimes very loud accompanied with vigorous hand, arm, and body gestures.

Those folks are viewed by some as being off balance or crazy, and it is this view which has wrongly stigmatized normal everyday, garden variety, positive self-talk.

As you will see later, controlled self-talk is a God-given tool, and it is the most powerful weapon in your arsenal to produce growth and change in your life. It is your controlled self-talk that will provide the means for you to receive your covenant inheritance of wealth and riches in this New Millennium.

In fact, the words that you self-talk can cause sickness and poverty to overtake you. Or your self-talk can cause you to prosper and be in good health and wealthy and rich.

Death And Life Are In The Power Of The Tongue

> *Death and life are in the power of the tongue, and they who indulge in it shall eat the fruit of it (for death or life).* Proverbs 18:21, Amp.

The Word of God is unveiling to us how powerful our tongues can be. It can cause life and it can cause death. Think about it, anything that has that kind of power in our lives demands that we fully understand its workings and how to control it.

We give this power to our tongues through our self-talk. Uncontrolled negative self-talk is disabling, destructive and as the Scripture says, it can cause death. The words that we self-talk make us or break us. Words heal us or make us sick. We can speak life to ourselves or we can speak death to ourselves.

Words create things in your life. In fact, spiritual things and natural things are created by words. Words can curse and words can bless. Words can cause poverty to overtake you, and they can keep you bound in poverty. Words can keep you living from paycheck to paycheck.

Conversely, words can cause you to prosper in every area of your life. They can cause your covenant inheritance of wealth and riches to overtake you.

What You Say Is What You Get Sooner Or Later

There is a saying that we have heard quoted from time to time that goes like this, "What you see is what you get." Flip Wilson, the sidesplitting comedian popularized this saying when performing on television as the character Geraldine. Geraldine would say, "What you 'sees' is what you get!" This saying is generally quoted in a joking, light-hearted manner to denote "What you are looking at is all there is, there isn't any more."

I have a similar quote that goes like this. "What you say is what you get sooner or later!"

No harm intended to Geraldine, but her saying is based on the senses, it is based strictly on sight. The saying that I cited is based on the spiritual law of <u>sowing</u> and <u>reaping</u> which we discussed earlier. In fact, this law is based on the <u>unseen</u>, and not the things <u>seen</u> by the physical eyes. The Good News is that this law will work for you if you work the law. This law works when it is applied to spiritual or natural (physical) things. The secret is to manage and control your self-talk.

Personal Self-Talk Inventory List

It is said that, "One will never correct a problem if they are unaware that one exists." Unconsciously over the years, negative self-talk has infiltrated our (minds and) hearts, resulting in the negative unproductive ideas molding our beliefs and habits.

I have provided for you a Personal Self-Talk Inventory List which is designed to reveal to you the exact self-talk that is negative, unproductive and life-defeating. This destructive self-talk has been passed along from generation to generation in many families; resulting in children and their children's children living far below life's standard in sickness and disease, and/or poverty. In other words, living on the lower rung of society.

I urge you to look closely at the Personal Self-Talk Inventory List to see if you can locate any statements that you have used at one time or another when talking to yourself or to others. Also look for statements that you have heard others say from time to time.

Doctors have you take physical examinations (which is a form of inventory) to determine if there are areas that you may have a problem with in your body that may need treatment. Financial advisors require you to complete a financial worksheet (which is a form of inventory) to assist in identifying unsound money management and to recommend proven financial strategies.

Well, your self-talk professor is asking you to complete a Personal Self-Talk Inventory List to help you identify any of your self-talk that needs to be corrected.

Why Sears Conducts Annual Merchandise Inventories

I worked for Sears and Roebuck for ten years in the retail sales store as a Sales Development Training Manager. And every year, everyone in the store would be involved in a storewide merchandise inventory. These inventories were conducted to determine how much merchandise was actually in the store, both on the sales floor and in the stock rooms. The results of these inventory counts would be compared to the computerized records which show how much merchandise was shipped to the store and how much merchandise the store sold.

Main Benefits Of Sears Annual Merchandise Inventories

The following are the threefold benefits of Sears' annual merchandise inventories.

1. It's an effective means of accountability and purification of merchandise records.
2. It uncovers merchandise losses.
3. It identifies damaged, unusable, defective, junk merchandise that was occupying valuable storage space, which could be discarded.

Some of the junk merchandise may have been returned because of manufacturer defects, safety hazards or damage. Some of the junk merchandise occupying valuable space may be outdated, obsolete or simply not repairable and worthless.

This junk merchandise is identified and discarded to make room for current, viable, sellable merchandise.

The key benefit in your completing the Personal Self-Talk Inventory List is the same as Sears' benefit outlined in item number three.

The Personal Self-Talk Inventory List will identify unusable, defective, life-defeating, junk; self-talk that is occupying valuable storage space in your (mind and) heart memory file. Once the junk self-talk is identified, then your task is to get rid of it forever.

Developing A Sixth Sense

This Personal Self-Talk Inventory List is a vital and essential part of the principles and techniques present in this book. Therefore, I exhort you to take the necessary time and carefully read through the inventory list. This light exercise is designed to help you, and it is one of the building blocks that will help you build within you a sixth sense for detecting negative, life-defeating self-talk.

It is also a trigger tool designed to move you toward using new principles and techniques that are the vehicle for receiving your covenant inheritance of wealth and riches in this New Millennium.

Know that the enormous benefits to you far outweigh the small amount of time it will take to go through the Personal Self-Talk Inventory List.

Keep in mind that you are the only person that you are in competition with. And always remember, if someone is not aware or fully convinced that they have a problem, they will never, never rise above the problem.

As you read through the inventory list, keep count of the following:

1. How many of the statements or similar statements you have used in the past.
2. How many of the statements have you heard others use in the past?

A Personal Self-Talk Inventory Worksheet is provided for your use. It is located in Appendix C.

Personal Self-Talk Inventory List
Top 50

1. I can't seem to keep my head above water.
2. I generally get the flu around this time of the year.
3. It's impossible, I can't do it.
4. I get so depressed at times.
5. I can't get rid of my headache.
6. I never win anything.
7. I'm always living from paycheck to paycheck.
8. The only luck I have is bad luck.
9. It just makes me sick.
10. You make me sick.
11. My mom/dad had it, so I will probably get it also.
12. I can't seem to get there on time.
13. I am always running late.
14. It seems I'm always broke.
15. This thing is worrying me to death.
16. I just can't seem to quit smoking.
17. Looks like it is going to be a bad day.
18. I have a fear of heights.

19. I will try to eat less.
20. I am never able to keep my New Year's resolutions.
21. Sometimes I can't control my temper.
22. I have a really hard time remembering names.
23. At my age, I can't do that.
24. My color is one strike against me.
25. I've been down on my luck lately.
26. I'll never own a house at the rate I'm going.
27. It's a struggle every month for me to pay the rent, the car payment, and utilities.
28. I always end up with losers.
29. I can't get enough sleep.
30. I am so clumsy.
31. It seems I worry about the least little thing.
32. Someone is always trying to take advantage of me.
33. Nothing seems to satisfy me.
34. No one seems to care for me.
35. I'll try to attend.
36. I doubt if I'll be feeling well enough tomorrow.
37. It looks too difficult, I can't do that.
38. I have this terrible fear of having an automobile crash.
39. Sometimes I just hate myself.
40. I'm always feeling tired.
41. I know they won't approve my loan.
42. My credit is not the best.
43. I lose weight and I gain it right back.
44. I can't seem to get organized.
45. Why should I try; it won't work anyway.
46. I've always heard "No" and "You can't."
47. I get upset easily.
48. Sometimes people get on my nerves big time.
49. My dad and grandfather died of cancer, so I'm really worried now.
50. I know I'm just a worry wart.

This list of negative, life-defeating statements is a condensed version of some that I have compiled throughout the years of my interacting with other people. This list does not, by any means represent the sum total of all the negative statements people make. There may be some that you have used that were not on this list.

There are thousands of negative, life-defeating words and statements; far too many to record in this book. However, I believe you will agree that this inventory list serves to highlight some of the negative, life-defeating statements which you have used in your self-talk, or you may have used these statements when speaking to others.

I am sure you also identified statements which you have heard others use. I don't know about you, but when I read through the fifty statements, I sense a mental and physical pull or drain, from all the negative stuff.

This inventory list also served to illuminate the fact that you were able to recall your old negative talk and that of others. This further solidifies what we already know, and that is that the negative words and statements that hit your ear gates are recorded in your (mind and) heart memory file.

Uncontrolled Negative, Life-Defeating Self-Talk Is Stored In The Stockroom Of Your Mind And Heart

Let's go back to the Sears' annual merchandise inventory for a moment. First, the outdated, defective, damaged, unworkable, worthless merchandise detected during the inventory didn't just show up in the stock rooms overnight. No!

Some of the merchandise may have had tags showing that it was counted in a previous inventory inspection. But due to some reason (generally administrative) it was never discarded.

Generally, detailed directives are issued that indicate by what means junk merchandise should be discarded. As mentioned earlier, the purpose of the annual inventories at all of Sears retail stores is to insure that the physical count of the merchandise in the stockrooms and on the sales floor matches the computerized administrative records.

The results of the inventory should show that all merchandise is accounted for and all the records balance.

As stated, a very, very important part of the Sears inventory is to identify merchandise that is defective, damaged, unrepairable, and worthless, which clutter up the stock rooms using valuable space. Sears removes this junk merchandise and gets rid of it. From an accounting standpoint, this junk merchandise inflates the bottom line, dollar-wise. Hence, when this merchandise is properly classified, it provides the company officials with a true picture of the company's inventory.

The reliability of true inventory records is vital because the company bases its future merchandise-buying decisions on it.

How To Get Rid Of Your Old Negative, Life-Defeating Self-Talk

Some of the same reasons that Sears gets rid of the worthless merchandise are some of the same reasons we ought to get rid of old, negative, life-defeating self-talk.

1. The old negative self-talk is worthless and counterproductive.
2. It occupies and clutters up valuable space in your (mind and) heart memory files.
3. It unconsciously controls much of your conscious habits, thoughts, beliefs, and self-talk.
4. Your future development and growth depend on your getting rid of old, negative, life-defeating self-talk.
5. Your goal of receiving your covenant inheritance of wealth and riches in this New Millennium hinges directly on your burning desire to get rid of your old negative, life-defeating self-talk.

In the book of Proverbs, the Word of God warns us about the words on our lips.

> *You are snared with the words of your lips, you are caught by the speech of your mouth* (Proverbs 6:2, Amp.).

The key word in the above Scripture is the word "**snared**." It refers to a trapping device used for capturing birds or animals. It is something that serves to entangle.

It is essential; it is imperative that you fully understand the groundwork, the foundation, that has been laid thus far in the previous pages concerning the effects of negative, life-defeating self-talk. The reason why this is so important is that most people are not easily motivated to change old beliefs and habits, even when they know that the habits and beliefs are counterproductive.

We clearly see this with people who are smokers, drinkers, worriers, and over-eaters. These folks know that these creature habits (satisfying the flesh) are counterproductive but, for whatever reason, they are bound by these habits and they choose not to change.

I encourage you not to fall into the trap of complacency. Instead, fix your (mind and) heart on making lasting and meaningful changes in your life, in your self-talk, in this New Millennium. Fix your (mind and) heart on the principles, precepts, and techniques outlined in this book which are designed for your growth financially, spiritually, mentally, physically, domestically, and socially.

Fix your (mind and) heart on receiving your covenant inheritance of wealth and riches for the purpose of being a blessing to the Kingdom of God and to the poor and needy. Know this, as you sow financial seeds and share your inheritance, all of your needs and desires will be met. Brothers, sisters, and friends, this is Good News! I have provided a sample outline of how you can share your covenant inheritance, and still have plenty of wealth and riches left over to meet all of your needs and desires. This information is provided in Chapter 5, Part 3, under the subtitle, "What Is Faith."

As stated before, Sears issues directives to its people detailing by what means junk merchandise should be discarded. Well, in the next chapter, you will be given simple and easy-to-follow instructions on how to get rid of your old, negative, life-defeating self-talk.

Negative Self-Talk Is Your Worst Enemy

Let's return to your *Personal Self-Talk Inventory List.* Those negative self-talk statements that you identified as "my old, negative self-talk" are your worst enemies. And, as it was said earlier, these negative statements are stored in your (mind and) heart memory files, occupying valuable, valuable space.

This negative stuff stored in your memory files is poison to your spiritual, mental, and physical well-being. Man has not figured out exactly how it works, but we do know that it's based on the law of **sowing** and **reaping**. The negative things in your (mind and) heart build up and then unconsciously control your beliefs and habits in your everyday life.

Your (mind and) heart don't care what you tell them, whether it is true or false, real or unreal, good or bad. It accepts everything it receives as reality, and then works overtime to make it become a reality in your life.

We clearly see this law in progress when we plant a seed in the ground. The ground doesn't care what kind of seed you plant. It could be a seed from a poisonous plant, but like the (mind and) heart, it will work overtime to produce whatever seed was planted.

The growth of the seed and plant can be accelerated with proper sunlight, fertilizer and ongoing cultivation. The same holds true with negative self-talk. The more you say the same negative stuff, day after day, the faster it begins to unconsciously control your beliefs and habits on the conscious level. It's likened to a small drop of water that falls into a pail day after day. Eventually the pail will become full and overflow outside the pail. It started as a small drop of water on the inside of the pail, but with the continuous dropping of water over time, the pail overflows.

This is a simplified illustration of how negative, life-defeating words can build up in your (mind and) heart memory files, and this build-up causes the same words to overflow into your everyday habits, beliefs, expressions, and your actions.

In the book of Proverbs, the following is revealed:

For as he thinks in his heart, so is he (Proverbs 23:7, NKJV).

Guess who has the responsibility to control what self-talk goes into your (mind and) heart? YOU!

How To Shut Off Your Uncontrollable, Negative Self-Talk

Researchers indicate that 75 to 80% of what we tell ourselves (negative self-talk) is counterproductive and works against us. A simplified method that I developed and use to shut down negative thoughts and self-talk is given in this four-step procedure:

1. **Stop** - First, stop the thoughts, stop the flow of self-talk; shut it off the same way you would shut the water faucet off. Make your mind and your mouth obey your commands.
2. **Inhale** - Secondly, take a deep breath in, hold it, mentally count to three, and then exhale the air (completely out). This helps to clear your mind on the conscious level.
3. **Think** - Thirdly, think of how to self-talk the solution, the answer or the results desired and not the problem.
4. **Speak Aloud** - Fourthly, self-talk your statement in a bold, positive (as if it has already been accomplished) manner. Your self-talk may sound like this, "I refuse to let the present circumstances dictate my day. I'm believing for a safe, healthy, productive, and joyous day today!"

This four-step procedure works for me every time. It is simple and easy to do **(Stop, Inhale, Think and Speak)**. And it works for many, many others also.

Once you begin on a regular basis to renew your (mind and) heart with new, controlled self-talk, it will override, or record over the old junk until all of the old negative self-talk is erased. This leaves the new, positive self-talk in control, as it should be.

Step-by-step instructions on how to erase and get rid of the old, negative self-talk which is already stored in your (mind and) heart memory file is provided in the next chapter.

Coming up next is "What Is Controlled Self-Talk?"

Remember, the wise person stops negative, life-defeating words at their ear gates and, like a security guard, refuses to let them in.

CHAPTER 4

WHAT IS CONTROLLED SELF-TALK?

PART 1

Controlled self-talk is when an individual consciously manages the words that are released from his/her mouth. It requires an ongoing effort to purposely choose to use positive words when talking to self and to others. For controlled self-talk to be effective, it requires a "boy-scout-like oath" that you are committed to working overtime at eliminating negative, life-defeating words and statements from your speech. Controlled self-talk is the most effective tool available for getting rid of old uncontrolled, negative self-talk.

The way self-talk works is that when your controlled self-talk sends positive, constructive words to your (mind and) heart, the (mind and) heart goes to work double-time to manifest your words on the conscious level. This is another aspect of the spiritual law of sowing and reaping, which was discussed in the last chapter. When you self-talk positive words, you are guaranteed to reap the results of those words in reality.

The following are a few types of words that will produce great results on the conscious level; self-talk words that are caring, loving, strengthening, full of faith and high expectancy. Words that are spoken with strong faith for good health and prosperity will produce after their own kind on the conscious level.

Root Foundation Of *Self-Talk And Grow Rich*

Positive, controlled self-talk, along with faith-building confessions is the root foundation for this book. The principles, precepts, and techniques prescribed in this book are all entwined around positive, controlled self-talk, and faith-building confessions. It is the unveiling of these powerful principles that will provide the means for you to receive your covenant inheritance of wealth and riches in this New Millennium.

When doctors talk about cholesterol, they say that high-density lipoproteins (HDLs) are the good cholesterol, which promote good health, and the low-density lipoproteins (LDLs) are the bad cholesterol. The doctor will warn a patient who has a total cholesterol reading over 200 along with a high level of LDL, that they can be at risk for stroke, heart attack, or even death. To minimize these risks and lower the LDL level, the doctor may prescribe treatment, diet, and exercise. The same holds true for controlled, positive self-talk. It is the good kind of self-talk that produces life and life more abundantly on the conscious level. Conversely, uncontrolled negative self-talk produces negative, life-defeating results on the conscious level and it is definitely the bad self-talk.

As it was mentioned before, controlled self-talk expresses words that are positive, full of strong faith and high expectancy.

It is written in the book of Proverbs: *A good man thinks before he speaks; the evil man pours out his evil words without a thought.* Proverbs 15:28, TLB

Remember, your words have incredible power; words create; words influence; words activate; and words motivate; or they can devastate.

Think On And Self-Talk These Things

Follow closely with your eyes the following highly beneficial Scripture. It is a command from God.

> *Finally, brethren, whatsoever things are* ***true****, whatsoever things are* ***honest****, whatsoever things are* ***just****, whatsoever things are* ***pure****, whatsoever things are* ***lovely****, whatsoever things are of* ***good report****; if there be any* ***virtue*** *and if there be any* ***praise*** *think on these things (*Philippians 4:8, KJV).

This Scripture clearly tells us exactly what to think on, and since these are the things that the Holy Spirit directs us to think on, then these same things must be the things we are to also speak (self-talk) on.

Notice that there are eight key words in the above Scripture, and these words deserve your undivided attention:

True	**Just**	**Lovely**	**Virtue**
Honest	**Pure**	**Good Report**	**Praise**

What Is The Philippians 4:8 Assessment Test?

The eight key words in Philippians 4:8 are what I call the Philippians 4:8 Assessment Test. If you examine this Scripture, you will notice that it only contains positive words, words that build up, edify, honor, congratulate, and compliment. You pass the Philippians 4:8 Test when your self-talk and speech to others is positive, encouraging, loving, and edifying.

The Word of God clearly tells us what to think on. Therefore, we know that we are to think on and self-talk the eight key words outlined in the Scripture.

The utter importance of these eight key words can be compared to the following narrative: When soldiers train for combat, they are thoroughly trained on how to use their rifles. The proper use and operation of the rifle can mean the difference between life and death in combat.

As a drill instructor in the Army Signal Corps, one of the exercises that I conducted required that each soldier disassemble and then reassemble their rifle while blindfolded. This exercise was designed to familiarize the soldier with each part of his rifle, its operation, and how to properly maintain it. Also, in case they experienced a problem with the operation of the rifle, they could fix it, even in the dark. The last thing a soldier would ever want to happen is his rifle misfiring during combat due to poor maintenance. In fact, if this did happen, they may not live to tell about it.

The soldiers also received training on the weapons of the opposing forces; how their weapons functioned and their capabilities, such as range and effectiveness.

As a result of the intense preparation for combat, our soldiers were fully trained on how to use their weapons, and they had received general knowledge of the opposing forces' firepower. Armed with this combat training, our soldiers were ready to go out boldly and confidently to win the victory for their country.

The relationship to our Scripture outlined in Philippians 4:8, and the above narrative mirror each other. Let's unfold what some of the similarities are:

1. The eight key words are your weapons (rifle), and the proper or improper use of them could mean the difference between life or death on the battlefield of life.
2. Having full knowledge of what negative, unproductive, life-defeating words you need to avoid gives you a huge advantage in the everyday warfare of life.
3. Armed with full knowledge of your weapons and how to use them, you are then ready for combat day or night. You are ready to do battle with boldness and the confidence needed to win the victory over negative, life-defeating thoughts, self-talk, and Satan.

Be Your Own Top-Notch Quality Control Word Inspector In This New Millennium

Recently, I had an opportunity to go into the back warehouse of a popular fruit, vegetable, and health food chain store here in lovely San Diego. As I walked through the area, I noticed busy employees wearing white caps, aprons, and rubber gloves. They were standing on both sides of a slowly moving conveyor belt, and they were carefully inspecting fruit and vegetables for defects or any signs of unfreshness. They were throwing the bad produce into a large garbage container, while the good fruits and vegetables were placed in boxes and loaded on carts to go out to the customer sales floor. The workers were performing quality control (inspection) to ensure that items placed for sale are fresh.

I am writing this to encourage and inspire you to be your own top-notch quality control "word" inspector in this New Millennium. As a word inspector, your job will be to stand guard duty. Your duties will be to carefully inspect every word that is thought or spoken which hits your ear gates, with the Philippians 4:8 Assessment Test. This means that your self-talk must get inspected, as well as your thoughts and your speech to others. Also, the self-talk and conversational talk of others must be inspected at your ear gates. Every word that hits your ear gates must pass the Philippians 4:8 Assessment Test. Those words that don't pass the test will be yanked off the verbal conveyor belt before entering your ear gates. The quality control word inspector will label such words as negative and defective and immediately discard them into the garbage container.

Full-Time Duties – Guarding Your Ear Gates

Your task as a quality control word inspector is an on-going duty, 24 hours a day, seven days a week, 365 days a year.

Do you know that if you don't maintain your lawn, it will get out of hand? The grass and weeds will grow and grow; and if left undone, they will become overgrown and unsightly.

In most communities, when lawns are left unkempt, it violates local city laws which require owners or renters to keep the property tidy. I have personally known of some cases where people were cited for similar violations. On occasion, you will see newspaper accounts of absentee landlords who are cited for these sorts of violations.

Overgrown lawns create another major problem because they are very difficult to cut. They require extra work and sometimes require special tools and heavy-duty machines to get the job done. What all this means is that it would have been much better to have maintained the lawn on a consistent basis, rather than let it get out of hand and go unattended. The results of which caused extra effort, extra time, extra labor, and in most cases, extra money to clear the overgrown lawn.

No Vacations For The Quality Control Word Inspector

Let it be known that similar occurrences will inevitably happen to your self-talk if you let it go unattended and uncontrolled. The negative, life-defeating influences will begin to grow larger and larger in your (mind and) heart and will spread themselves out to your conscious reality. You cannot afford to take a vacation and leave your inspector job unattended.

Like the overgrown lawn, when your self-talk is not controlled over a period of time, it takes additional effort and time to reprogram and renew all the negative things in your (mind and) heart. Just as the unkempt lawn violates civil law, the negative, life-defeating self-talk violates God's law governing speech.

Look and see what the Word of God commands on this subject:

> *Let no foul or polluting language, nor evil word nor unwholesome or worthless talk (ever) come out of your mouth, but only such (speech) as is good and beneficial to the spiritual progress of others, as is fitting to the need and the occasion, that it may be a blessing and give grace (God's favor) to those who hear it* (Ephesians 4:29, Amp.).

It is imperative that you control your self-talk and guard your ear gates from others, negative talk. Negative talk from others is the same as second-hand smoke, it has an adverse affect on the listener as well.

Always remember that your present self-talk and the talk of others will determine your future.

Practice the Philippians 4:8 test daily, and remember to always speak on and listen for the good report. An excellent biblical example of men with a good report is seen in the Caleb and Joshua narrative which is written in the Old Testament. To get a better understanding of a good report and an evil report, I encourage you to stop now, get your Bible, and read Numbers, chapters 13 and 14.

Now, let's resume our discussion on good reports and evil reports. As you have read, Caleb and Joshua's report was bold, fearless, and confident; their trust (faith) was in the Lord. They brought back a good report and the other ten spies brought back an evil report laden with negativity, fear and faithless words. Fear is the opposite of faith and when fear comes on the scene, faith leaves. And **without faith it is impossible to please God.**

The people of Israel rejected the good report because they were operating on fear transmitted by the ten spies who gave the evil report. The people of Israel's choice to accept (the majority report) the evil report caused them to suffer immensely for forty years. God said that all the people 20 years old and older who accepted the evil report of the ten spies would never see the promised land. They were doomed to laborious suffering in the wilderness for forty years. And He said that none of them would live to see the promised land. Instead, they would all die in the wilderness.

The ten spies who brought the evil report, inciting, the rebellion against God by striking fear in the hearts of the people were struck down. They died of a plague before the Lord, but Joshua and Caleb who brought the good report lived still.

The moral of the Joshua and Caleb narrative is to inspire you to fix your self-talk and your speech on words that line up with the Philippians 4:8 key words. Also, it was definitely revealed in this narrative that the majority report is not always the correct report. Some people like to side with the majority (go along with the crowd), but you need to have the courage and faith of Joshua and Caleb to speak good reports and accept good reports even when it is unpopular.

By speaking and seeking after the good reports, you will triumph in every area of your life in this New Millennium, and the God of peace will be with you! Further, be forewarned to never, never accept an evil (negative) report. Instead, rely on the Word of God concerning the situation.

Control Your Self-Talk First

I sincerely urge you not to rush out and attempt to change others, based on this new information you have received thus far. Your task and your priority is to develop yourself first. Control your self-talk first, by fully utilizing the principles, techniques and exercises prescribed in this book.

Those of you who are fed up with living from paycheck to paycheck, pension check to pension check, social security check to social security check, or those who desire change in other areas of your life are not reading this book by accident. It has been preordained that the instructions and knowledge in this book come upon you.

Those of you who master the principles and techniques prescribed in this book are well on your way toward receiving your covenant inheritance of wealth and riches in this New Millennium.

Remember this...your faith and your possessions will never rise above the level of your self-talk. By controlling your self-talk, you can control your destiny. The sky is the limit!

I exhort you to begin immediately reading **aloud** the following self-talk (faith-building) confession before each meal and snack, before bedtime, in the morning, and throughout the day when possible, season after season after season.

Self-Talk (Faith-Building) Confession:

I obey God's Word. I think on and I self-talk things that are true, honest, just, pure, lovely, things that are of good report, and things that have virtue and praise. I self-talk these things consistently, and my God, the God of peace is with me at all times. I make this (faith-building) confession under the authority, and in the mighty Name of Jesus Christ of Nazareth! SO BE IT! Philippians 4:8-9

PART 2

BENEFITS OF GOD'S LIVING WORD. IT IS THE SAME YESTERDAY, TODAY, AND FOREVER

When you self-talk your faith-building confessions, your words become one with God's Word. Your words create a match in your (heart and) spirit with His Word, and the Holy Spirit within you steps in and acts favorably on your behalf.

The Bible says,

> *The rain and snow come down from the heavens and stay on the ground to water the earth. They cause the grain to grow, producing seed for the farmer and bread for the hungry. It is the same with my Word. I send it out, and it always produces fruit. It will accomplish all I want it to, and it will prosper everywhere I send it* (Isaiah 55:10-11, NLT).

You are empowered and exhorted to confess God's Word to your situation and it will always produce fruit. His Word will cause you to flourish and prosper in every area of your life.

I earnestly encourage you to read aloud and study God's Word. His Word abiding in you gives you authority in heaven, which is an awesome and thrilling fact. Another outstanding fact is that God the Father loves you very much. He desires that you step up to the plate and receive all of your covenant blessings, so that you can be a blessing to others (which glorifies Him).

Jesus Christ of Nazareth says in the book of John...

> *If you abide in Me, and My words abide in you, you will ask what you desire, and it shall be done for you* (John 15:7, NKJV).

The word "if" in this Scripture identifies it as a conditional Word of God. It is a cause and effect principle. If you abide in, live in, and unite with Him, and His words remain in you (in your heart and spirit), then you will ask (confess) whatever you will, and it shall be done for you. Moreover, the Word of God that you self-talk builds strong faith, and it causes His Word to abide in your (heart and) spirit and dominate your members as it should. God rewards faith!

Your self-talk confession of faith in the Word of God produces supernatural bionic power to cause things that are invisible to become visible and tangible.

I challenge you to reverently and consistently self-talk the faith-building confessions prescribed in this book, then patiently wait while continuing to self-talk your confessions and watch God the Father, God the Son, and God the Holy Spirit, and all of God's heavenly army of angelic beings, do mighty works on your behalf.

Brothers, sisters, and friends, self-talk faith-building confessions work! In fact, down through the years, Christianity has been called the "Great Confession." Salvation is gained by confessing with the mouth (Romans 10:9-10).

I have personally practiced (daily) what I am writing for nearly two decades and the results have been utterly astounding. You can literally predict the outcome of your confessions, which is "You possess what you confess." I will share the results of some of my self-talk (faith-building) confessions and the testimony of others in Chapter Eleven, Part 2.

Moreover, faith-building confessions work because they are backed up by the Word of God which has withstood the tests of time and has never been proven wrong by anyone.

Jesus Christ of Nazareth said the following for your understanding of the power of His words...

> *It is the Spirit who gives eternal life. Human effort accomplishes nothing. And the very words I have spoken to you are spirit and life* (John 6:63).
>
> *If you live in me (abide vitally united to Me) and my words remain in you and continue to live in your hearts, ask whatever you will, and it shall be done for you* (John 15:7).

How To Abide In Jesus Christ Of Nazareth

When you persistently self-talk the faith-building confessions prescribed in this book, you will be acting on the Word of God; you will be abiding in Him and His Words will be abiding in you, when you remain united to the vine which is Jesus Christ. Notice that this Scripture does not say that you can ask whatever you want. No, the word "can" expresses an ability. This Scripture is a command. It says to ask whatever you will, and it will be done for you.

Also notice that this Scripture is conditional. The first word in the verse is "if." The word "if" is a conjunction, which means a process or result of combining things. Hence, if you abide in Him and His words abide in you (conditional/conjunction), then ask whatever you will...and it shall be done for you.

This is awesome authority that is available to you, and the way to step into your authority is by persistently self-talking the faith-building confessions prescribed in this book.

You Are A King Or A Queen And Member Of The Royal Family

As a king or queen, you are a member of the royal family. You have supernatural power, influence, and status among men and God. You reign as king or queen in this life, on the top and not on the bottom. You are the lender and not the borrower. Wealth and riches are in your house, not poverty. As a king or queen, you live a balanced life of victory; you are not controlled by the circumstances.

As king or queen, you travel first class, not coach (second class) or you own your own plane. And when you walk into a store to buy goods, you do not worry if you have enough money to buy the things you need and desire or that your family needs and desires. As king or queen, you have the same love in your heart and spirit as the King of Kings, Jesus Christ of Nazareth. You possess the same heart and spirit of giving and compassion for others as Jesus did. As king or queen, you live in the best home, own the best automobiles, wear the best clothes, and your children attend the best schools. As a king and queen, you fret not about doctor or medical bills because all your needs and desires are met; and by Jesus' stripes you are healed and made whole. As a king or queen, you are above and not beneath; you are like the eagle, you soar above the circumstances of life because you are a member of God's Royal Family. You are a king or queen, you are royalty! You are greatly blessed by God the Father to be a blessing to others. It is written in the book of Romans:

> *For if because of one man's trespass (lapse, offense) death reigned through that one, much more surely will those who receive (God's) overflowing grace (unmerited favor) and the free gift of righteousness (putting them into right standing with Himself)* ***reign as kings in life*** *through the one man Jesus Christ (the Messiah, the Anointed One)* (Romans 5:17, Amp.).

Another rendering of this Scripture says...

> *The sin of this one man, Adam, caused death to be king over all, but all who will take God's gift of forgiveness and acquittal are* ***kings of life*** *because of this one man, Jesus Christ. Romans 5:17, TLB*

The word "reign" in the first Scripture means royal power. My paraphrase of this is...because of one man, Jesus Christ of Nazareth, the believer has been given royalty (befitting a king or queen) status, and royalty power in this life!

Please notice closely that this Scripture does not say that they reign as kings in the life to come in heaven (eternal life). No! It says...reign as kings in life; this life, which means physically alive and living in this earthly realm, is where you reign as a king or queen. Praise the Lord!

Your mouth is the master key to life.

By controlling your self-talk you control your destiny.

CHAPTER 5

THREE KINDS OF FAITH

In this section, we will dissect the word "faith" and then, later on, the word "confession." But first, you must have a solid, unwavering understanding of the word "faith."

I have discovered in my own personal experiences, my interactions with others, and in my research and study of the Bible that there are three kinds of faith. They are sense knowledge faith, natural human faith and revelation faith.

PART 1

WHAT IS SENSE-KNOWLEDGE FAITH?

You have probably heard someone say, "I'll believe it when I see it." This person is definitely walking in sense-knowledge faith. Sense-knowledge faith is based upon physical evidence. One must see it to believe it; one must hear it before they believe it. In other words, sense-knowledge faith must have logical proof or material evidence gained through the five senses; seeing, hearing, feeling, smelling or tasting.

The following are a couple of sense-knowledge faith slogans, which I am sure you have heard: "Experience is the best teacher." "Seeing is believing."

Be forewarned that these slogans are deadly, poisonous arrows designed to contaminate by transmitting a disabling virus to your (mind and) heart memory file.

This sense-knowledge faith is in total opposition to God's Word and it stops God's blessings, period!

A clear-cut example of sense-knowledge faith unfolds in the following narrative involving doubting Thomas:

Jesus Appears To Thomas

One of the disciples, Thomas (nicknamed the Twin) was not with the others when Jesus came. They told him, "We have seen the Lord!" But he replied, "I won't believe it unless I see the nail wounds in his hands, put my fingers into them, and place my hand into the wound in his side."

Eight days later, the disciples were together again, and this time Thomas was with them. The doors were locked; but suddenly, as before, Jesus was standing among them. He said,

> *"Peace be with you." Then he said to Thomas, "Put your finger here and see my hands. Put your hand into the wound in my side. Don't be faithless any longer. Believe!"*
>
> *"My Lord and my God!" Thomas exclaimed.*
>
> *Then Jesus told him,* ***"You believe because you have seen me. Blessed are those who haven't seen me and believe anyway."*** John 20:24-29, NLT

Thomas showcased his sense-knowledge (evidential) faith when he said, "Unless I see in His hands the marks made by the nails and put my finger into the nail prints and put my hand into His side, I will never believe it."

Another example of sense-knowledge faith is revealed in the following narrative where Jesus Christ of Nazareth raised Lazarus from the dead:

> *They told him, "Lord come and see." Then Jesus wept. The people who were standing nearby said, "See how much he loved him." But some said, "This man healed a blind man. Why couldn't he keep Lazarus from dying?"*

Jesus Raises Lazarus From The Dead

> *And again Jesus was deeply troubled. Then they came to the grave. It was a cave with a stone rolled across its entrance. "Roll the stone aside," Jesus told them.*
>
> *But Martha, the dead man's sister, said, "Lord, by now the smell will be terrible because he has been dead for four days." Jesus responded, "Didn't I tell you that you will see God's glory if you believe?" So they rolled the stone aside. Then Jesus looked up to heaven and said, "Father, thank you for hearing me. You always hear me, but I said it out loud for the sake of all these people standing here, so they will believe you sent me." Then Jesus shouted, "Lazarus, come out!" And Lazarus came out, bound in graveclothes, his face wrapped in a headcloth. Jesus told them, "Unwrap him and let him go!"*
>
> *Many of the people who were with Mary believed in Jesus when they saw this happen* (John 11:34-45, NLT).

Notice that the Scripture says that the people believed when they saw with their eyes. This also reveals that before they saw Jesus raise Lazarus from the dead, they did not believe, and this is 100%, sense-knowledge and sense-evidence faith. This reveals that the Jews faith in Jesus was based on seeing (sense-evidence faith). They believed, after seeing Jesus raise Lazarus from the dead.

The apostle Paul, inspired by the Holy Spirit, provides the following spiritual food for you to chew on and digest slowly.

> *Since we consider and look not to the things that are seen but to the things that are unseen; for the things that are visible are temporal (brief and fleeting), but the things that are invisible are deathless and everlasting* (2 Corinthians 4:18, Amp.).

I will always remember an incident some years back in Ohio. It was early Sunday morning; and when I got up to prepare for church, I looked outside and there was a huge blanket of snow covering everything. Looking out my front window, I couldn't tell where my driveway ended and where the street began. It looked like we had about two feet of snowfall overnight. I lived in Bedford Heights, which is a suburb of Cleveland; and it was known as the snow belt, which meant that the snow was always much heavier in our area.

At that time, I was a member of Christian Fellowship Center. It was under this ministry that I was ordained as an Elder in 1989. The church was seventeen miles from my home and it was located adjacent to Lake Erie. In fact, it is called The Church on the Lake.

When I saw all the snow outside, immediately sense-knowledge thoughts (all negative) began to come into my (mind and) heart like a flood. These thoughts were: It is too bad to drive in all that snow; you won't be able to get out of the driveway, and if you do, you'll get stuck. Then the thought came that since it was Sunday, the roads had not been snowplowed or salted, so the highway to church would be treacherous. The sense-knowledge thought said that the road would be slick with ice, and that I would probably have an accident with my car. Then the thought came to call and have someone substitute for me.

But, I resisted all that negative sense-knowledge faith and began to get ready for church. My plan for getting out of my driveway was to open the garage door, start the car and accelerate fast out of my 30 foot driveway to the street, and use the remote garage door opener to close the garage door. Once on the street, I would use the low speed to ease out onto the main street where there should be some traffic movement.

Well, to make this short, it all worked out fine; and the closer I got to my church the less and less snow there was. The sun began to shine and when I arrived at church, there was no sign of snow anywhere and the sun was brightly shining! It was a gorgeous Sunday morning and church school and the church service was spirit filled! I marked this experience up as a win-win for revelation faith and a defeat for sense-knowledge faith.

The following precepts decree how believers' daily lives are to be lived and by what creed:

> *For we walk by faith (we regulate our lives and conduct ourselves by our conviction or belief respecting man's relationship to God and divine things, with trust and holy fervor; thus we walk) not by sight or appearance* (2 Corinthians 5:7, Amp.).

I believe that you will agree that these Scriptures have clearly shown that sense-knowledge faith of seeing is believing is in total opposition to God's instructions to us.

In fact, the Word of God instructs us to consider not, and look not to the things that are seen, but to the things that are unseen. When you look to the unseen, you are majoring in the God-kind of faith, which is revelation faith.

I urge you to resist sense-knowledge faith every time it tries to vex and entrap you. Instead, rely totally and confidently on what God's Word has to say about the situation.

A word of caution to the wise. Never, never walk by sight, never self-talk the problem or the circumstances. Instead, walk and self-talk the solution, strive to always focus on the answer, the desired results, which temporarily reside in the unseen spirit realm. Furthermore, sense-knowledge faith is ungodly.

The late Dr. E.W. Kenyon was a renowned man of God, pastor, teacher, and author of many inspiring books. He wrote the following in one of his books entitled, *The Two Kinds of Knowledge.*

> "We are to cast down the world mind and all its knowledge and accept the revelation of God in its place. You cannot build faith as long as sense knowledge sits upon the throne of your reason (mind and heart). As long as you listen to the reasons derived from the senses, you will never believe the Word. You will never walk by faith, you will never see the triumphs of faith in your life."
>
> He went on to say... "Sense knowledge will not give God the credit. The only thing to do with sense knowledge is 'to cast it down.'And let revelation knowledge, the Word of God take its place. Sense-knowledge faith is in what man is, can do, and has done. Revelation faith is in the Word of God that liveth and abideth."

PART 2

WHAT IS NATURAL-HUMAN FAITH?

Natural-human faith does not require sense-evidential proof, but it is based on something that is believed, especially with strong conviction. It is void of belief in Jesus Christ of Nazareth. It does not depend upon God the Father, but rather its belief is in the natural course of things.

This kind of faith is presented and glossed over in most secular self-improvement, self-help, motivational seminars, books, materials and tapes.

As it was stated in the introduction section of this book, the actual groundwork for *Self-Talk And Grow Rich* started back in early 1982, almost two decades ago. I was attending a company-sponsored seminar designed to enhance staff management personnel's teaching, interactive and personal development skills. I held a position on the corporate staff of the then Ohio Bell Telephone Company which had its headquarters in downtown Cleveland, Ohio.

The material presented at this particular seminar was different. I had attended many other management-training courses, some that focused on management by objectives; others emphasized listening, speaking, and hands-on and feedback techniques. My training records reflected a potpourri of courses, all of which definitely sharpened my management and teaching skills. But in this particular seminar, there was a strong emphasis on treating your co-workers, subordinates, and others as you would want to be treated. This kind of training was different coming from a company-sponsored seminar. This material also zeroed in on developing self before setting out to develop others.

Most all of the other training courses I had attended focused on how to get others motivated to meet company objectives and maintain good performance reports and quality service.

The one thing that loomed big in my mind as I sat through those daily class sessions was that the material was being presented from a secular viewpoint, but most of the principles that were presented could be found in the Bible.

Although the material wasn't presented from a biblical perspective, it had Bible written all over it. For instance, the strong emphasis on treating others as you would want to be treated is a carbon copy of THE GOLDEN RULE.

In the book of Matthew, Chapter 7, verse 12, Jesus says, "*Do for others what you would like them to do for you. This is a summary of all that is taught in the law and the prophets.*"

The apostle Paul issues the following command in the book of

Galatians, Chapter 5, verse 14. He says, *"For the whole law can be summed up in this one command, Love your neighbor as yourself."*

One of the growth exercises presented during the personal development sessions of the seminar has stuck with me ever since. In fact, I have used this exercise many, many times during workshops that I have conducted and in seminars and corporate training sessions. Also I use this particular exercise when training one-on-one. This growth exercise is presented in this book in two other locations, first in the Author's Notes, and then in chapter 11.

This growth exercise required the participants to examine themselves closely, and then indicate in writing what areas in their life needed change; growth, development, and improvement.

We were given a handout that had six categories listed, and we were to select from those six categories which areas we needed improvement.

The six categories were:

1. Physically	4. Financially
2. Mentally	5. Domestically
3. Spiritually	6. Socially

We were all given adequate time to make our selections. I gave the six categories some very serious thought and decided that I needed to grow spiritually and domestically. At that time, I was not a consistent churchgoer.

I felt a strong tug to select spiritually and a small inner voice from my human spirit posed this question to me, "Are you a worker in the church or do you just attend?" Well, that question sealed spiritually as an area I needed to grow. Also, there was something else that fit into this decision; it was thoughts I had about some bachelor partying habits that I needed to shed. These two things galvanized my decision.

My selection of improvement domestically was centered around my daughter who was not living with me at that time. I had been divorced two years and my daughter, Juliana Marie was seven years old.

The decision to select domestically as an area that I needed improvement came about when that same small inner voice from my spirit said, "Spend more time with your daughter." Well, ironically, I had been thinking about spending more weekends keeping my daughter and taking her places. I can still remember that feeling of peace that overtook me after making these selections.

We were then instructed on how to write an affirmation for each area we selected for growth and improvement. The affirmations were to be written in a positive, personal, present-tense statement.

My Affirmations Read Like This:

<u>Affirmation No. 1</u>

My daughter and I now attend church school and church services on a regular basis. We are active in the church and we enjoy attending each Sunday.

<u>Affirmation No. 2</u>

I enjoy spending more quality time with my daughter. We do fun things together on a regular basis. She enjoys our time together and I eagerly look forward to picking her up for the weekend or on Sunday mornings.

The instructor explained in detail that we should read our affirmation aloud in the morning when we get up, at night right before we go to bed, and throughout the day when possible.

We were told that each time we read our affirmation we should close our eyes and visualize the affirmation as being already accomplished. In other words, we were to paint a mental picture of the growth and improvement for each affirmation as having already taken place, and then feel the emotion associated with the accomplishment.

As an example, in my mental pictures, I would see my daughter in church school on Sunday morning, sitting with other youngsters being taught Bible lessons. Then, I would see myself participating with the adult class. Then I would see the two of us standing together in the main sanctuary singing praise and worship songs with the congregation. In my mental picture, I would feel joy with a smile on my face as the result of being in church and being with my daughter.

We were told that the reading aloud, visualizing and feeling the emotions associated with each affirmation would program our "sub-conscious" on the inside to bring about the desired change on the outside. We were told to write our affirmations down on a 3 x 5 index card, so that we could carry the card with us and read our affirmations at every opportunity.

We were also instructed not to go out and deliberately try to make our affirmations come true, or try to create the outcome on our own. But rather that we should regularly read our affirmations and then leave it up to our sub-conscious and to a power much greater than man to make our affirmations become reality.

Results Obtained Using Natural-Human Faith

I read my affirmations enthusiastically each day and, lo and behold, after reading, visualizing, and feeling the emotions for 2 1/2 months, suddenly one day, as I was sitting down for a few minutes of quiet time, I realized that my daughter and I were attending church each Sunday. She was a member of the Children's Choir and I was a member of a Special

Projects Committee at church. I also realized how unexpectedly smooth the arrangement was with my ex-wife for picking my daughter up every other weekend, and every Sunday.

I fully realized that the exact things that I was affirming had come to pass. The amazing part of all this was how smoothly and effortlessly things seemed to fall into place. The things I was affirming actually came true.

At this point, I said to myself, "Wow, this stuff works! I am attending and working in the church regularly, and I am spending more quality time with my daughter. She is active in church with me."

By the way, Juliana Marie is a fine young woman now. She holds a Bachelor's Degree and Master's Degree in Special Education and will obtain her Doctor of Philosophy Degree (Ph.D.) within 12 months. She and her husband, Roy, are active in youth affairs at their church. Juliana still sings in her church choir, praise the Lord!

Secular Training Concepts Similar To Biblical Precepts And Principles

I will pause here and let's rewind to the beginning of this topic, which was "What is Natural-Human Faith."

I mentioned earlier that I had attended a company-sponsored seminar that was different from all the others I had attended. The material presented in the training was from a secular viewpoint, but the overall presentation had Bible written all over it. Hence, for your perusal, below are some of the glaring similarities to what is written in the Bible, and what was taught in the training sessions I attended:

1. The initial emphasis and instructions on treating others as you wanted to be treated is parallel to the biblical Scripture called the "Golden Rule" found in Matthew 7:12. It says, *"Do to others what you would like them to do for you."*
2. The word "affirmation" used frequently during the class presentations means to assert positively. It is generally used in secular training books and tapes. However, the biblical word "profession" which is translated confession (not to be confused with confession of sin) in more recent translations is a word used most often in Christian training, books and tapes. As an example, in Hebrews 10:23, believers are told, *"Let us hold fast the confession of our hope without wavering, for He who promised is faithful."*
3. The instructions given to write our affirmations down on a 3 X 5 index card for easy access throughout the day, mirrors God's instructions which He gave to the prophet Habakkuk. The

Amplified Bible gives this account in Habakkuk 2:2, *"And the Lord answered me and said, write the vision and engrave it so plainly upon tablets that everyone who passes may (be able to) read (it easily and quickly) as he hastens by."*

4. The instructions to read our affirmations aloud three or more times each day is set forth by David in the book of Psalms. He said, *"As for me, I will call upon God, and the Lord shall save me. Evening and morning and at noon I will pray and cry aloud, and He shall hear my voice"* (Psalm 55:16-17).
5. The instructions to visualize the results as if they were already accomplished are exactly what God used with Abram (whose name was later changed to Abraham by God). It is written, *"Then He brought him outside and said, Look now toward heaven, and count the stars if you are able to number them. And He said to him, So shall your descendants be. And he (Abram) believed in the Lord, and He accounted it to him for righteousness"* (Genesis 15:5-6).
6. The instructions given in the class to mentally and physically feel the emotions (joy and excitement) of having already achieved that which you were affirming is likened to David, the shepherd boy, when he was convincing King Saul that he would go and destroy the Philistine giant, Goliath. David told the King, *"I have been taking care of my father's sheep, and when a lion or a bear comes to steal a lamb from the flock, I go after it with a club and take the lamb from its mouth.. If the animal turns on me, I catch it by the jaw and club it to death. I have done this to both lions and bears, and I'll do it to this pagan Philistine too, for he has defied the armies of the Living God! The Lord who saved me from the claws of the lion and bear will save me from this Philistine"* (1 Samuel 17:34-37).

David borrowed the emotions of being victorious from his past experiences of killing vicious animals with his hands and a club. And he transferred those emotions of being victorious, knowing that the Lord had saved him from the claws of the lions and bears. He also filled himself with the same emotions, knowing that the Lord would save him in his fight with giant Goliath.

I invite you to read 1 Samuel, chapter 17, to get a full understanding of the powerful truths revealed in this exciting chapter. Also, if you don't know the outcome of this saga, then this chapter is a must read for you.

There were far too many other similarities in this training session that I attended to record in this book, but I believe that the six similarities outlined previously, along with many others not mentioned in this book, didn't fall out of the sky. Since these secular concepts came after the Bible, I am fully persuaded that they were lifted from the Holy Scriptures.

The rationale given for presenting this particular training from a purely secular viewpoint would probably be that corporate America stays clear of religious issues fearing backlash from customers, employees, and the American Civil Liberties Union (ACLU).

Natural-Human Faith Works: But There Is A Higher Dimension, A Higher Calling And Greater Rewards

As it was stated before, this seminar that I attended was presented on a secular level and, therefore, void of any mention of faith in God the Father. However, the concepts and techniques presented during the seminar worked for me. After seeing them work in my situation, I began to enthusiastically share the concepts and techniques with others. The feedback from those who followed the concepts and techniques were overwhelmingly positive. Why was this so, in their case and in mine?

Well, the spiritual law of sowing and reaping was at work. The (mind and) heart is like the ground, it doesn't care what kind of a seed you plant. You can plant flower seeds, vegetable seeds, or deadly poisonous bush seeds and the ground will work overtime to produce whatever seed is planted (after its own kind).

The reason why my affirmations and those of the others worked, is because we were operating in the spiritual law of sowing and reaping, which works equally in natural things and spiritual things.

The spiritual law of sowing and reaping is revealed in the Scriptures as follows: *"Do not be deceived; God is not mocked; for whatever a man sows, that will he also reap"* (Galatians 6:7, NKJV).

Another Powerful Spiritual Law That Works With Natural Things

During the time I was repeating aloud my affirmations, and during the time the other people that I mentioned earlier were repeating their affirmations, there was another spiritual law at work, although we were affirming through natural human faith.

To provide a clearer understanding of this next spiritual law and how it works with "natural-human faith," I need to ask some pointed questions first:

1. Why do you think American and some foreign companies paid $1.6 million for a 30-second television commercial during the 1998 Super Bowl (football) game? Now hold on to your seat! Why do you think dot.com internet companies paid an average price of $2.2 million for a 30-second

commercial during the 1999 Super Bowl game on the American Broadcasting Company Television Network (ABC)? This amounted to an amazing $73,333 per second, and it represented a whopping, thirty-eight percent increase from the previous $1.6 million price for a 30-second commercial. Don't you just wonder why they pay so much money for commercials?

2. Why do you think companies paid the American Broadcasting Company (ABC) $800,000 for a 30-second television commercial on "20/20," which featured a Barbara Walter's interview with Monica Lewinsky?
3. Why do you think General Motors Corporation (Corp.), the leading advertiser for the period of May 1997 to April 1998, spent about $2,293,746,000 in total advertising expenditures; but 84.5% of the company's total advertising expenditures was for television and radio commercials? The remaining 15.5% of the company's advertising expenditures was spent in consumer magazines, Sunday magazines, newspapers, national newspapers and outdoor advertising.
   Source: 1999 Standard Directory of Advertisers Volume 1
4. Why do you think that PepsiCo, the number seven leading advertiser, spent an estimated total of $808,863,000 in advertising expenditures; and of that amount, $778,308,000 (96.2%) was devoted to television commercials, but only 3.8% was spent on radio?
   Source: 1999 Standard Directory of Advertisers Volume 1
5. Why do you think that the hamburger folks at McDonald's Corporation (Corp.), the number sixteenth leading advertiser, spent an estimated total of $582,309,000 in advertising expenditures (96.3%) on television, but no advertising dollars were devoted to radio?
   Source: 1999 Standard Directory of Advertisers Volume 1
6. Why do you think companies like General Motors Corporation never produce a television or radio commercial and run it one time only?
7. Why do you think that during a Super Bowl football game you may hear and see the same television commercial half a dozen times or more during the game?

I suspect that one of your answers to these questions I raised might be that television and radio reach very large audiences of listeners and reviewers. My reply to that answer is, you are exactly right! However, there is another major underlying reason why companies spend hundreds of millions and even billions of dollars on television and radio commercials. The other answer that I want to amplify is revealed in the book of Romans. It is spiritual law governing faith, which is unfolded in the next topic.

Hidden Secret Unveiled: Spiritual Law Governing Faith Works In The Spiritual As Well As The Natural Realm.

The other answer to the seven questions which were previously asked, is found in the spiritual law governing faith.

This spiritual law states:

> *So then faith comes by hearing, and hearing by the Word of God.*
> Romans 10:17, NKJV

What this Scripture reveals is that you must hear the Word of God in your ears and that's how faith comes. Notice that it doesn't say faith comes by reading, lip-syncing, thinking, or meditating, No! The Word of God says that **faith** comes by **hearing**.

Kindly take notice of the key word in this Scripture, "hearing" which has "ing" at the end of the word denoting an active, ongoing process. The emphasis here is not on just hearing it once and that's it, but the hearing must be a continuous process of hearing for faith to come.

Corporate executives and advertising firms have long ago discovered that faith for their products comes by the consumer hearing their commercial messages in the ear. If this spiritual law governing faith gained by hearing did not work, you can be sure that the corporate executives of major companies would drop their TV and radio advertising campaigns like a hot potato. Instead, most Fortune 500 companies increase their television advertising budgets each year.

Hence, we know that faith for natural things can be obtained in the same way that faith for spiritual things is obtained, and that's by hearing the words, the message, the commercial in the ear.

Now let's see how this hearing and believing works. Let's say it's a Sunday afternoon in January and the Super Bowl (football) game is on TV. The first commercial is a General Motors Corporation, 30-second spot that features its new, elite (top of the line) Cadillac Seville STS (sports touring suspension). This elegant Seville is a gold on gold, 4-door, luxury sedan with plush complimentary interior, and the announcer says it provides the ultimate experience in driving comfort, safety, and benefits.

This commercial will run a total of eight times during the football game. The viewers at home watching and listening to the Cadillac commercial each time it runs are seeing and hearing it, seeing and hearing it. After seeing and hearing the same Cadillac commercial, time after time, the (mind and) heart is busy at work directing your conscious mind to accept and move toward what was said and demonstrated in the TV commercial as reality.

This strong influence (push) by the (mind and) heart is the main reason why some people will go to the local Cadillac dealer to see this new Seville STS. Some will end up buying the car on the spot, and others will eventually purchase it later. And some will elect not to purchase it for reasons due to needs and personal preference, etc.

Answers Provided For The 7 Questions Previously Asked

Question No. 1

Answer — Super Bowl games have a history of attracting millions and millions of viewers. It provides the advertiser with the opportunity to reach the maximum number of viewers within a two-hour time frame with their commercial message.

The ultimate reason companies spend mega-bucks on television commercials is because it is a medium that can effectively impact the major two of the five senses, which are hearing and sight.

It also transmits the body language of a speaker, which accounts for 58% of the effectiveness of the speaker; 35% of effectiveness is associated with the tone of voice (reflection in pitch or loudness); and just 7% is based on what the speaker is saying. In other words, the effectiveness of what someone is saying depends almost totally on body language and tone of voice.

We have all seen and heard politicians on TV who lack cheerful facial expressions who go on and on, speaking in boring monotone voices. We generally either click off or over to something else.

Television commercial producers capitalize on the hearing aspects, the body language, and movement aspects when producing a television commercial. In addition, television captures things in living color, which has a profound lasting and easy recall impact on the mind of the viewer.

These are some of the reasons why advertisers spend $1.6 million or even $2.2 million on a single 30-second TV commercial. But keep in mind that it is the "hearing" part that is the main ingredient that makes an effective TV commercial. They want to get their message in your ear gates. How many times have you watched TV with the mute on? Or how many times have you rented a silent movie?

Question No. 2

Answer - High profile individuals, which Monica Lewinsky certainly was at that time, generally attract a large number of television viewers.

Especially in her case because at that time, the general public had not heard her speak before. Advertisers want to reach the largest audience possible.

Question No. 3

Answer - Same answers as given for Question No. 1.

Question No. 4

Answer - Same answers as given for Question No. 1, plus television is more effective because it impacts two of the viewers senses, sight and hearing, where radio only impacts one, hearing.

Question No. 5

Answer - Same answers as given in Question No. 4.

Question No. 6

Answer - The spiritual law governing faith says that faith comes by hearing, which means an ongoing process of hearing the same thing repetitiously. Remember that the corporate executives are wise as the owl. They set their advertising budget to get maximum television commercial spots and yet keep within their budget. In other words, the greatest bang for the buck. Furthermore, it would not be cost-effective to produce a commercial and run it one time only.

Question No. 7

Answer - The more times that the viewer hears and sees the same commercial on television, the greater the impact on the (mind and) heart of the viewers and on their conscious reality, either positively or negatively.

Spiritual Law Governing Faith Works In The Natural Realm

Think about this, if television and radio commercials were not effective mediums to influence viewers' and listeners' attitudes, desires, and buying habits, then the corporate executives are unwise. They would be wasting millions and billions of their stockholders' dollars in advertising expenditures. However, they are not wasting their stockholders' money; in fact, they are wise to the bone. They are using a spiritual law to acquire billions and billions of dollars in profits in the natural (physical) realm.

Although I exercised natural human faith (by reading my affirmation) and it produced positive results, I soon realized that this kind of faith was divorced from any mentioning or belief in God the Father. I also realized that the Bible commands us to trust in the Lord with "all" our heart. It doesn't say trust in your own natural-human faith.

Rededicated My Life To Jesus Christ Of Nazareth

In the late summer of 1982, I attended a Dr. Frederick K.C. Price, Ever Increasing Faith Ministries Crusade in Long Island, New York. It was there that I rededicated my life to Jesus and was filled with the Holy Spirit. It all happened at this crusade. I had been seeking a church home, as I had been led by the Holy Spirit to leave the United Church of Christ that my daughter and I were attending. Ironically, I was told by a person at the crusade about a good church in Cleveland. A church whose ministry was similar to Dr. Price's teachings. I had never heard of the church, so when I arrived back in Cleveland I was excited about checking out this church.

Well, the rest is history. My daughter and I attended Christian Fellowship Center for about six months and then joined the fellowship. My daughter sang in the youth choir and I served as a Sunday School teacher and Administrator, Deacon, Special Projects Coordinator, and I was ordained Elder on February 10, 1989.

Soon after I had returned from the New York crusade, there was a tug on my spirit concerning the growth affirmations I was reading each day. I was moved to find Bible Scriptures to support my desires to grow in different areas of my life. One specific desire of mine was for a wife. Wow! How excited I was when I found the Scripture that said, *"And the Lord God said, It is not good for the man to be alone,"* and I found another Scripture that said, *"The man who finds a wife finds a treasure and receives favors from the Lord."* This was truly Good News for me! I immediately sat down and wrote my faith-building confession for a wife.

I found Bible Scriptures to support my need and desires, and began to rewrite my affirmations around what the Word of God says about who I am, what the Word of God says about what I can do, and what it says I have as a believer. I chose to walk in and confess "Revelation Faith" and not natural-human faith. I had to get my act together as I was rapidly learning that there were tremendous earthly and spiritual benefits available to me as a believer. I had also come into the knowledge that there is "supernatural bionic power" in the Word of God. When the believer speaks the Word of God through his/her lips, that supernatural bionic power is planted in the believer's heart and spirit, and that same supernatural power will manifest on the conscious level of the believer's life. Praise the Lord!

Guaranteed Protection Under The Revelation Faith Umbrella

The Traveler's Insurance Company trademark is an open red umbrella. The meaning that company promotes is that when you have insurance coverage with Travelers, you are protected under their red umbrella when the storms of life come pouring down. As long as you stay under their red umbrella, your medical bills, house, property, and automobile are covered. Also, damage due to accidents, fire and theft are covered. You and your family are covered in case of death, as long as you remain under their red umbrella.

My decision to change from natural-human faith to revelation faith was because I wanted to be under God the Father's glorious umbrella of protection and blessings. I didn't, for one minute, want to take a chance on being out from under His umbrella due to disobedience to His Word (out of fellowship).

I have set up permanent residence under His glorious umbrella and I will not be moved. Praise the Lord!

If you are not sure whether you are under His glorious umbrella of divine protection and blessings, or if you are unsure of what will happen to you when you die, then there's Good News for you! There is plenty of room for you under His umbrella. I invite you now to come under His glorious umbrella of protection and blessings in this life and also receive eternal life. God loves and values you so much, He made a way for you to be saved.

I encourage you to turn now to Appendix A. There you will find some valuable information that will get you under God's glorious umbrella of protection and blessings. Turn now and receive your gift of a lifetime!

> ***"The time to repair the roof is when the sun is shining."***
> ***John F. Kennedy, American President***

There Is A Better Way

For those individuals who are tired of living from paycheck to paycheck, pension check to pension check, social security check to social security check, then there is a better way.

I urge you to be as wise or wiser than the corporate executives whom we discussed earlier. You can be, by doing the following:

1. Maximize the use of the spiritual law governing faith (faith comes by hearing) to produce meaningful and lasting changes in your spiritual, financial, physical, mental, domestic, and social life in this New Millennium.
   Use the self-talk (faith-building) confessions prescribed in this book, and make your own reality commercial by confessing and visualizing the things that you need or desire as though they already were a reality. In doing so, you will make your way prosperous in this New Millennium.
2. Diligently and persistently read **aloud** the self-talk (faith-building) confessions prescribed in this book to help you grow

and develop strong faith in the Word of God. Keep your (faith-building) confessions before your eyes, and program these reality commercials in your (mind and) heart every chance you get.

3. Set your goals high! Aim to be a self-talk (faith-building) confessaholic in this New Millennium, and remain steadfast in your goals.
4. Fix your heart, your spirit, and your self-talk on receiving your covenant inheritance of wealth and riches in this New Millennium, for the purpose of giving into the Kingdom of God and sharing it with the poor and needy. Also, to meet your own needs and desires, and the needs and desires of your family. Praise the Lord!

In the book of Galatians, the apostle Paul writes the following word of wisdom to you.

> *And let us not lose heart and grow weary and faint in acting nobly and doing right, for in due time and at the appointed season we shall reap, if we do not loosen and relax our courage and faint* (Galatians 6:9, Amp.).

In summary, yes, natural-human faith works, but there is a higher dimension, a higher calling, and greater rewards when you put your trust in revelation faith, the God-kind of faith. I am a witness to this.

The following is one of my self-talk (faith-building) confessions. It has been revised throughout the years, and I will share it with you. It has helped to keep me under my Heavenly Father's glorious umbrella of protection and blessings. I urge you to add this faith-building confession to your daily menu of confessions.

Self-Talk (Faith-Building) Confession:

I put total trust and dependence on my Heavenly Father and His Word. I lean not to my own understanding. I am not moved by how I feel. I am not moved by the present circumstances. I am not moved by what I see. I am not moved by what I hear. I am only moved by what I believe and act upon. If the Bible says it, I rightly divide it and if it's a statement of truth, I believe it. I believe it! And I act upon it, and that settles it. I stagger not at the promises of God, for I am fully persuaded that what the Word of God promises me, my Heavenly Father will perform. I confess this under the authority and in the wonderful Name of Jesus Christ of Nazareth! So Be It! (2 Corinthians 5:7; John 20:29; 2 Corinthians 4:18; 2 Timothy 2:15).

In the next section, Revelation Faith will be unveiled.

PART 3

WHAT IS REVELATION FAITH?

Revelation faith does not rest on logical proof or material evidence. It puts no reliance upon things that are seen with the natural eye or the things perceived by the other four senses (hearing, feeling, tasting, and smelling).

Revelation faith relies totally on the Word of God as the undisputed proof and evidence in every situation. It unwaveringly fixes complete confidence and trust in God the Father, God the Son, God the Holy Spirit, and total dependence on the revealed Word of God (as stated in the Holy Bible).

Master Key That Unlocks The Treasure Of Faith. The Spiritual Law Governing Faith

The apostle Paul unveils the biblical road map that believers are to live by. The leading of the Holy Spirit establishes the following spiritual law governing faith. *"For we walk by faith, not by sight"* (2 Corinthians 5:7, KJV).

To walk by faith means we are to self-talk, speak to others, act on, do, and walk by the Living Word of God in our everyday life. This Scripture provides the key to unlock the treasure of faith.

Know this, that your major task in receiving your covenant inheritance of wealth and riches in this New Millennium will be to devote quality time, effort, energy, and passion toward building strong faith. Also know that you can build strong faith by diligently, reverently, and persistently self-talking the (faith-building) confessions prescribed in this book, or by writing your own faith-building confessions and adding them to your daily menu.

It is written:

> *So you see, it is impossible to please God without faith. Anyone who wants to come to him must believe that there is a God and that he rewards those who sincerely seek him.* Hebrews 11:6, NLT

Concerning faith, you have two choices. One is to please God, and you please Him when you trust in the Living Word of God, self-talk His Word and do His Word by walking in faith. The other choice is to please Satan by walking by sight, putting your faith in man and the things that man does, which are all perceived through the five senses. Individuals who are ruled by their bodies or ruled by their senses are walking by sight. And indeed, they are displeasing God and pleasing Satan.

As for me, I refuse to please anything or anyone that is a killer, a destroyer, a thief, the father of lies, and a deceiver; these are all character traits of Satan and his modus-operandi.

What Is Faith?

Before we proceed further, let us closely examine five modern versions of Hebrews 11:1 which provide the Biblical definition of faith.

King James:	*Now faith is the substance of things hoped for, the evidence of things not seen.*
Living New Testament:	*What is faith? It is the confident assurance that something we want is going to happen. It is the certainty that what we hope for is waiting for us, even though we cannot see it up ahead.*
New International Version:	*Now faith is being sure of what we hope for and certain of what we do not see.*
New Living Translation:	*What is faith? It is the confident assurance that what we hope for is going to happen. It is the evidence of things we cannot yet see.*
Amplified Bible:	*Now faith is the assurance (the confirmation, the title-deed) of the things (we) hope for, being the proof of things (we) do not see and the conviction of their reality – faith perceiving as real fact what is not revealed to the senses.*

I favor the Amplified Bible's rendering of the definition of faith. The very first word "now" reveals an extremely valuable component of faith! Look for a moment at the words on both sides of the word "faith." The apostle Paul says "**Now faith is**..." The word "now" is an adverb which means "at the present time," as opposed to in the past or in the future. In this setting, the phrase "at the present time" is synonymous with being present tense. Hence, faith is always **now**, not in the past, and not in the future. Faith is now, present tense.

The word "is" on the other side of the word "faith" is a verb which expresses actions or existence. It too is a present tense word.

Faith that is the substance of things hoped for is always "now" faith. The word "substance" means that the thing you hope for already exists (has substance) in the spiritual realm. If faith is not "now," it's not faith.

The word "hope" is a goal setter. It identifies those things that you need or desire. The things that you are praying for, believing for, and confessing for. Hope is always out there in the future. Hope says, "I hope that I will have enough money to meet my bills."

Faith says, "I believe in my (heart and) spirit that my bills are paid. My God supplies all my needs according to His riches in glory by Christ Jesus."

Rather than saying "I hope" which is not faith, I always say "I'm believing," or "I'm confessing," which demonstrates faith.

The word hope is a hindrance to faith. We have a hope of heaven, and when we reach heaven we shall hope no longer. In most cases, the needs and desires of believers are things that they need now, today. I am not hoping for my covenant inheritance of $167,800,000 sometime in the future. No! I'm confessing that I believe that I have received my covenant inheritance of $167,800,000.

I will quickly pause here again, before the spirit of criticism engulfs the mind of some who are reading this. That spirit would say, "Why does he need so much money?" Well, there are a number of reasons why:

1. In this New Millennium, we need to renew our (minds and) heart concerning wealth and riches. Our possession of wealth and riches will never rise above the level of our mind set concerning how much money represents being wealthy.

   Many years ago, a loaf of bread cost 10 cents and a person with holdings of $100,000 would be considered wealthy. However, in our fast paced cyberspace economy, we have seen young men under 30 years of age become millionaires overnight.

   Think about this: Bill Gates, the richest man in the world at last count was worth $85 billion plus. His home cost $75 million. He is the world's icon of computer software. As a teenager in high school, he dreamed, believed, and often self-talked and said to others that computers should be available to everyone. They would provide functions that would benefit and enhance the way we do things. He also dreamed and believed and said that lots of money could be made designing and producing personal computers and software. Gates taught himself much about computer programming along the way. He studied hard and he worked hard at his trade. He made it, and he deserves it.

   It's all relative, when we think of money. What was big money yesterday is considered peanuts today. It's like age; if you think you are old, you will act and be old. If you think $250,000 is a lot of money, then chances are you will never accumulate anywhere near that amount. It's as if you have installed a governor in your mind which controls your ability to rise above the level of that which you have knowledge of or faith for.

2. When I went to my Heavenly Father in prayer and asked Him how much money He had bequested to me, and He told me $167,800,000, I didn't tell Him that it was too much. I told Him that I would be a good and faithful steward over what He had given me.
3. Another very important factor to remember is that you are entrusted with God's money to distribute it according to His plan and purpose. For example, if your covenant inheritance is $100 million, taxes (federal, state, and city), could take upward of 55%; the government could get $55 million, which would leave you with $45 million.

   Your covenant mission and purpose is to share a minimum of 30% of your remaining covenant inheritance of $45 million with God's storehouse, your local church. Your local church gets $13.5 million. Also, your covenant mission and purpose is to share a minimum of 40% of your covenant inheritance with the poor and needy. The poor and needy get $18 million (as directed by the Holy Spirit).

   This leaves you with $13.5 million of which your covenant mission and purpose is to invest wisely 10%, which means you will invest $4.5 million. The remaining 20% of your covenant inheritance, $9 million, is yours to meet your needs and desires, and the needs and desires of your family; which includes leaving an inheritance to your children and your children's children.

   This then confirms and brings into reality that which you had been confessing for, and that was "I believe in my heart and spirit by faith that I have received my covenant inheritance of $100 million." Praise the Lord! I have figured it out, and my covenant inheritance of $167,800,000, along with what I have already been blessed with, works out just fine in my case. Of course, my Heavenly Father had already figured that out long before I did. Everyone's situation is different. Your age, number of dependents, and the number of your family members whose needs are not met, are all part of figuring your covenant inheritance. **SO THINK BIG!!**

   Forbes Magazine indicated that it has found some 470 billionaires. Think about this, if 470 people are billionaires, it means that it is possible that you can be one also. Surely you and thousands of other believers with the Holy Spirit can close the "wealth divide" and become abundantly rich and wealthy within the next decade or two.

Your covenant inheritance could be much, much more than $167,800,000 or it could be less. It could be $500 billion. Ask your Heavenly Father and wait. He will let you know the amount. Praise the Lord!

Your Covenant Inheritance Of Wealth And Riches Is A Done Deal

Before we took the side tour of discussing the amount of my covenant inheritance, we were discussing faith and the word "hope." Let's resume where we left off. Many people confuse hope and faith. They say, "Well, I believe that God is going to do this for me sometime or sooner or later" or "I hope God will do this or that."

But God has done all that He is ever going to do about your covenant inheritance of wealth and riches. He has done all He will ever do about your healing. He has done all He will ever do about your salvation and your eternal life. It was done when Jesus Christ of Nazareth took upon Himself the great substitutionary sacrifice for our sins, sickness, spiritual death, and poverty.

Upon His death, He met our adversary, Satan, and conquered him, stripped him of his authority, defeated him in open combat, and took from him the armor of which he had robbed Adam in the Garden of Eden.

When He conquered the adversary, we conquered the adversary in and through Him. He conquered the adversary on our behalf. It was done when He bore our sickness and carried our disease. He substituted Himself so that with His stripes we are healed from sickness and disease. It was done when He took it upon Himself to become poor that through His poverty you might become rich.

Jesus conquered the adversary on our behalf and with His victory, we today are conquerors and victorious because of His substitutionary sacrifice for us. The promises of God have already been spoken. God's will is His Word; His Word is His will. The New Testament is the last will and testament of Jesus. He has already said yes to it. It's not a matter of what He is going to do someday, it is a matter of us acting on our faith and receiving what He has already done. Praise the Lord!

The Scripture that we are focusing on says, *"Now faith is the assurance (the confirmation, the title-deed) of the things (we) hope for, being the proof of things (we) do not see and the conviction of their reality"* (Hebrews 11:1).

Your faith in the Word of God is the title-deed. The Word of God is the bona fide evidence that God the Father has already legally granted the things that you hope for. The things that you pray for, believe for and confess for are already yours (tangible) in the spiritual realm. It is your persistent reading aloud of your self-talk faith-building confessions that will cause those same things to become tangible in the physical realm.

Remember this always: Your confession is the expression of your faith; you rise or fall to the level of your confession!

The Word Of God Is Your Title-Deed

Let's see if we can bring this subject of faith into clearer focus with the following illustration.

A man passed away and he had bequested a lovely white, ten-room bungalow house to his only grandson. The grandson had just left the ABC Title-Deed Warranty Company and had the legal papers (the title-deed) in his name showing that he was the legal owner of the ten-room house which his grandfather left to him.

Although the grandson was not yet physically living in the house, the title-deed was the evidence that the house belonged to him. It didn't matter whether he moved in or not, the house still belonged to him. His title-deed was a legal document that would stand up in any court of law.

Remember this, that the Word of God and the Name of Jesus Christ of Nazareth are the title-deed (the evidence) to whatever things you're confessing for, and the evidence that you already have ownership or possession of those things (present tense) by faith. It is your persistent, reverent acting on God's Word, by applying it to your situation and reading aloud your faith-building confession, that will cause the thing to become reality.

The written Word of God is your title-deed and it will stand up in God's court of law, with full backing by all of God's heavenly forces. Praise the Lord!

His Words written in the Holy Bible are your title deed, your guarantee that you already have everything that He promises in His Word. Sad to say, many believers beg, plead, cry, and pray for things that are already theirs.

If a father called his son, who had just turned 21 years old, to come and sit down and talk; and the father then told him that he had been a good son, and he was gifting him with the keys to a brand new sports car, fully insured...Do you think the son would go back to his father the next morning, begging, pleading, crying, and asking his dad to please buy him a new sports car? No, the son would confidently, thankfully, and patiently wait until the father finalized the car sale and handed him the key. The father's word is the title-deed until the keys are handed to the son.

The same holds true in spiritual things; the Word of Father God is the title-deed to everything He has promised you in the Holy Scriptures. It is your confident, persistent, and thankful self-talk (faith-building) confessions, along with patience, that will cause the things that you confess to be tangible in your life.

Caution – Never Give Up

Don't let other people derail you with their negative comments. Hold fast to your planned destiny.

Frederick W. Smith is a man who held fast to his ideas and dreams. Federal Express Corporation was founded by Frederick W. Smith, Chairman and President of FDX Corporation. In 1965, as a Yale undergraduate, Smith wrote a term paper about the passenger route systems used by most air freight shippers, that he viewed as economically inadequate. Smith stated that what was needed was a system designed specifically for airfreight that could accommodate time-sensitive shipments such as medicines, computer parts and electronics. Smith received a C on that term paper.

It has been said that Smith's professor told him that his idea of time-sensitive shipments of goods via special air freight carriers would not work; therefore, he gave Smith a C. But this didn't stop Smith. Federal Express was incorporated in June 1971, officially began operations on April 17, 1973, and the rest is history. Federal Express revenues for fiscal 1999 were $14.0 billion (U.S. dollars). Source, Fed Ex Fast Facts.

Be aware. Do not let the adversary (Satan) deter you from receiving your covenant inheritance of wealth and riches. Revelation knowledge (revealed in the Scriptures) cautions us not to lose heart, grow weary, or faint in acting nobly, and doing right; for in due time and at the appointed season, you shall reap, if you do not loosen and relax your courage, and faint.

Developing Strong Faith Is The Greatest Challenge

Earlier, it was stated that developing strong faith will be your greatest challenge in receiving your covenant inheritance of wealth and riches in this New Millennium. The apostle Paul, inspired by the Holy Spirit penned the following revelation knowledge for us to grasp.

> *"For in it the righteousness of God is revealed from faith to faith; as it is written,* ***the just shall live by faith.****"*
> Romans 1:17, NKJV

The message that the apostle Paul is revealing is that the only way the believer should live is by faith (revelation faith) in the Word of God.

The faith life is the most beautiful life in the world. It is the life that God has designed for us. He wants us to walk by faith and not by sight (2 Corinthians 5:7). He wants us to enjoy all of the benefits He promised in this life.

You must work overtime at letting both your words and your actions line up and agree with the Word of God. The two must be the same as wet is to water. In other words, if you self-talk faith, you must act on faith. Your words and your actions ought to coincide. It is like a hand and a glove, the glove is no good without a hand.

It is worthless to self-talk faith and not have corresponding action. You may have heard someone say, "I am trusting God to meet my needs." Later on, or the next day, they say, "I don't know how I am going to pay my car payment. It looks like I may lose my car. It will probably be repossessed."

In this case, the individual is mentally asserting that He is trusting God to meet his needs. His second statement is a confession of doubt, and doubt is the opposite of faith; it hinders faith. The Word of God tells us clearly that the just shall live (walk) by faith and not by sight (the five senses) or mental assertion. The just shall live by revelation faith, which is the written Word of God.

Sorrow looks back, worry looks around, faith looks up.
Guidepost

Faith declares what the senses do not see.

CHAPTER 6

WHY DO PEOPLE PUT GREAT TRUST IN MAN AND LITTLE TRUST IN GOD?

We put inordinate trust or faith in man and his abilities. We do this blindly, without thinking; we put faith in man without weighing minor logical terms, without investigating the reality of this incredible and valuable trust which we freely allow ourselves to have for man. We put unwarranted faith in doctors, dentists and others. For some people, their doctor is like a god. In fact, we put our life and the lives of our loved ones in man's hands without doing some simple, basic, logical thinking and investigating. Our owner's operating manual (the Holy Bible) clearly instructs us not to put trust in man.

It says, "*It is better to trust and take refuge in the Lord than put confidence in man*" (Psalm 118:8, Amp.).

Let's step back and take a real look at how the reality of this trust in man plays out in our everyday life.

1. How many times have you asked to see and read your primary care doctor's board certified certificate? The emergency room doctor? Your surgeon? Your dentist? Or others?
2. How many times have you asked to see and read the personal background record similar to a resume of any of the doctors listed above?
3. How many times have you read the doctor's or dentist's board certified papers and personal background records, and you did some follow-up investigation to insure that the doctor's or dentist's papers were valid?
4. How many times have you requested that a test be redone two or three times, even if the results show negative?
5. How many times have you had a second, third, or fourth (independent) opinion done before taking strong medication, treatments, or surgery?
6. If you or a member of your family were recommended for surgery, how many times did you request to see the hospital's success records (in writing) for the type of surgery being proposed?
7. And how many times have you requested to see (in writing)

> the surgeon's success rate for the type of surgery being proposed? In other words, how many patients recovered from the surgery? And of those who recovered, how long did they live? One year? Three years? Five years, etc.

I believe that most individuals would agree that unless you have full disclosure, clear-cut intelligent answers (in writing) to the above questions, it would not be wise to proceed with strong medication, treatments, or surgery. Otherwise, you are placing an awesome amount of unintelligent faith in doctors, surgeons, dentists, the hospital, and the like. I guarantee you that doctors themselves would not allow someone to put them under anesthesia and cut them open, without first having full creditable information on the qualifications and track record of the hospital, the doctors involved, and the staff.

Even with our automobiles, we want the best auto shop and the best mechanic to work on and fine-tune our automobile. Our bodies are the temple of God, and far more important and valuable than any machine.

Beware Of Quacks And Kooks On The Loose

We have come to learn from investigative reporting on television that quacks have been identified and put in prison for practicing medicine, treating patients, and even performing surgery with no license or with an expired or invalid license. Some of this quackery occurred at major hospitals here in the good old USA.

In a number of cases, we have come to know that certain caregivers who were supposed to administer care and treatment to keep people alive were, in fact, psychopathic serial killers who were giving patients poison or injecting them with overdoses of substances that resulted in deaths.

When we go to the Word of God, we will always find the answers we need to keep us wise. The answer that God gives concerning putting trust in man is very stern. This is what the Lord says:

> *Cursed are those who put their trust in mere humans and turn their hearts away from the Lord* (Jeremiah 17:5).

We have also come to learn from investigative reporting on television and in the printed media that countless doctors who were addicted to drugs and alcohol, suicidal, and sex offenders were practicing medicine with a license and others were practicing medicine illegally.

Most people put so much faith in their doctor that they don't even ask for copies of their own test results, which they have paid for with their hard-earned cash. They simply accept brief, and sometimes hurried, verbal comments from the doctor or his/her staff member concerning test results.

I always request written copies of my test results and those of my family members for our personal file.

I always strongly urge second and third opinions when strong medications or treatment are prescribed, or when surgery is being recommended. News reporting has revealed faulty and improper testing of blood and body tissues at (production type) laboratories, which have produced incorrect test results.

The experts warn, poor regulation lets life-altering errors occur. An incident that was reported in the print media revealed that a gene test provided results that showed a woman was at greatly increased risk of getting breast and ovarian cancer. This woman's mother and aunt had both died of cancer, so she had her ovaries removed. Months later, she got more devastating news. The company that tested her genes had made a mistake, she didn't have the cancerous genetic defect after all.

Arecent report revealed that as many as 98,000 American lives are lost each year due to what is now called medical errors, which occur at hospitals throughout America. Medical errors are a soft term which masks pure negligence and in some cases, criminal acts on the part of some caregivers who are paid hefty fees to provide life and not death. The 98,000 lives lost each year is equivalent to a jetliner crash every day.

A New York Times News Service recently reported "Veterans Hospitals Mistakes Kill 700." The federal investigators documented almost 3,000 medical mistakes in less than two years. More than 700 patients died in those cases. Mistakes ranged from prescribing and dispensing wrong drugs, to errors in blood transfusions and operations on wrong body parts.

In obedience to the Word of God, I strongly urge that unless it is a case of life or death, whenever surgery is being considered, a second or third independent source should be used to duplicate previous tests before surgery. However, ongoing self-talk (faith-building) confessions for divine redemptive health is the optimal.

How Much Trust Do You Put In Airline Companies?

1. How many times have you asked to see the maintenance records for the airplane that you are going to travel on, to insure that all the Federal Aviation Administration (FAA) recommended modifications and maintenance procedures were being followed?
2. How many times have you asked to see the pilot's safety and performance records to determine if the pilots had any job performance reprimands in the past?

3. How many times have you asked how many hours of rest is required for pilots between flights, and if the pilots have met the required rest periods?
4. How many times have you asked to see (in writing) the airline safety record? Runway? In-flight and landing?
5. How many times have you asked to see (in writing) the air traffic controllers' safety records at the departure and arrival airports?
6. How many times have you asked your travel agent about the safety record of the airlines, and of the specific airplane which they are scheduling you on?

When we plan to drive for a long distance, one of the first things we want to make sure of is that our automobile is thoroughly checked out and is operating properly.

We have come to learn that many of the commercial airplane accidents on the ground and in the air are related to safety guidelines and maintenance procedure errors. Sad to say, but these airplane accidents cause hundreds of deaths, loss of life which may have been prevented if someone had been **bold** and taken the time to ask questions, rather than putting complete trust in the airlines.

How Much Trust Do You Put In Restaurants?

1. How many times have you requested to see the Health Department Records of each person who handles your food to insure that they have met all of the required health standards?
2. How many times have you asked to see the Health Department Records which will show if the restaurant has any outstanding violations? Also, how many times have you requested to see records that would show if the restaurant meets required standards in cleanliness, food preparation, food storage, etc.?
3. How many times have you asked to see the restaurant's policy (in writing) which covers employee's sanitation procedures? Are employees required, under strict supervision to wash their hands thoroughly after using the restroom? When employees begin their duty or if they were engaged in another work activity, are they required to wash their hands thoroughly before handling your food?

Some of these questions may sound frivolous, but we have come to know of outbreaks of food poisoning and even deaths resulting from improper handling of food and from contaminated food. It has also been discovered that an employee of an eating facility who had a contagious disease passed the disease along to patrons of the restaurant.

San Diego County has an outstanding record when it comes to public safety and protection. I have lived in paradise (the golden triangle) of sunny San Diego for almost two years now. Here in San Diego, all restaurants are inspected four times a year by the Health Department and rated either A, B, or C, based on meeting state and local health requirements.

You will see a sign posted in every restaurant window which reflects how they are rated, "A" being the best rating. My family and I always choose to eat at "A"-rated restaurants. This rating system provides some means of screening for the public, but the ultimate responsibility remains with each individual to check things out for themselves.

Indeed, it is not wise to put complete trust in restaurants, or anything or anyone else, unless you have checked it out first. Remember, your body is the temple of God. He needs a healthy, strong body to work through.

Why Do People Put Trust In Astrology, Psychic Readers, And Necromancers?

In most communities you will find neon signs flashing (with much written advertising) urging folks to come on in and get their fortunes told, palms read, or for a tarot reading. Television is bombarded with psychic hot line commercials. The people who make their living doing this kind of thing are making big money, otherwise they would not stay in business. This means that they have substantial amounts of customers to keep their doors open. Some are located at prime real estate spots in downtown and upscale suburban areas.

Some people will not make any decisions unless they confer with a psychic hot line first, or they have to check with their astrologer or read their horoscope to see if the moon or Pluto is in the right position before they engage in a business transaction or take a trip.

Well, for those folks who partake in these things, I must burst their bubble; these things are an abomination to the Lord.

The Lord God says:

> *For example, never sacrifice your son or daughter as a burnt offering. And do not let your people practice fortune telling or sorcery, or allow them to interpret omens, or engage in witchcraft, or cast spells, or function as mediums or psychics, or call forth the spirits of the dead. Anyone who does these things is an object of horror and disgust to the Lord. It is because the other nations have done these things that the Lord your God will drive*

> *them out ahead of you. You must be blameless before the Lord your God. The people you are about to displace consult with sorcerers and fortune tellers, but the Lord your God forbids you to do such things (*Deuteronomy 18:10-14, NLT.).

God's Word clearly tells us that anyone who does these things is an object of horror and disgust to the Lord. God's Word commands us to be blameless before the Lord our God. Since God hates these things, then, as believers we are to act like and imitate Him; we ought to hate these things also. Please notice I said we are to hate the things (sin) and not hate the people who partake in such things. It is God's job and He will take care of those who disobey His commandments.

I must repeat again, that believers are not to hate anyone. The Word of God reveals to us that our hate and our fight is not against people, but it is against the evil spirits that cause people to sin.

God's Word reveals the following:

> *For we are not fighting against people made of flesh and blood, but **against** the evil rulers and authorities of the unseen world, **against** those mighty powers of darkness who rule this world, and **against** wicked spirits in the heavenly realms. Ephesians 6:12, NLT*

The Good News is that in spiritual warfare, believers win with the Name of Jesus. As for the sinner, believers should pray that the sinner will see the light and that the Lord our God will draw the sinner to come from the kingdom of darkness into the kingdom of light.

The Word of God does not instruct us to trust in psychics, fortune tellers, witches, black magic, astrologers, horoscope, and the like. No! The Word of God says to:

> *Trust in the Lord with all your heart; do not depend on your own understanding. Seek His will in all you do, and He will direct your paths (*Proverbs 3:5-6).

Think about this, if God does not want you to depend on your own understanding, He for sure does not want you to depend on a psychic reader, astrologer, fortune teller, and the like.

The Word of God says, "He will direct our paths."

There are far too many other areas where we put enormous trust in man, far too numerous to record in this book. The last one that we will discuss is the use of credit cards. We have come to know that giving credit card numbers over the telephone and over the internet can be very risky.

It was recently uncovered at some restaurants that the waiters would take the customer's credit card to go ring up the sale and, while doing so, they would capture the credit card number and information illegally, to sell to a third party, or for the waiters to use fraudulently.

Well, some may say, "Brother Jim, what does all this stuff have to do with my receiving my covenant inheritance of wealth and riches in this New Millennium?"

My reply is:

My sincere desire is that this information highlights how much faith we put in man and in man's abilities. I challenge you to transfer your faith from man to the Word of God, and act on the Word in the same fashion that you act on what man says and does. In doing so, you benefit because you put yourself in a position to become a spiritual giant having strong faith in God's Word, which is "Revelation Faith."

Also, you will more than qualify for another benefit, which is your covenant inheritance of wealth and riches, when you have a relationship with God the Father, and when you are in fellowship with Him. When you trust in Him and His Word completely, you are then operating in the God-kind of faith, "Revelation Faith," which pleases God the Father.

With God, all things are possible.
Matthew 19:26

CHAPTER 7

PART I
WHAT IS A FAITH-BUILDING CONFESSION?

In the previous pages, we discussed the different kinds of faith and, in particular, revelation faith which is the God-kind of faith. Now in this section, we will dissect the word "confession."

Different Uses Of The Word "Confession" Revealed

This word "confession" is a troublesome word because the results of its usage can reflect a positive outcome or a negative outcome. For example, one definition of the word "confession" is to "acknowledge or disclose one's misdeed, fault, or sin." Another meaning is to "declare faith in." It is the latter meaning that I am prescribing.

Christianity is called "the Great Confession." Confessing is affirming something that we believe. It is testifying of something that we know. It is witnessing for a truth that we have embraced. The right confession is the means by which a sinner is born again (Romans 10:9), and the right confession is the key to receiving your covenant inheritance of wealth and riches in this New Millennium. To get a clearer understanding of this often misunderstood word, I will do what I call the "flip flop method" to unveil the different uses of this word "confession."

First, we will look at some usages of the word "confession" which are not the meanings that I am prescribing for self-talk (faith-building) confessions.

Faith-Building Confession Is Not A Confession To Crime

Recently, an article appeared in the USAToday newspaper and the title of the article read "Handyman's Confession Launches FBI Inquiries." The word "confession" in this case is used relative to a person confessing to a crime or crimes committed. This is most certainly not the meaning of the word "confession" that I am advocating.

Faith-Building Confession Is Not A Confession To A Priest

Another usage of the word "confession" occurs when a parishioner confesses (reveals) their sins to a priest and asks forgiveness. This confessing of sin to a priest is **not** the kind of confession that is under examination in this topic.

Faith-Building Confession Is Not A Confession Of Sins Associated With Baptism

The first mentioning of confessing, in the New Testament appears in the book of Matthew, and this event unfolds thusly.

John the Baptist Prepares the Way

> *John's clothes were woven from camel hair, and he wore a leather belt; his food was locusts and wild honey. People from Jerusalem and from every section of Judea and from all over the Jordan Valley went out to the wilderness to hear him preach. And when they confessed their sins, he baptized them in the Jordan River.*
> Matthew 3:4-6, NLT

This Scripture gives an account of God's covenant people, the Jews, confessing their sins, and then being baptized by John the Baptist in the Jordan River.

At this point in time, Jesus had not died and risen again. Therefore, the Jews were still operating under the law. This act of confessing sins, when associated with baptism, has no reference for New Testament believers today.

The confessing of sins mentioned in this Scripture is most certainly **not** the self-talk (faith-building) confession that I am prescribing for your growth, development, and your prosperity in this New Millennium.

Faith-Building Confession Is Not the Sinner's Confession To Obtain Salvation

Another mentioning of confessing is found in the book of Romans, and this Scripture is the key reason why Christianity is called the Great Confession. It is one of the most widely-referred-to Scriptures in the Bible, other than John 3:16. I exhort you to read this Scripture aloud, then study and digest each word and its meaning.

> *That if you confess with your mouth the Lord Jesus and believe in your heart that God has raised Him from the dead, you will be saved. For with the heart one believes unto righteousness, and with the mouth confession is made unto salvation.*
> Romans 10:9-10, NKJV

The sinner is guilty of only one sin and that is the rejecting of Jesus Christ as Lord over his/her life (see John 16:7-11; 1 John 2:2).

God the Father designed His system whereby a sinner (a non-believer) could be saved (born again).

Jesus Himself told the Jewish religious leader named Nicodemus, a

Pharisee, *"I assure you, unless you are born again, you can never see the Kingdom of God."* The sinner is required to make only two confessions. He is not required to confess sins to be saved. Jesus' substitutional sacrifice for the world has already taken care of the sin problems, the poverty problems, the sickness problems, and the spiritual death problems. I have often heard believers requiring sinners to confess sins as part of their confession for salvation.

The confession that God the Holy Spirit requires of the sinner is clearly spelled out in the Scriptures we just read.

1. Confess with your mouth that Jesus is Lord...(confession of Lordship of Jesus Christ in one's life).
2. Believe in your heart that God raised Him from the dead; you will be saved.

Golden Nugget Revealed - Please notice with a keen eye and ear that to be born again, to get into God's Kingdom, one must "confess with the mouth."

As it was discussed earlier, this is why Christianity is called the Great Confession. We see in this Scripture that the confessing with the mouth and believing with the heart are the two prerequisites required to leave Satan's kingdom of darkness and enter into God's Kingdom of light.

This is an awesome, invaluable supernatural Scripture. It is where God the Father, God the Son, and God the Holy Spirit perform spiritual surgery to bring new birth to all who confess with the mouth that Jesus is Lord, and who believe in their heart that God raised Him from the dead. They will be saved.

As great as this Scripture is, the word "confess" mentioned here is **not** the one that I am prescribing for self-talk (faith-building) confessions.

I will pause again right here, to make a very, very important announcement. The two most important questions of your life are:

1. Are you fully persuaded that you are born again?
2. What will happen to you when you die?

If you are unsure of the answers to these questions, or if you are afraid you will not spend eternity in Heaven, there is Good News for you because God loves and values you so much that He made a way for you to be saved. You can settle these most important questions of your life. Turn now to Appendix A, pray the prayer provided, and receive Jesus as your Savior.

Faith-Building Confession Is Not Believers Confessing Sins To Each Other

Another reference of the word "confess" appears in the book of James.

James, the writer, exhorts believers in the following manner:

> *Confess your sins to each other and pray for each other so that you may be healed. The earnest prayer of a righteous person has great power and wonderful results* (James 5:16, NLT).

The exhortation to "confess your sins to each other" does not mean that believers are to indulge in indiscriminate public or even private confessions. In fact, one must exert keen discernment when selecting a prayer partner. And certainly this passage has nothing to do with secret confessions to a priest.

Believers are to confess their sins (faults) to others only that they may pray one for another.

Without a doubt, the reference to the word "confess" in this passage is **not** the same as the self-talk (faith-building) confessions that I am prescribing. In fact, the author strongly advocates not sharing certain ones of your faith-building confessions with anyone.

Faith-Building Confession Is Not The Confession Of Sins To God The Father

Our Heavenly Father is merciful and He has provided us with a wonderful Scripture that allows believers to confess their sins to Him, and He will forgive them of every wrong that they have done. The apostle John, inspired by the Holy Spirit, wrote the following which is an awesome benefit for believers.

> *If we (freely) admit that we have sinned and confess our sins, He is faithful and just (true to His own nature and promises) and will forgive our sins (dismiss our lawlessness) and (continuously) cleanse us from all unrighteousness (everything not in conformity to His will in purpose, thought, and action)* (1 John 1:9, Amp.).

This Scripture is often quoted in Christian settings and in prayer. It is very popular as it is the one Scripture that provides a means for believers to confess their sins to our Heavenly Father and be forgiven, allowing the believer to remain in fellowship with Him.

This is a wonderful Scripture! However, this is **not** the confession that I am prescribing in this topic for self-talk (faith-building) confessions.

Golden Nugget Revealed — Please make a mental note of this fact.
A confession of the mouth is required to be born again (saved), and a confession of the mouth is required for a believer to have sins forgiven.
The Holy Spirit is telling us something.

Unveiling The $500 Billion Dollar Scripture

The word "confession" in its positive meaning in the Bible is defined as affirming what God has said in His Word. It is witnessing to His Word by declaration (to make known openly). It is testifying to truths revealed in the Bible. The hallmark of those men and women whose names made the "Hall of Faith" chapter in the book of Hebrews was that they had unwavering, steadfast faith in God and in His Word. They often confessed God's Word as can be seen with Moses, Noah, David, and others; they were obedient and they acted on God's Word.

What is a faith-building confession? It is saying what God has said in His Word (the Bible) about a certain thing. It is agreeing with God. It is saying the same thing the Scriptures say about what you can do in Christ, who you are in Christ and what you have in Christ.

PART 2

Author Reveals $500 Billion Scripture That Defines The Word "Confession," That Builds Strong Faith

The word "confession" that is prescribed to build strong faith is unveiled in the book of Hebrews in the New Testament. I estimate that the revelation knowledge of God's Word flowing from this Scripture is worth around $500 billion to you. Well, right away, I know some may be thinking..."Has Brother Jim gone off the deep end and lost it?"

My reply is, no, I didn't go off the deep end, and yes, you read it right; the Scripture that I am about to share with you is priceless. In fact, $500 billion is a mere pittance in God's economic system.

Think about this, people during World War II thought that ten cents for a gallon of gas was too much. But with today's price averaging around $1.50 per gallon it makes ten cents per gallon look small. It is almost unbelievable that a gallon of gas could cost so little.

Bill Gates, the world's richest man and Microsoft Founder, was recently the keynote speaker here in America's finest city, San Diego, at a Microsoft Windows on Healthcare Conference. A local newspaper article indicated that according to the most recent estimates, Bill Gates is worth $105 billion. Indeed, we can readily see that in the world's economic system, $500 billion in personal worth is obtainable. But in God's economic system, "the sky is the limit." For God creates it all.

I anticipate that Bill Gates's personal wealth will exceed the $500 billion mark very early in this New Millennium, and I base this on the fact that Bill Gates operates in a biblical and natural principle of sowing and reaping. His stated goal in life is to give away (to charity) 90 percent of his personal wealth.

Bill and his wife, Melinda, have established the Bill and Melinda Gates foundation with assets of 17 billion, and it is the second largest philanthropic foundation in the world, behind London-based Wellcome Trust. Since 1997, it has given more than $2.4 billion, primarily for global health and education. Bill and Melinda will reap the harvest from their giving, as it is stated in the Scriptures...*"He who sows sparingly will also reap sparingly, and he who sows bountifully will also reap bountifully."* (2 Corinthians 9:6).

Generous giving sets a reciprocal flow in motion that is inherent with giving and sharing. It is a spiritual law that works in spiritual things as well as natural/physical things.

Trillionaire Believers

I am boldly believing that many who are reading this book will become multimillionaires and super billionaires who are possessed with a spirit of bountifully sowing into the Kingdom of God and sharing bountifully with the poor and needy. In fact, I believe that we will begin to see trillionaire believers surface as groups and as individuals in this New Millennium.

I sincerely desire that something that has been written thus far has pricked your heart/spirit and inspired you to take up the challenge to carry the torch for Jesus Christ of Nazareth. Your torch would be a flaming light that reflects a generous heart and spirit of giving to help spread the Good News of the gospel and bountifully sharing with the poor and needy. Our Heavenly Father's agenda consists of these things.

The $500 billion Scripture is found in the book of Hebrews and without fanfare, this is what it says:

> *Let us hold fast the confession of our hope without wavering, for He who promised is faithful* (Hebrews 10:23, NKJV).

Another translation amplifies and illuminates this valuable Scripture thusly:

> *So let us seize and hold fast and retain without wavering the hope we cherish and confess and our acknowledgment of it, for He who promised is reliable (sure) and faithful to His word.*
> Hebrews 10:23, Amp.

The noted and revered man of God, Rev. Kenneth E. Hagin, prophet, preacher, teacher, author, and founder of Kenneth Hagin (worldwide) Ministries and Rhema Bible Training Center, said the following during one of his Bible teaching series:

"The subject of holding fast to our confession of faith in the Word of God is one of the most important, one of the most significant and one of the most valuable teachings of the New Testament."

When Rev. Kenneth Hagin speaks, it is likened to E.F. Hutton, everyone listens! When he speaks, you can be sure that his message is auspicious and beneficial to the hearer. I have seen and heard him speak in person and he is a powerful teacher of the gospel. I personally own a collection of his books and tapes on biblical teachings, along with books and tapes from other biblical scholars.

In his remarks on the previous page, he places strong emphasis on holding fast to our confession of faith in the Word of God. Notice that he says that this is one of the most important, most significant, most valuable teaching of the New Testament. His choice of such weighty words got my attention in a big way, and I was moved to further study this Scripture that speaks of holding fast to our confession.

> *Let us hold fast the confession of our hope without wavering, for He who promised is faithful* (Hebrews 10:23, NKJV).

Because this Scripture is so valuable and so beneficial to you, we need to examine it closely for clear meaning and total understanding. It provides the key for bountiful sowing and reaping. It provides the key for receiving your covenant inheritance of wealth and riches in this New Millennium. It also provides the key for you to be prosperous in all areas of your life, spiritually, physically, mentally, domestically, and socially.

The word "confession" as it is used in this text is the correct usage that has been prescribed to build strong faith. This word "confession" has three meanings:

1. Affirming 2. Testifying 3. Witnessing

It is affirming (to state positively) something that you believe; it is testifying of something you know, and it is witnessing for a truth you have embraced.

What Is The Confession Of Hope?

The word "hope" is a verb, an action word which means to "desire with expectation of receiving or achieving." What I am going to do now is paraphrase our $500 billion Scripture and make it a faith-building confession.

First remove the word "hope" and then insert whatever promise the Word of God has made that provides for your needs or desires. It would then read like this: "I hold fast to my confession for a lovely home of my own (fully paid for and fully insured). I confess this without wavering, for He Who promised is faithful!"

Faith-Building Confession Is Covered In Your Spiritual Insurance Policy

When you self-talk your faith-building confessions daily, you are making payments on your spiritual lifetime insurance policy. Hence, whenever the storms of life come your way, you are fully covered under God's umbrella of protection and the storms of life must pass you by. Moreover, your faith-building confessions are akin to a health insurance premium; when you self-talk your faith-building confessions daily, you are making payments on your supplemental spiritual lifetime insurance policy. This supplemental coverage takes care of wellness, medicine, preventative measures, testing and trials, treatment and healing. It provides a total health care plan.

Remember, your insurance plans cover you as long as you pay the premiums. If you don't pay your insurance premiums, your insurance coverage will lapse, leaving you unprotected. Think about this, in the worldly realm, you must pay money to have insurance coverage of any kind. In some states, car insurance, business, and other kinds of insurance are mandated by law; it is illegal not to have certain kinds of insurance.

Indeed, our Heavenly Father's insurance plan provides the best coverage in the world and you are in good hands when you are protected by Him. The Good News is you don't have to pay any money to be insured under God the Father's Insurance Plan. Simply keep your policy in force by saying your self-talk (faith-building) confessions each day.

Self-Talk (Faith-Building) Confessions Are Guaranteed to Work

Let's read aloud and digest the Scripture that establishes the unconditional lifetime warranty covering your self-talk (faith-building) confessions. It is revealed in the book of Hebrews as:

> *Seeing then that we have a great High Priest who has passed through the heavens, Jesus the Son of God, let us hold fast our confession. For we do not have a High Priest who cannot sympathize with our weaknesses, but was in all points tempted as we are, yet without sin. Let us therefore come boldly to the throne of grace, that we may obtain mercy and find grace to help in time of need* (Hebrews 4:14-16, NKJV).

First, notice that we see the exhortation again to "Let us hold fast our confession." Moreover, our Lord and Savior, Jesus Christ the Son of God is our great High Priest. He is our advocate Who pleads for us before our Father. It is like having your big brother go to your biological father with an issue on your behalf.

You are guaranteed under our conditional lifetime warranty, that when you hold fast to your self-talk (faith-building) confessions without wavering, that He Who promised is reliable (sure) and faithful to His Word. In due season, your faith-building confessions will become a reality in your physical life.

Remember...nothing in the world can take the place of persistence and determination. Calvin Coolidge

Let us return to our $500 billion Scripture because it is conditional. Therefore, you have a responsibility to do something and then God the Father is committed to do something.

This is a magnificent covenant that God the Father has put together for our benefit. It is great because it involves just you and God the Father, hence no one else can get involved and mess things up unless you allow it.

> *Let us hold fast the confession of our hope without wavering for He who promised is faithful* (Hebrews 10:23, NKJV).

Let's look at the responsibilities:

Believer's Responsibility

If you notice closely, the believer has two things that he/she is responsible for:

1. Hold fast the confession of your hope...
2. ...without wavering.

In the first responsibility, the phrase "hold fast" means to hold onto tightly and do not let go. In the second responsibility, we see the word "wavering," which is a very appropriate word that harmonizes perfectly with the two words "hold fast."

The phrase "without wavering" means under no circumstance should you ever fluctuate, hesitate, or vacillate in your opinion, your allegiance or your faithfulness.

Father God's Responsibility

Our $500 billion Scripture commands the believer to hold fast the confession of our hope without wavering. Hence, when the believer holds fast to the confession of his/her hope, then Father God steps in.

His Word says that *"He who promised is faithful."* My paraphrase for this statement is "He who promised is trustworthy, credible, and His track record is perfect; His Word is guaranteed, you can take it to the bank."

The Word "Hope" Gets Transformed

Notice with me the word "hope." This word is on my "Hit List" of words not to use when making self-talk (faith-building) confessions, because the word "hope" denotes future tense and faith is now, present tense. A faith confession says, "I believe that I have it." It does not say, "I hope to have it." I am a believer not a hoper. My desire is that you are a believer too. Instead of using the word "hope," begin to say "I believe..."

Under the provisions of God's promises, made available to us through Jesus Christ, the things that you confess that line up with God's Word, you already have ownership of in the spiritual realm. It is the holding fast of your confession without wavering, regardless of the circumstances (sense knowledge) that causes that which you are confessing to become a reality in your physical life. Praise the Lord!

Remember, self-talk your faith-building confessions the way you would like to be and you will become the way you self-talk in due season, when you hold fast to your confessions. I encourage you to add the following faith-building confession to your daily menu of confessions.

Self-Talk Faith-Building Confession:

The King of Kings, Jesus Christ, is my great High Priest Who is an advocate on my behalf with my Heavenly Father; with His grace, all my needs and desires are met. And I reign as king/queen, prosperous in every area of my life. I confess this under the authority and in the wonderful Name of Jesus Christ of Nazareth! SO BE IT! (Hebrews 4:14-16).

If you don't like your past, confess your future.

CHAPTER 8

FOUNDING FATHERS HAD IT RIGHT

President William Jefferson Clinton said on a CBS Television 60 Minute II interview that, "The Founding Fathers who wrote the Constitution of the United States were smart people." I agree with the president, especially those Founding Fathers and patriots who had courage and took an open stand to help promote our country as a non-heathen nation.

Let's read some of the notable statements that some of the Founding Fathers made publicly:

"It is impossible to rightly govern the world without God and the Bible."
George Washington (1732-1799), First President of the United States

"I believe the Bible is the best gift God has ever given to man. All the good from the Savior of the world is communicated through this book...All things desirable to men are contained in the Bible."
Abraham Lincoln (1809-1865), 16th President of the United States

"When you read the Bible, you will know it is the Word of God, because you will have found it the key to your own heart, your own happiness, and your own duty."
Woodrow Wilson (1856-1924), 28th President of the United States

One of the foremost Founding Fathers of morality, wisdom, and godliness made the following notable statements:

> *The good influence of godly citizens causes a city to prosper, but the moral decay of the wicked drives it downhill.*
> Proverbs of Solomon, Proverbs 11:11, TLB
>
> *Righteousness exalts a nation, but sin is a disgrace to any people.*
> Proverbs of Solomon, Proverbs 14:34, NIV
>
> *When there is moral rot within a nation, its government topples easily. But with wise and knowledgeable leaders, there is stability.*
> Proverbs of Solomon, Proverbs 28:2, NLT
>
> *God blesses those who obey Him; happy is the man who puts his trust* in the Lord (Proverbs of Solomon, Proverbs 16:20, TLB).

All of the Founding Fathers' statements are words of wisdom to those who have an ear to hear.

Shortly, you will realize how President Clinton's statement about the Founding Fathers ties into the keys for your covenant inheritance of wealth and riches in this New Millennium, and how the framers of the United States Constitution were very wise when it came to whom and what we should put our trust in.

We will pick up on President Clinton's comments about the Founding Fathers a little later. But now, let's read some of the other enlightening statements he made during the interview.

Excerpts From TV Interview
With President Clinton - Impeachment Woes

On March 31, 1999, President Clinton was interviewed on CBS Television News 60 Minutes II, by Dan Rather. At the beginning, the interview focused on the crisis in Kosovo and the role of the United States and the North Atlantic Treaty Organization (NATO) in that area.

Further in the interview Mr. Rather said,

"Mr. President, you know Americans like to know that the first family is OK, that they're doing all right. Given the year, plus what you and our first family have been through, tell us what you can about how the three of you are doing."

President Clinton responded:

"Well, I think given what we've been through, we're doing reasonably well. And, you know, we're not a large family, but we do love each other very much, and we work hard to support one another."

The President continued:

"And I think that this trip to North Africa has been a good thing, not only for our country, because I think Hillary's done a great job on it. And I think it must have been good for Hillary and Chelsea, too, to have that time together to do some exciting things, to be in a different environment, and I believe they really enjoyed it. But I think we're doing quite well considering what we've been through and, God willing, we'll keep after it."

Indirect Question Concerning President
Clinton's Impeachment Woes

Mr. Rather said,

"Well, I asked you about the first family; how about yourself? You know, we're here in a room with pictures of Lincoln, Washington, the Continental Congress. When you look back over this year plus, I mean — you know, what's the moral of it? Does it have a moral?"

President Clinton answered:

"Oh yes, I think there is more than one lesson here. I think first of all, the moral is there's a personal moral, which is that every person must bear the consequences of his or her conduct. And when you make a mistake, you pay for it, no matter who you are. And it's true, whether or not it's made public or whether or not what's made public is exactly an accurate reflection of what, in fact, happened, that's not the important thing. The important thing is that there are consequences in people's personal lives no matter who they are."

Note: This interview with the president will resume later on in this chapter.

Brief Sidebar: To Discuss President Clinton's Acquittal

President Clinton's impeachment trial ended with his acquittal on Friday, February 12, 1999. The Senate voted 55-45 to reject the perjury charge and split 50-50 on the obstruction of justice allegation. To convict President Clinton and remove him from office would have required a two-thirds vote, or 67 votes.

The Senate was comprised of: 45 Democratic Senators
55 Republican Senators

Tally Of Votes Cast by Both Parties:

Perjury Article

	Guilty	Not Guilty
Republican	45	10
Democrat	0	45
Total Votes	45	55

Obstruction of Justice Article

	Guilty	Not Guilty
Republican	50	5
Democrat	0	45
Total Votes	50	50

As you can see the votes were cast, by far, along party lines. It is hard for me to understand (in fairness) how all the Democrat Senators concluded that the president was not guilty, and how the overwhelming majority of the Republican Senators determined that the president was guilty. Something smacks of being fishy.

I sincerely hope that no future president or anyone else, will ever have to stand trial before the Senate Chambers and be subjected to a verdict dictated wholly by political affiliation.

After his acquittal, Clinton again apologized, saying he was "profoundly sorry" for what he had put the nation through. "This can be and this must be a time of reconciliation and renewal for America."

The moral issue of President Clinton's conduct with Miss Monica Lewinsky is a no-brainer. According to the Scriptures we are to:

> *"Abstain from all appearance of evil"* (1 Thessalonians 5:22, KJV).

Jesus Christ of Nazareth said, *"He who is without sin among you, let him throw a stone at her first!"* (John 8:7, NKJV).

The weightier question concerning moral conduct/sin is repentance. In such matters, I choose to step back and let God do His work. The resolution of immoral or sinful conduct is between man and God, his family, and between those against whom the immoral or sinful act was committed. And citizens can voice their opinion on Election Day, as the president and senators are elected by the people.

As for the president, anyone who has valid civil or criminal charges can file them in a court of law after the President has left the presidency position.

Urgent Sidebar: For all believers and the unsaved.

While we are still on the subject of voting and the presidency, and the Founding Fathers, I want to take this opportunity to offer what I believe are very worthwhile exhortations.

The Bible says, *"when there is moral rot within a nation, its government topples easily. But with wise and knowledgeable leaders, there is stability."* I firmly believe that this Scripture is timely revelation knowledge for us today. It prompts us to get busy and elect wise and knowledgeable leaders. We live in the greatest nation in the world and during the latter part of the twentieth century, we have enjoyed the best economy in the world. However, during the same time we have seen a rise in moral rot at every level and station in our society. We see the divorce rate at 50% and above, for believers as well as non-believers, and a decrease in family values.

We see an increase in hate crimes, workplace violence, domestic violence, child abuse, road rage, and drive by (senseless) shootings. We see moral rot as the root cause of the Oklahoma Federal Building bombing, the shooting at Columbine High School in Littleton, Colorado, and the shooting massacre at Wedgewood Baptist Church in Fort Worth, Texas, to mention a few.

I submit to you that if those elected to public office were wise and knowledgeable of God's Word, and stood for Christian principles, we would begin to see moral stability in our nation again, as the Founding Fathers meant it to be. After the fifty-six Founding Fathers signed the

Declaration of Independence of the Thirteen Colonies in Congress on July 4, 1776, they left Philadelphia and went back to their newly-founded states, and created their states' constitutions. The state constitutions reflected the spirit of the Declaration of Independence.

The Founding Fathers from Delaware were George Read, Caesar Rodney, and Thomas McKean. They went back to the state of Delaware and created their state constitution. The following are excerpts from the Delaware Constitution:

> Everyone appointed to the office must say, "I do profess faith in God the Father, and in the Lord Jesus Christ, His Son, and in the Holy Ghost. One God and blessed forevermore. And I do acknowledge the Holy Scriptures of the Old and New Testaments to be given by divine inspiration."

The Founding Fathers from North Carolina were William Hooper, Joseph Hewes, and John Penn. The following are excerpts from the North Carolina Constitution:

> "No person who should deny the being of God, or the truth of the (Christian) religion, or the divine authority of either the Old or New Testaments, or who shall hold religious principles incompatible with the freedom and safety of the state, should be capable of holding any office or place of trust in the civil government of this state."

Patrick Henry, lawyer, patriot, and orator said:

> "It cannot be emphasized too strongly or too often that this great nation was founded, not by religionists, but by Christians; not on religions, but on the gospel of Jesus Christ."

Well, I believe you can clearly see which way the Founding Fathers intended this nation of ours to be governed. Their intent was that these United States of America be governed and based on biblical creeds and principles. Keep in mind that the State Constitutions required Christian principles, not denomination or religious (man-made) doctrines.

Vote The Way Jesus Would Vote

My final point and my exhortation to you is that you can make a difference in this great nation of ours. You can help change the moral decaying of our nation in this New Millennium. Someone may ask, "How can I make a difference?" My response to that question is:

1. Do what the Founding Fathers intended you to do, and

that is to carefully study candidates at all levels who seek your vote, to insure that they believe and stand for biblical principles and values.

2. Equally important, I strongly urge you to ask yourself this question concerning every candidate running for public office, from school board to President of the United States. "Would Jesus Christ of Nazareth pull the lever or punch the hold in the card to cast His vote for this candidate?" If your spirit and the Holy Spirit say no, then you should obey the Holy Spirit.

Whenever you are faced with the dilemma of who to vote for, go into prayer and/or fasting, and ask the Holy Spirit's guidance and direction in the matter, and He will provide you with the right answers.

Word of Caution: Don't Be Deceived

Look beyond the double tongue of those political candidates who follow the same old concocted rhetoric (of saying a whole lot of nothing) to get your vote. Listen attentively for the candidates who stand on Christian principles. Ascertain whether or not their past and present actions demonstrate pro-Christian principles. Don't be deceived!

I firmly believe that believers have an obligation to vote in elections in which the results can have an impact negatively or positively on their lives, children, family, church, community, or their country. Your vote is precious; countless men and women have died so that you could have the right to vote. When you vote, don't vote for the man or woman, but vote for the Christian principles that the man or woman upholds. Whenever you cast your vote, it should be dual casing, one vote that you cast for yourself, and one vote for Jesus Christ of Nazareth. Remember that your vote counts, and it will make a difference.

People are influenced by their leaders, whether political, spiritual, or otherwise. We need the Founding Father's kind of leaders today!

Note: The interview with President Clinton resumes.

President Clinton Applauds The Founding Fathers And The American People

President Clinton continued by saying,

"The second lesson is that the Constitution works. The Founding Fathers were smart people. They understood that partisan passions would (very often get carried away and the temptation to seize on events of the moment would be too great, and that's why they wrote the Constitution the way they did. And they were awfully smart.

"The third thing that I think we learned this year is that American people almost always get it right if you give them enough time to think through things and really work on it."

The thing that stuck in my mind the most was when the President said, **"The Founding Fathers were smart people."** And in this same statement the President again says, **"And they (the Founding Fathers) were awfully smart."**

The Founding Fathers of this great country were smart people. In addition to having the foresight to establish viable legislative guidelines for the impeachment of a sitting president, they also enacted other laws that have stood the test of time. One such law was the implementation of the National Motto of the United States along with the Coinage Act.

By now you may be wondering, "Brother Jim, what does all this about the Founding Fathers have to do with the keys to my covenant inheritance of wealth and riches in this New Millennium?" My response to that is...exercise a little patience. This brief history tour is beneficial, as it reveals the minds of the Founding Fathers for our nation. And it sets the foundation for the introduction of the unveiling of the hidden keys, which guarantee wealth and riches in this New Millennium for those who are bold, determined and unwavering in their quest.

In God We Trust (The National Motto Of The United States Inscribed On Coin)

The National Motto of the United States is "In God We Trust." The first Coinage Act was passed by the United States Congress on April 22, 1864; and the motto "In God We Trust" first appeared on the 1864 two-cent coin. I wholeheartedly applaud the Founding Fathers for the stately courage and their foresight in getting the motto "In God We Trust" inscribed on United States coins.

The religious proponents of the motto suggested that without this motto "would not the antiquaries of succeeding centuries rightfully reason from our past that we were a heathen nation?" The proponents emphasized that the recognition of Almighty God in some form on United States coins would relieve us from the ignominy of heathenism.

I am very grateful to the framers of the United States Constitution. I definitely would not want history to reflect that my earthly citizenship was in a pagan country. However, had I been at the Congressional Round Table with the Founding Fathers, when the Coinage Act legislation was being discussed, I would have argued for the motto to be worded as follows: "In God The Father We Trust."

I do believe that I could have passionately convinced them that my version was the best.

Paper Currency Gets The National Motto

A law was passed by the 84th Congress and approved by President Lyndon Baines Johnson, on July 30, 1956, declaring "In God We Trust" as the National Motto of the United States. And "In God We Trust" was first used on paper money and put into circulation on October 1, 1957.

Note: The history of the motto "In God We Trust" can be found in Appendix D.

Glorifying God doesn't stop at the doors of the church. As God's ambassadors, believers represent God in the earth. So we should make God look good in everything that we do!

CHAPTER 9

4 KEYS TO RECEIVING YOUR COVENANT INHERITANCE OF WEALTH AND RICHES IN THIS NEW MILLENNIUM

PART I

How To Use Self-Talk (Faith-Building) Confessions To Build A Strong Godly Foundation

This remarkable foundation Scripture below reveals one of the hidden keys needed to gain your covenant inheritance of wealth and riches in this New Millennium.

The idea for the National Motto of the United States was more than likely taken from this powerful passage of the Bible, which reads as follows:

> *Trust in the Lord with all your heart, and lean not on your own understanding; In all your ways acknowledge Him, and He shall direct your paths* (Proverbs 3:5-6, NKJV).

Master Key #1 Build a strong godly foundation.

Master Key #1 unlocks heavenly treasure and reveals how to build a strong godly foundation.

My favorite translation of this passage reads like this:

> *Don't ever trust yourself. In everything you do, put God first, and he will direct you and crown your efforts with success.*
> Proverbs 3:5-6, TLB

Wisdom On A Tree Waiting To Be Plucked

Our foundation-building Scripture is like a tree full of ripe, luscious fruit waiting to be plucked. When the fruit is taken and eaten, it is sweet as honey and delicious to the taste buds. It provides vital nutrients needed by the body to develop and grow, and maintain a healthy lifestyle. It is very good food for the body. Likewise, when you take our foundation-building Scripture and persistently read it, speak it aloud, visualize it, and show joyous emotions about this Scripture each day, you are feeding your human spirit with God's Word. It is sweeter than honey; it builds mountain-moving faith that causes those things that are not, to be as though they were. It implants untold wisdom in your spirit that will be immovable by your adversary (Satan) and all his cohorts (evil, demonic spirits).

Foundation-Building Scripture Has A Guarantee Clause

Let us take a closer look at our foundation-building Scripture. First, whenever I see the word "all" a red flag goes up and I always try to closely discern what the "all" is all about. In our foundation scripture, the word "all" appears twice. The word "all" means without exception, every one of, the whole of it, includes every constituent element or individual; and it means the total supply or whole amount. In other words, nothing left out.

Another element of this Scripture text is that it is a binding agreement. There are two parts to this agreement. Part one is your responsibility and part two is God's responsibility.

Your Responsibility And God's Responsibility

Let us dissect your responsibility first. It is similar to a lease agreement on an apartment or an automobile. The lessee agrees to pay so much per month on time, and agrees to abide by the other terms of the agreement. The lessor provides you with the key to the apartment or automobile, and the lessor agrees to meet the terms set forth in the lease agreement. As long as you make payments on time, chances are you will never hear from the lessor. However, if you are late with your payment or miss a payment, or if you damage the lessor's property, or default in some other way, then you are in violation of the lease agreement and may be subject to financial penalty.

Or in the worst case scenario, if the defaults continue, the lessor could take action to have you vacate the apartment or the lessor could take action to recover his automobile.

The good news in the above illustration is that as long as you do your part, the lessor will do his/her part. The same holds true with our foundation-building Scripture. However, it is more reliable than any man-made lease, because it was drafted by God, and His Word shall stand forever, and will not return to Him void.

Your Responsibility Under This Agreement

1. Trust in the Lord with all your heart.

> The word "trust" means that you are to rely totally on, to place your confidence totally in the Lord. In the remaining part of this text, the red flag goes up because the word "all" appears, which means nothing is to be left out. It continues "with all your heart."

The trust that you must have in the Lord must be deeply rooted in your heart, which is the seat or center of secret thoughts and emotions. And it must be deeply rooted in your spirit, which is your inner self. I will explain later how to use your self-talk (faith-building) confessions to get this Scripture deeply rooted in your (heart and) spirit.

2. Lean not to your own understanding.

A complete book could be written about this subject alone. It is an area where most of us lack revelation knowledge. And, therefore, we operate on our own mind, and will, and on our emotions which are controlled by our souls (sense realm) rather than our spirits.

The Word of God right now is exhorting us to lean not to our own understanding (the five senses; sight, hearing, smell, touch and taste). The five senses are very useful in our everyday life as they are sensors, and they transmit good and bad information to our soul realm (mind), our heart/spirit realm and to our bodies. However, the five senses are imperfect and the Word of God warns us not to rely on our own insight and understanding. Your five senses are not reliable and they will fail you; they will leave you out in the boat without oars in the middle of the water.

Hidden Dangers Of Leaning To One's Own Understanding

Earlier in this book, I mentioned that in early 1982, I attended a company-sponsored training seminar designed to enhance corporate staff training facilitators in teaching skills. The then Ohio Bell Telephone Company (now renamed Ameritech) had strong goals regarding employee training at all levels. The frequent training seminars were mandatory for our group (management staff training).

I will always remember this segment of the seminar because it dealt with the pitfalls of assumption. Assuming things and leaning to one's own understanding are cousins.

Do Not Assume Anything

I vividly remember watching a video that showed a small, cozy Italian restaurant with people seated at six to eight tables all covered neatly with white linen tablecloths, beautiful vases of flowers and candlelight. A waitress was gracefully and cheerfully moving from table to table taking orders and pouring water.

Acouple walked in, casually dressed, and they looked to be in their early thirties. The hostess directed them to a table that was somewhat in the middle of the seating area, in full view of most of the other people. The thoughts that flashed in the hostess's mind as she seated the couple were... "They sure look good together; their chemistry seems to flow as one. I wonder how long they have been dating?"

The waitress greeted the couple and took their order for drinks. The waitress overheard their names; the man's name was Jeff and the woman's name was Bernice. As she left their table, the thoughts that flashed in her mind were..."They are surely into each other; they were looking each other directly in the eyes. They were having an intense conversation, and they tuned everything and everyone else out. I had to interrupt them several times to get their complete order."

Seated at a table across from the couple were a middle-aged man and his wife. The wife's thoughts about the couple were..."It sure would be nice to be young like they are again; they are a loving couple."

Then, in walked a breathtaking, very attractive young woman with a beautiful face and the body of a Ford Agency model. She caught everyone's attention. She spoke to the hostess and then headed toward the powder room. The eyes of most of the folks in the restaurant were glued to her as she moved very sensuously; she walked like a professional model.

Almost immediately, Jeff got up from his table and walked to the area near the powder room, and stood there as if he were waiting for someone. Most of the people in the restaurant were watching Jeff and they were curious. As the young woman with the beautiful face was leaving the powder room, Jeff engaged her attention and their conversation appeared to be mutually participatory, but somewhat on the serious side.

Those in the restaurant, by now, were preoccupied with what was going on with Jeff and this attractive woman. Then Jeff handed the woman what looked like a business card. Smiling, she took it, nodding her head as if to say, "See you later." By now, most of the folks in the restaurant were fuming inwardly and outwardly at Jeff as he walked back to the table where Bernice had been patiently waiting.

The thoughts of the hostess after closely observing Jeff's encounter with the attractive woman were.."That man ought to be ashamed of himself, bringing a nice young woman out to dinner, having the nerve to flirt with another woman in public, in full view of his date." The waitress was so taken aback by Jeff's actions that she wanted to tell him off, but she remembered the restaurant's policy about dealing with customers. (The customer is always right.) Her thoughts were..."Why would a nice young woman like Bernice get involved with a womanizer like Jeff. If I were she, I would walk out on him."

The middle-aged couple, especially the wife, had been nosily eyeing Jeff and the goings on with the attractive woman. The wife told her husband, "I can't believe that someone would be as bold as that man (pointing in Jeff's direction). I know that that nice woman with him is very embarrassed and hurt because of what he just did. If I were she, I would be fighting mad."

A Mind Can Be A Terrible Thing When It Is Uncontrolled

There were some classic assumption errors made in this scenario involving Jeff, Bernice and the attractive woman.

First, Jeff is a very successful artist who had been commissioned by a very wealthy client to paint the face of a woman-of-color with unique features and impeccable beauty. Bernice works for Jeff as his secretary, and had arranged this meeting with the attractive woman as she had done many times before. For some unknown reason, Jeff preferred to meet potential models in a public setting initially.

As you can clearly see, when the mind is left to wander, uncontrolled, it can be very dangerous; especially when people start to outwardly act out their assumptions with negative body language, or acting out verbally and/or physically.

Know that this same truth revealed in this account with Jeff is equally true when it pertains to leaning on your own understanding.

Choice Between God's Kingdom Or Satan's Kingdom

God's Word commands us to lean not to our own understanding. You have a choice. You can obey the Word of God and benefit from the wisdom and blessings that accompany obedience to His Word. Or you can move into this New Millennium carrying the same old baggage of being sense-and-self-ruled instead of being ruled by God's Word in your spirit.

Believe this, God the Father would not tell us in His Word to do something that would be harmful or destructive to us, but what He tells us is just the opposite. His Word is to enlighten and to edify us. We benefit when we obey His Word.

3. In all your ways acknowledge Him.

The key words in this part of your responsibility are "all" and "acknowledge." The red flag goes up whenever we see the word "all" because it means: everything, every bit, every one, and as it was stated before anything was left out.

The word "acknowledge" has three meanings according to my Merriam Webster Computer Dictionary:

1. Admit as true or valid
2. Admit the authority of
3. Express thanks for

Without a doubt, Jesus Christ of Nazareth is our example of how this third responsibility should be practiced. There are far too many Scriptures to write them all. But as you will see, Jesus Christ of Nazareth always acknowledged God the Father at every opportunity.

> Jesus Christ of Nazareth said, *"If anyone acknowledges me publicly here on earth, I will openly acknowledge that person before my Father in Heaven. But if anyone denies me here on earth, I will deny that person before my Father in Heaven."* Matthew 10:32-33, NLT
>
> Jesus Christ of Nazareth said, *"For I have not spoken on My own authority; but the Father who sent Me gave Me a command, what I should say and what I should speak. And I know that His command is everlasting life. Therefore, whatever I speak, just as the Father told Me, so I speak."* John 12:49-50, NKJV

These Scriptures clearly show a definite pattern of Jesus Christ of Nazareth acknowledging the Father (our Heavenly Father). To bring this third responsibility (in all your ways acknowledge Him) into clearer focus and understanding, let's read what God and others have to say concerning acknowledgement.

> God said, *"You shall have no other gods before or besides Me... You shall not bow down yourself to them or serve them; for I the Lord your God am a jealous God"* (Exodus 20:3,5, Amp.).
>
> It is written: *So they took away the stone and Jesus lifted up His eyes and said, "Father, I thank You that You have heard Me."* John 11:41, Amp.
>
> It is written: *At that time Jesus began to say, "I thank You Father, Lord of heaven and earth (and I acknowledge openly to Your honor), that You have hidden these things from the wise and clever, and learned, and revealed them to babies (to the childish, untaught, and unskilled)"* (Matthew 11:25, Amp.).
>
> The apostle Paul wrote in a letter to Timothy, *"Now to the King of eternity, incorruptible and immortal, invisible, the only God, be honor and glory forever and ever (to the ages of ages). Amen (so be it)"* (1Timothy 1:17, Amp.).

"In all your ways acknowledge Him" is a command from God. In today's way of doing things (dog-eat-dog world), we often see individuals

eager to unjustly take the credit for this achievement or that achievement. Oftentimes others have devoted many work hours and sometimes financial support toward a project or program, but they are not given credit at all. Sad to say, but this occurs in the religious community as well as it does in the business sector.

Individuals who have huge ego problems also have huge appetites for wanting to be first to shine (look good) before men and women. They not only fail to acknowledge their co-worker, but they fail to acknowledge God. They either knowingly or unknowingly fail to realize that God the Father is the source and cause of man's achievements in every walk of life; in every project and in every program. Those who unjustly seek and take all the credit for achievements and success are sinning against their fellowman. And worst of all they are sinning against God.

The Word of God commands: *"In all your ways acknowledge Him."*

Notice that the word "ways" is plural, which denotes more than one. I submit to you that "in all your ways" means we are to leave nothing out. The word "all" is the qualifier which means "everything." Knowing this, we should program ourselves, whenever the opportunity arises, to acknowledge Him first (our Heavenly Father) both in our self-talk and publicly.

Professional Athletes Got The Message

I applaud those athletes: basketball, football, baseball, boxers and others who seize the opportunity and evade the sportscasters' first question. And then proceed to acknowledge God, to give Him the thanks and the glory on nationwide TV for their victory.

Now, let's get a glimpse of John the Baptist and see how he insistently explained Who should be acknowledged.

> *One day someone began an argument with John's disciples, telling them that Jesus' baptism was best. So they came to John and said, "Master, the man you met on the other side of the Jordan River—the one you said was the Messiah—he is baptizing too, and everybody is going over there instead of coming here to us." John replied, "God in heaven appoints each man's work. My work is to prepare the way for that man so that everyone will go to him. You yourselves know how plainly I told you that I am not the Messiah. I am here to prepare the way for him—that is all. The crowds will naturally go to the main attraction—the bride will go where the bridegroom is. A bridegroom's friends rejoice with him. I am the Bridegroom's friend, and I am filled with joy at his success.* ***He must become greater and greater and I must become less and less.****"*
> John 3:25-30, TLB

I like what the King James Bible says..."He must increase, but I must decrease."

How Tragedy Struck King Herod — He Failed To Express Acknowledgment

While he was in Caesarea, a delegation from Tyre and Sidon arrived to see him. He was highly displeased with the people of those two cities, but the delegates made friends with Blastus, the royal secretary, and asked for peace, for their cities were economically dependent upon trade with Herod's country. An appointment with Herod was granted, and when the day arrived he put on his royal robes, sat on his throne and made a speech to them. At its conclusion the people gave him a great ovation, shouting, "It is the voice of a god and not of a man!"
Instantly, an angel of the Lord struck Herod with a sickness so that he was filled with maggots and died—because he accepted the people's worship instead of giving the glory to God. Acts 12:20-23, TLB

Do Not At Any Time Follow In King Herod's Footsteps

If you will examine those statements concerning acknowledgment given earlier by Jesus Christ of Nazareth, and those of the apostle Paul, and John the Baptist, you will find a consistent acknowledgment of God the Father as the supreme deity. These statements admit the authority of God, and the unwavering willingness to obey His Word. The open expressions of thanks show their devoted, sincere gratitude to our Heavenly Father.

God's Responsibility - Guarantee Clause

In our foundation-building Scripture, the Word of God is saying: If you trust in the Lord with all your heart and lean not on your own understanding; and in all your ways acknowledge Him — then, He will direct your paths.

I call your attention to the word "paths." Notice that it has an "s" at the end which means it is plural, denoting more than one path. I submit to you, if you do your part of this foundation-building Scripture, then you can be assured that your Heavenly Father will direct all of your paths, if you yield to His leading. Also, look closely at the word "shall," it is a verb which expresses action. So we can say that God will take some action on your behalf. It doesn't say that He may direct your paths, or that there is a 50/50 chance that He may direct your paths. No, the Word of God says "He shall/will direct your paths." This is awesome when you think about it; all you have to do is your part and then stand back, get out of the way, and let your Heavenly Father do His part.

Think on this: Doing your part means you have God the Father, God the Son, God the Holy Spirit, and God's host of angelic beings working on your behalf; a tremendous amount of supernatural power and authority, paused and ready to go to work for you.

How To Carry Out Your Responsibility That Is Outlined In Our Foundation-Building Scripture.

Someone may ask, "How do I carry out my responsibility?" This is a very good question, especially since the aim of this book is to focus on the "How To" aspect of receiving your covenant inheritance of wealth and riches in this New Millennium. I have read far too many books that tell you what to do, but they don't fully and clearly tell you how to do it. The two previous books that I wrote contain a strong blend of "How To" throughout each book in clear and easy-to-understand language. This, too, is the goal of *Self-Talk And Grow Rich.*

The answer to the above question is twofold. The first answer is to just do it the same way Daniel and David did. Imitate them, follow their examples when it comes to prayer time and self-talk (faith-building) confession time.

In the book of Daniel it says:

> *When Daniel knew that the document had been signed, he went to his house where he had windows in his upper chamber open toward Jerusalem; and he got down upon his knees three times a day and prayed and gave thanks before his God, as he had done previously (*Daniel 6:10, RSV).

This Scripture tells us that Daniel prayed three times a day, and the writer was inspired to let us know that he had prayed three times a day previously. This highlights regularity; as one translation states:

> *But though Daniel knew about it, he went home and knelt down as usual in his upstairs bedroom, with its windows open toward Jerusalem, and prayed three times a day, just as he always had, giving thanks to his God* (Daniel 6:10, TLB).

There are two statements to focus on in this passage. First, he went home and knelt down as usual and secondly, it was just as he always had. Both of these statements emphasize regularity. It was a daily habit for Daniel to get down on his knees three times a day and pray and give thanks before his God.

Note: I encourage you to read all twenty–eight verses in Daniel, chapter 6 to get a full understanding of the occurrences involving Daniel during this period.

The second answer and example is set for us by David in the book of Palms. David says, *"I will pray morning, noon, and night, pleading* ***aloud*** *with God; and He will hear and answer"* (Psalm 55:17, TLB).

Hidden Secret Revealed

Click on (with a keen eye) the word "aloud." David prayed morning, noon, and night, and he tells us that he pleaded aloud with God. The word "aloud" in this text is a tremendous revelation as it unveils one of the hidden secrets that are uncovered throughout this book.

Let's read what Jesus Christ of Nazareth has to say:

> *Now it came to pass, as He was praying in a certain place, when He ceased, that one of His disciples said to Him, " Lord teach us to pray, as John also taught his disciples." So He said to them, "When you pray, say:*
> *"Our Father in heaven, Hallowed be Your name, Your Kingdom come. Your will be done on earth as it is in heaven."*
> Luke 11:1-2, NKJV

Now look closely at Jesus' instructions to His disciples. He told them, "When you pray, **say**..."

My Merriam-Webster Franklin Computer Dictionary definition of the word "**say**" is: It's a verb, which means it's an action word; it means to express in words, to state positively, to form speech sounds. My definition of the word "say" is to open your mouth and speak words aloud. Kindly notice that Jesus didn't say to pray silently, He didn't say to think on this, He didn't say to meditate on this. No, He said that when you pray, "**say**," which means to express in words, aloud. I have known individuals who prayed silently or at least they said they were praying. I wonder if this is the reason some prayers go unanswered? The wrong key will never unlock the door.

Jesus Christ of Nazareth tells us that when we pray we are to "say," open our mouths and speak aloud.

Some may say, "Well Brother Jim, why are you making such a big issue about this speaking aloud?" My reply to this question is twofold:

1. If you want God's best and if you want Him to answer your prayers, then you must be willing to obey His instructions and then you can expect your prayers and confessions to be answered.

2. You have a choice to either do it God's way, or do it Satan's way. I choose to do it God's way and get my prayers and faith-building confessions answered. I hope you agree.

Biblical Law Governing Faith By Just Saying It

Now let's look at another powerful revelation that Jesus Christ of Nazareth unveils:

> *So Jesus answered and said to them, "Have faith in God. For assuredly, I say to you, whoever says to this mountain, be removed and be cast into the sea, and does not doubt in his heart, but believes that those things he says will be done, he will have whatever he says"* (Mark 11:22-23, NKJV).

You Will Have Exactly What You Say

Let's dissect this powerful Scripture to get the full meaning, so that we can thereby benefit. First, in verse 23 the word "say" appears three times and the word "believe" appears once. Many believers have focused on the believing part and have neglected the weightier part which is the saying. The word "mountain" in this text symbolizes whatever is hindering your progress or prosperity in wealth and riches, health, family, business, ministry or whatever.

Notice closely that Jesus says that you are responsible to do three things:

1. **Say** to the mountain (the circumstances or problems)
2. **Not doubt** in your heart
3. **Believe** that those things you say will be done

When you have done the three things outlined, then Jesus guarantees that the following will occur...**you will have whatever you say**.

Brothers, sisters, and friends, the hidden secret is in the **saying**. Self-talking your (faith-building) confessions is the secret for building a strong godly foundation and it's the secret to receiving your covenant inheritance of wealth and riches in this New Millennium.

Now look closely with me; what is it that Jesus says you shall have? What you pray for? No. What you believe for? No. Jesus did not say, "He will have whatever he prayed." He did not say, "He will have whatever he believeth." He said..."He will have whatever he says."

Saying It Or Praying It

Self-Talk And Grow Rich is based on the biblical law of saying it, believing it, and receiving it as set forth in Mark 11:23, which we just reviewed. Faith will work by saying it without praying (notice Mark 11:23

doesn't mention praying at all). But faith most certainly works by prayer also. However, when you pray it, you still have to open your mouth and say (or confess) it.

It is of the utmost importance that you fully understand that faith will work by saying it or it will work by praying it; but when you pray it, you still have to say it. I personally spend about 25% of my devotional time in praying and 75% in saying my faith-building confessions. The reason is that God has already provided for all my needs and most of my desires in His Word. Therefore, I don't have to pray and ask for something that's already available to me. I simply exercise my faith by self-talking my (faith- building) confession until it becomes a reality in my life.

Strong Faith Builds A Strong Foundation

Jesus Christ of Nazareth is the Master when it comes to discussing building strong and weak foundations. This is how He unfolded this subject:

> *"All who listen to my instructions and follow them, are wise like a man who builds his house on solid rock. Though the rain comes in torrents and the floods rise and the storm winds beat against his house it won't collapse. For it is built on rock.*
> *"But those who hear my instructions and ignore them are foolish like a man who builds his house on sand. For when the rains and floods come, and storm winds beat against his house; it will fall with a mighty crash"* (Matthew 7:24-27).

God's Instructions For Those Who Have Ears To Hear

Our foundation-building Scripture is God's instructions to us to be wise and build a strong, godly foundation of strong faith in Jesus Christ of Nazareth and in the Living Word of God. And as we obey God's instructions to trust in the Lord with all our heart, and lean not to our own understanding, we place ourselves on a successful path toward receiving our covenant inheritance of wealth and riches in this New Millennium.

Small Sacrifice Considering The Huge Benefits

Think about this, there are people who systematically pray and confess to their god, five, seven or more times a day. Each time they pray, they remove their shoes, they get down on their knees and bow their faces to the floor repeatedly, while sometimes chanting, but always facing a certain direction. Honestly, they are to be commended for their steadfastness and devotion to their god.

Surely, for those who love the Lord Jesus Christ of Nazareth, the reading aloud of your self-talk (faith-building) confessions three times a day or more is a very small sacrifice. Especially, when you consider the enormous earthly benefits of prosperity in health, family, wealth and riches, business, ministry and whatever else you desire that's in line with God's Word. In addition, your heavenly rewards are being laid up for you to enjoy in eternity. Praise the Lord!

Set your goal to become a self-talking (faith-building) "confessaholic." I am already addicted and there is no turning back for me. For the very best results, you should read each faith-building confession ten times daily, which is the optimal, The more the better!

Self-Talk (Faith-Building) Confessions Contain Supernatural Power

You can have exactly what you say. If you are not satisfied with what you have in life, then I urge you to give serious thought to what you have been saying or what you haven't been saying. The weightier questions are: Is your self-talk destroying your faith for good health and prosperity? Or is your self-talk building strong faith for good health and prosperity in this New Millennium? Is your self-talk building a strong, godly foundation within your heart and spirit? Do you lean not to your own understanding? Do you trust in the Lord with all your heart?

Only you have the answers to those questions, and only you can choose to remain the same or step out in faith to the next level and begin to enjoy the good life of health, wealth and riches provided for you under God's covenant. Know this, all that you have accomplished in life and all that you are today are direct results of what you said yesterday and yesteryear. Always, remember that you are already greatly blessed by God to be a blessing to the Kingdom of God and to the poor and needy!

Don't forget, you shall have whatever you say!

Faith-building confessions are the secret to building a strong, godly foundation and to receiving your covenant inheritance of wealth and riches in this New Millennium. Add the following faith-building confessions to your daily menu of confessions.

Faith-Building Confessions:

Take two Gospills before each meal and snack, before bedtime and in the morning and throughout the day.

Begin reading aloud these (faith-building) confessions immediately:

I purpose in my heart and in my spirit, by faith, that I will read aloud my faith-building confessions at least three times a day. I believe that my appetite for saying my (faith-building) confessions is stronger than my appetite for food for my physical body. I know that it is easy and a joy to say this confession aloud three times each day!

It is written that I can do all things through Christ Who strengthens me. I make the time to say this confession and others on a systematic basis because I know of the wonderful benefits. I confess this in the mighty Name of Jesus Christ of Nazareth! SO BE IT! (Philippians 4:13)

Faith-Building Confession:

I do trust in my Lord with all my heart, and I do not lean to my own understanding; in all my ways I acknowledge my Lord, and I know that He directs my paths. I speak this confession under the authority, and in the Mighty Name of Jesus Christ of Nazareth! SO BE IT! (Proverbs 3:5-6)

PART 2

How To Use The Cornerstone Scripture To Build A Strong Godly Foundation

Master Key #2 Seek God First.

Master Key #2 provides entry to the cornerstone Scripture that unlocks the heavenly treasures, guaranteeing that every need is met.

Jesus Christ of Nazareth unveils this priceless cornerstone Scripture in the book of Matthew in this way...

> *But seek first the kingdom of God and His righteousness, and all these things shall be added to you* (Matthew 6:33, NKJV).

I exhort you to examine Matthew chapter 6, starting at verse 25. You will see that the word "things" mentioned in this cornerstone verse are all material things.

It is very interesting when we contrast human behavior in reacting to certain situations in life. We find that when peoples' automobiles are cutting off or running erratically, they first seek a mechanic to fix it without batting an eye. It is the natural thing to do.

When they have a toothache, they first seek a dentist; and when they need legal advice or representation, they first seek an attorney. And also, when they need financial advice, they first seek a financial planner.

But when it comes to spiritual matters, the things that are unseen, problems that are unresolved in the physical realm, and when it comes to seeking God first and putting His promises to the test in our lives, most people would receive a D or F on their report card. Because most people strive to use sense knowledge to resolve spiritual matters.

The Cornerstone Scripture Is Conditional

Please notice closely that our cornerstone Scripture is conditional which simply put, means the ball is in your court. Your responsibility is to seek first, not second, not after everything else has failed, but seek first the Kingdom of God and His righteousness, and then God promises you that all (not some but all) these things (material and financial) shall be added to you; not subtracted from you, but added to you.

The companion Scripture to our cornerstone Scripture is revealed in the book of Philippians, and it says the following...

> *And my God shall supply all your need according to His riches in glory by Christ Jesus* (Philippians 4:19, NKJV).

God Will Supply All Our Needs

People in the world are always uptight about money and having their needs met. In fact, they spend much of their time and energy in pursuit of security. They will cheat, lie, steal and kill in their pursuit for money and material things.

The believer in Jesus Christ is to live a life free from the fear of lack of finances or of anything. God has promised in His Word that He will take care of our needs through His infinite resources.

When life's circumstances make victory seem impossible, remember that "With God, **all** things are possible!" Not some things, but **all** things are possible!

However, as long as you choose to be stressed, worried and hold on to those things that keep you in bondage, God can't do anything about your situation because you've still got it. Let's say you were struggling to pay your house payments and you still owed $15,000. And let's say your biological father said to you, "Give me the bill that shows the total remaining balance you owe on your house." Further, he says, "I've been led by God to pay off the balance on your house."

Question, would you cast the bill onto your father or would you continue to worry and fret over trying to make the payments?

Well, if it were me, I would gladly give the house bill to my father; and at that point, I would no longer have any worries or stress. The ball is then in my father's court to do what he promised. And I would have put my total trust in him and in his word.

Far too many times, believers try to solve spiritual problems with natural thinking; but we should seek first the Kingdom of God and His righteousness, and all these things (prosperity wise) - spiritual, material, financial, physical, mental, and domestic shall be added to you.

Some may be thinking, "Brother Jim, how do I seek first the Kingdom of God and His righteousness?" I'm glad that someone was thinking of this question. The answer is found in the following Scripture:

> *You lust and do not have. You murder and covet and cannot obtain. You fight and war. Yet, you do not have because you do not ask. You ask and do not receive, because you ask amiss, that you may spend it on your pleasures* (James 4:2-3, NKJV).

It is a known fact that in the natural realm, if you want something, you must ask for it boldly and confidently if you expect to receive. And it works the same way in spiritual things. You must open your mouth and ask God to bring about His promises in your life. But your asking must be in line with His will and not amiss.

Jesus Christ Of Nazareth Spoke These Words In The Book Of Matthew

> *Ask, and it will be given to you; seek and you will find; knock, and it will be opened to you. For everyone who asks receives, and he who seeks finds, and to him who knocks it will be opened.*
> *Or what man is there among you who, if his son asks for bread, will give him a stone? Or if he asks for a fish, will he give him a serpent? If you then, being evil, know how to give good gifts to your children, how much more will your Father who is in heaven give good things to those who ask Him!* Matthew 7:7-11, NKJV.

The following Scripture is loaded with rich instructions on how to seek first the Kingdom of God and His righteousness:

> *This Book of the Law shall not depart out of your mouth; but you shall meditate on it day and night, that you may observe and do according to all that is written in it. For then you shall make your way prosperous, and then you shall deal wisely and have good success* (Joshua 1:8, Amp.).

We can seek first the Kingdom of God and His righteousness by praying to God, by confessing God's promises into our life and by obeying His Word. And we should go to the Bible, the Word of God, and let the Word lead and guide us, because the Word of God is mighty and powerful and it always works! Praise the Lord!

Jesus Christ of Nazareth says that if we ask anything in His Name, *"I will do it."*

> *And whatever you ask in My name, that I will do, that the Father may be glorified in the Son. "If you ask" anything in my name, I will do it* (John 14:13-14, NKJV).

Jesus revealed a powerful Kingdom key, which says that believers have the privilege of asking God for what they need in prayer. Believers are not alone in the universe. We have a loving Heavenly Father to whom we can come with our needs. If we are walking with Jesus and asking or confessing according to God's will, He will grant us anything that we ask of Him in the Name of Jesus.

Listed Below For Your Perusal Are Shining Examples Of Two Individuals Who Sought God First.

In her autobiography titled *Mary Kay, The Success Story of America's Most Dynamic Businesswoman* by Mary Kay Ash, she writes...

"Mary Kay Cosmetics was founded on Friday, September 13, 1963. And through the ensuing decades it has been my joy and honor to watch it grow. With the help of God and my wonderful family, friends, and associates, we have evolved from a little storefront company with nine saleswomen to an international family of hundreds of thousands of Beauty Consultants — each controlling her own independent business."

God First, Family Second, Career Third

She continues....

"Over the years, I have found that everything seems to work out if you have your life in the proper perspective; God first, family second, and career third. I truly believe the growth of Mary Kay Cosmetics has come about because the first thing we did was to take God as our partner. If we had not done that, I don't believe we would be where we are today. I believe He has blessed us because our motivation is right. He knows I want women to become the beautiful creatures He created, and to use the wonderful God-given talents that lie within each of us.

"I've found that when you just let go and place yourself in God's hands, everything in your life goes right. When you try to do everything alone and rely on yourself, you begin to make major errors."

More than 325,000 Mary Kay Beauty Consultants and Directors serve customers in twenty-three countries worldwide today. All of them are independent business people operating their own Mary Kay businesses – in essence, presidents of their own companies.

In 1993 Mary Kay Cosmetics had wholesale sales of more than $735 million, which equates to well over $1 billion in sales at the retail level. In 1992, the company qualified for inclusion on the 1993 Fortune 500 list, and in 1993, Mary Kay Cosmetics again made the list, advancing fifty-seven spots on the 1994 Fortune 500 list.

Clearly we can see the benefits of Mary Kay's passion to put God first in her life. It has produced divine intervention in her life and in her business, which continues to flourish abundantly today.

Mary Kay states:

"There are four kinds of people in this world:

- Those who make things happen
- Those who watch things happen
- Those who wonder what happened
- Those who don't know that anything happened!"

She says that she knew from an early age that she wanted to be first on that list. And in the years since, she has learned that people who do succeed are set apart by their personalities, objectives, and abilities. Specifically this means that they have enthusiasm (with purpose), discipline, willingness (to work, to serve, and to learn), determination and appreciation of others.

Seek God First

Reverend Kenneth E. Hagin, a man mightily used of God in teaching, preaching and spreading the Good News of the gospel unveiled this enlightening account in his booklet titled, *Faith Foods*. He states...

"I knew a man down in East Texas whose family was so poor that he didn't have a pair of shoes until he was 12 years old. He had only a fifth-grade education. But way back when money was money, he had $2 million. He made his money in investments.

"Two people who had been frequent guests in his home told me that he had said, 'In many years of investing, I've never lost a dime.'

"Here's how he did it. He told my friend, 'When someone comes with an idea and wants me to invest in something, my first reaction is mental. So, I have a big closet. I go into it and pray about it. I wait long enough to hear what my spirit says.'

"'My head may say, "You'd be a fool to invest in that," but if my heart says, "Go ahead," I do. Or, my head may say, "You'd better get in on this one," while my heart tells me, "Don't do it," so I don't. I don't pay any attention to my head, I just get in that closet and wait - all night sometimes.

And sometimes I'm in and out of it for three days, just praying and reading my Bible, getting quiet so I can hear what my heart says.'"

What an awesome testimony! This millionaire said, "In many years of investing, I've never lost a dime." His track record in investing was perfect because he would always go into his closet and seek God first.

Know this, God the Holy Spirit always contacts men through their human spirit. He doesn't contact men through the senses (the mind). Jesus Christ of Nazareth told the disciples these truths concerning the Holy Spirit, and He is also speaking to us today.

> *But when the Father sends the Counselor as my representative - and by the Counselor I mean the Holy Spirit - he will teach you everything and will remind you of everything I myself have told you (*John 14:26, NLT),
> *When the Spirit of truth comes, he will guide you into all truth. He will not be presenting his own ideas; he will be telling you what he has heard. He will tell you about the future. He will bring me glory by revealing to you whatever he receives from me. All that the Father has is mine; this is what I mean when I say that the Spirit will reveal to you whatever he receives from me (*John 16:13-15, NLT).

As for me, every time I seek God first in prayer or when I go to the Word of God and study, meditate, and say my confessions, my track record is perfect. I always get an answer. After I pray, I immediately write out a faith-building confession and start confessing the answer (the results/the solution).

In 1989, my worth of nearly 3/4 million dollars (liquid) from AT&T and Baby Bell stock splits, as well as a hefty lump sum buy-out, were the direct results of my faith-building confessions. The money to publish my first book in 1990, and the money to publish my second book in 1997 came as a result of my prayers, the Holy Spirit's guidance, and my daily faith-building confessions. Both of my books were successful! Praise the Lord! I am believing and confessing that *Self-Talk And Grow Rich* will also be an overwhelming success, and that it will glorify my Heavenly Father as well as enhance the lives of many people.

I sincerely encourage you to safeguard Master Key #2, for it is the cornerstone Scripture that will help you build and maintain a strong godly foundation.

Worrying Is Ungodly

Anxiety, stress and worry are not supposed to conquer the Christian. Jesus Christ gave us a brand new way of looking at life that is designed to overcome the habit of worry. First, Jesus told His followers they should look at nature to see how God (our Heavenly Father) takes care of the birds, flowers, and grass (Matthew 6:26-30).

Then, He said that if God can take care of nature (and He can) then He can certainly meet our needs. Finally, Jesus Christ taught His followers to have a divine perspective on life. He promised that those who seek God and put His Kingdom first will have their needs met (Matthew 6:30-33). Therefore, don't worry! **Seek God first!**

Add this faith-building confession to your daily menu of confessions. Take one Gospill before each meal and snack, before bedtime, in the morning and throughout the day. Read this faith-building confession aloud!

Faith-Building Confession:

I do seek first the Kingdom of my God and His righteousness, His way of doing things. I obey His Word, and He directs my paths; He adds good health, wealth, riches, and a long joyous life to me! I confess this under the authority, and in the matchless Name of Jesus Christ of Nazareth! SO BE IT! (Matthew 6:33)

PART 3

Master Key #3 Develop and maintain a good relationship with God.

Master Key #3 opens the heavenly door to a good relationship with God the Father.

Relationship Required To Qualify For An Inheritance

When you were born again, you were immediately adopted into the royal family of God as one of His very own children, to reign as king or queen in this life.

The Bible says,

> *For all who are led by the Spirit of God are sons of God. For (the Spirit which) you have now received (is) not a spirit of slavery to put you once more in bondage to fear, but you have received the spirit of adoption (the Spirit producing sonship) in (the bliss of) which we cry, Abba Father!* (Romans 8:14-15, Amp.)

In the natural, when a man adopts a son, that son has the same legal rights as a biological son. He takes on the father's name and is entitled to a share of all property and possessions and inheritance, the same as the biological son. Let's see what Jesus Christ of Nazareth had to say about sons and their inheritance in this upcoming parable.

What Is A Parable

Jesus Christ told the Parable of the Lost Son to tax collectors and other notorious sinners who often came to listen to Him teach. A parable is an earthly story with a heavenly or spiritual meaning. This parable that Jesus told is widely referred to as the Parable of the Prodigal Son. However, let us note that the Bible does not call the son who left home a prodigal.

The word "prodigal" means recklessly extravagant or wasteful. And in this parable, Jesus is the Master speaking about earthly things that reveal heavenly meaning. He so eloquently unfolds the recklessness and wasteful lifestyle of the son who left home. But more importantly, we get a glimpse into the heart of God! It reveals His eagerness to welcome (His son) the returning, repentant sinner, therefore He goes more than halfway to meet him.

Some parables are in question form but in this one, Jesus speaks in a positive narrative form, relating an incident probably from common daily life. He might have had in mind a father and two sons, of whom He knew only too well. This parable could better be called the Parable of the Lost Sons, or the Parable of the Wonderful Father.

Bible scholars have hailed this parable as the crown and pearl of all parables. "It stands alone at the apex as one of the finest short stories every written," said Charles Dickens. This parable remains unequaled in literature for tenderness, love, grace and pathos. The King James Bible refers to this parable as the Parable of the Lost Son. I employ you to read all of this short story aloud studiously (Luke 15:11-32). We will examine one verse for relationship and fellowship, which are the two basic elements required for a son to receive an inheritance from a father.

Also, we will mine this parable for many hidden nuggets. This premier soul-winning parable unfolds with Jesus Christ of Nazareth speaking these words:

> *"A man had two sons. The younger son told his father, 'I want my share of your estate now, instead of waiting until you die.'So his father agreed to divide his wealth between his sons."*
> Luke 15:11–12, NLT

The word "relationship" means the state of being related or interrelated in kinship or connected by blood or marriage. An inheritance is generally left to kinfolk. Notice closely, the relationship in this parable is that of a wealthy father and two biological sons. It's a father-son's relationship and both sons are heirs to their father's wealth and possessions. And this is the same relationship that believers have with our Heavenly Father. It's a Father-son or/and a Father-daughter relationship.

Law Of Inheritance

Now, let's take a closer look at the bold request made by the youngest son for a portion of his father's estate. He probably knew that his father would grant his request, based on the law (Deuteronomy 21:15-17).

According to an ancient Jewish law of inheritance, under certain conditions an heir was entitled to claim his share of an estate during his father's lifetime if he wished to do so. The elder would receive a two-thirds portion, the younger a third of all movable property. A man could, during his lifetime, dispose of all his property by gift if he chose.

The Wealthy Man's Sons Received A Pre-Inheritance Allotment

Under the law, when the share of the younger children was to be diminished by gift or taken away, the disposition had to be made by a person presumably near death. No one in good health could diminish, except by gift, the legal portion of the younger son. In this parable, without a doubt, the younger son was thus entitled by law to his share of his father's estate. However, he had no right to claim it during his father's lifetime, unless his father was near death. This parable gives no such indication.

Therefore, this nervy request on the part of the younger son must be regarded as asking a favor, which the father graciously granted, with both sons receiving their lawful portion in advance. I named this a pre-inheritance allotment. Born-again believers have a relationship with their Father God. It is a Father-son and Father-daughter relationship, which is required for receiving your covenant inheritance of wealth and riches.

PART 4

Master Key #4 Develop and maintain a good fellowship with God.

Master Key #4 opens the heavenly door to a good fellowship with God the Father.

Fellowship Required To Qualify For An Inheritance

The word "fellowship" means an association or friendship between individuals, especially on pleasant or intimate terms. Thus far, the parable we read earlier clearly shows a pleasant fellowship between the father and his sons. I firmly believe that the key reason the father granted the early request from the younger son was because of a good father and son relationship.

In this eloquent earthly story, Jesus Christ of Nazareth reveals two of the essential keys required to receive an inheritance from a biological father, and they are **relationship** and **fellowship**.

Heavenly Meaning To This Parable Of The Lost Son Revealed

The heavenly or spiritual meaning of this parable is that we see in the wealthy father a warmhearted, caring father who graciously agreed to divide his estate with his sons without questions. The father of these sons represents our loving and caring father, our Heavenly Father, Who tells His children (believers) to *"Ask, and it will be given to you; seek and you will find, knock and it will be opened to you. For everyone who asks receives, and he who seeks finds, and to him who knocks it will be opened."* Matthew 7:7-8, NKJV

Every believer, through Jesus Christ, has been adopted into the royal family of God as one of His very own sons or daughters. Therefore, under spiritual law, all believers have relationship with our Heavenly Father. However, it is the **relationship** and the **fellowship** that make believers eligible for their covenant inheritance of wealth and riches.

We see boldness in the younger son, which is a characteristic of the righteous. The Bible says,

> *The wicked flee when no man pursues them, but the (uncompromising) righteous are bold as a lion.*
> Proverbs 28:1, Amp.

True fellowship with God comes about when you trust in Him with all of your heart and seek Him first; when you allow Him to direct your paths. Likewise, maintaining strong faith and applying His Word to your daily life will keep you in good fellowship with your Heavenly Father. Believers must be bold and relentless in their pursuit of the covenant blessings that God the Father has decreed for His sons and daughters.

Believer's Covenant Inheritance of Wealth And Riches Temporarily Resides In Their Heavenly Bank Account

The Bible says...

> *How we praise God, the Father of our Lord Jesus Christ, **who has blessed us with every spiritual blessing in the heavenly realms because we belong to Christ**. Long ago, even before he made the world, God loved us and chose us in Christ to be holy and without fault in his eyes. His unchanging plan has always been to **adopt us into his own family** by bringing us to himself through Jesus Christ. And this gave him great pleasure... Furthermore, because of Christ, we have received an **inheritance** from God, for he chose us from the beginning, and all things happen just as he decided long ago. God's purpose was that we who were the first to trust in Christ should praise our glorious*

> *God.* ***And now you also have heard the truth, the Good News that God saves you. And when you believed in Christ, he identified you as his own by giving you the Holy Spirit, whom he promised long ago. The Spirit is God's guarantee that he will give us everything he promised and that he has purchased us to be his own people****. This is just one more reason for us to praise our glorious God* (Ephesians 1:3-5, 11-14, NLT).

It is written in the book of Galatians...

> *And so it is: All who put their faith in Christ share the* ***same blessing*** *Abraham received because of his* ***faith****... Through the work of Christ Jesus, God has blessed the Gentiles with the same blessing he promised to Abraham, and we Christians receive the promised Holy Spirit through faith... There is no longer Jew or Gentile, slave or free, male or female. For you are all Christians - you are one in Christ Jesus. And now that you belong to Christ, you are the true children of Abraham. You are his* ***heirs****, and* ***now all the promises God gave to him belong to you*** (Galatians 3:9, 14, 28–29, NLT).

It is written in the book of Proverbs...

> *The blessing of the Lord makes a person rich, and he adds no sorrow with it* (Proverbs 10:22, NLT).

The apostle Peter seals the fact that believers, through faith in Jesus Christ are heirs of welfare (prosperity), happiness and protection. He writes the following...

> *Never return evil for evil or insult for insult (scolding, tongue-lashing, berating), but on the contrary blessing (praying for their welfare, happiness and protection and truly pitying and loving them). For know that to this you have been called, that you may yourselves* ***inherit a blessing*** *(from God - that you may obtain a blessing as* ***heirs****, bringing welfare and happiness and protection) (*1 Peter 3:9, Amp.).

Relationship, Fellowship And Strong Faith Guarantee Your Inheritance

The Bible says...

> *Whatever may be your task, work at it heartily (from the soul), as (something done), for the Lord and not for men.*
>
> ***Knowing*** *(with all certainty) that it is from the Lord (and not from men) that you* ***will*** *receive the* ***inheritance*** *which is your*

(real) reward. (The One Whom) you are actually serving (is) the Lord Christ (the Messiah) (Colossians 3:23-24 Amp.).

The word "welfare" is used twice in this Scripture, and it means prosperity. My paraphrase of this Scripture reads like this: You have been called to obtain a blessing of an inheritance of wealth and riches, happiness and protection.

Our covenant inheritance of wealth, riches, good health and divine protection is available to us. But it requires strong faith, the same faith that Abraham had. We must let God's Word and His Holy Spirit radically transform our way of thinking, renewing our minds to know and do the will of God and giving our bodies as a living sacrifice. In doing so, you can be assured of your right **fellowship** with your Heavenly Father.

The principles and techniques revealed in *Self-Talk And Grow Rich* are designed to help you build strong faith in God's Word, which will result in your becoming a world-class overcomer with victory in every area of life.

The self-talk faith-building confessions prescribed in this book can create the supernatural power needed to get things done in the spiritual realm; speaking these confessions aloud over a prolonged period of time is an excellent (spiritual) preventative medicine. Faith-building confessions can and will move the mountains of trials, troubles, poverty, sickness, and disease from your life. Faith-building confessions are the key to receiving your covenant inheritance of wealth and riches.

I have personally used these faith-building confessions for almost two decades with amazing results.

The United States Government Recognizes The Power Of Prayer And Confession

The National Institute of Health (NIH) has established a National Center for Complementary and Alternative Medicine (NCCAM). On the NCCAM classification list of alternative medicine practices, prayer therapy is listed under the mind/body control category. The classification list was developed by the Ad Hoc Advisory Panel (professional health care providers) to NCCAM and NIH for alternative medicine researchers and practitioners. Praise the Lord! The scientific world finally got it right.

This Ad Hoc Advisory Panel undoubtedly spent millions and millions of tax-payers' dollars studying and researching prayer, while all along the data was listed right in the Bible concerning prayer therapy and its awesome power.

PART 5
THE SECRET TO RECEIVING YOUR COVENANT INHERITANCE OF WEALTH AND RICHES REVEALED

The secret to developing strong faith and receiving things from God is to repeatedly speak God's Words (faith-building confessions) into your ear gates. Your spoken words are transmitted from your eargates to your (mind and) heart (not the heart that pumps blood throughout your body). But figuratively, it is the seat of feelings, emotions, thoughts, and intentions; it is the central or most vital part of man's being.

Proverbs 23:7 says, *"For as a man thinks in (speaks to) his heart, so is he."* The heart is like the ground; it produces whatever seed is planted. Once your (mind and) heart memory files are overflowing with your faith-building confessions, a divine connection takes place with your human spirit (Ephesians 3:16,17). And when your faith-building confessions line up with God's Word, it supernaturally causes a harvest in the life of a believer.

Jesus Christ of Nazareth said in the book of Matthew:

> *Either make the tree sound (healthy and good), and its fruit sound (healthy and good), or make the tree rotten (diseased and bad), and its fruit rotten (diseased and bad); for the tree is known and recognized and judged by its fruit. You offspring of vipers! How can you speak good things when you are evil (wicked)?* ***For out of the fullness (the overflow, the superabundance) of the heart the mouth speaks.*** *The good man from his inner good treasure flings forth good things, and the evil man out of his inner evil storehouse flings forth evil things. But I tell you, on the day of judgment* ***men will have to give account for every idle (inoperative, nonworking) word they speak. For by your words you will be justified and acquitted, and by your words you will be condemned and sentenced*** (Matthew 12:33-37, Amp.).

My paraphrase of these Scriptures is: Out of the fullness (the overflow, the superabundance) self-talk faith-building confessions stored in the heart, the mouth speaks, and causes those self-talk faith-building confessions to fling forth and produce a supernatural harvest in the natural realm.

Jesus Christ of Nazareth tells us how God's system works. Jesus said...

> *Here is another illustration of what the Kingdom of God is like; A farmer planted seeds in a field, and then he went on with his other activities. As the days went by, the seeds sprouted and grew without the farmer's help, because the earth produces crops on its own. First a leaf blade pushes through, then the heads of wheat*

> *are formed, and finally the grain ripens. And as soon as the grain is ready, the farmer comes and harvests it with a sickle.* Mark 4:26-29, NLT

In this parable (remember, a parable is an earthly story with a heavenly meaning), Jesus said that you are the one planting the seed. You speak it (faith-building confessions) out of your mouth. When you speak it, it is a seed: it goes into your ear gates and into your (mind and) heart, which represents the field or ground. And there it begins to supernaturally grow and produce. The Kingdom of God (God's way of doing things) is like a farmer planting seeds in a field or into the ground. Your words are your seeds which can produce a harvest.

Author Reveals The Secret Of How To Receive Your Covenant Inheritance Of Wealth And Riches

The Holy Spirit revealed to me what I am about to share with you. As you read these following instructions, don't throw the baby out with the wash water. And keep in mind what the Word of God says, *"For my thoughts are not your thoughts, neither are your ways my ways, saith the Lord."*

Another translation says...

> *"My thoughts are completely different from yours," says the Lord. "And my ways are far beyond anything you could imagine. For just as the heavens are higher than the earth, so are my ways higher than your ways and my thoughts higher than your thoughts.*
> *"The rain and snow come down from the heavens and stay on the ground to water the earth. They cause the grain to grow, producing seed for the farmer and bread for the hungry. It is the same with my word. I send it out, and it always produces fruit. It will accomplish all I want it to, and it will prosper everywhere I send it"* (Isaiah 55:8-11, NLT).

First, the Holy Spirit told me to write His instructions down this way, and specifically show believers how they are to receive their covenant inheritance of wealth and riches:

Step 1

Tell the believer to pray a petition prayer, asking their Heavenly Father to reveal to them what amount in money He has bequeathed to them (your inheritance).

Step 2

After you have prayed the petition prayer, then begin reading aloud before each meal, morning, noon and night, and as many times a day as possible, the following faith-building confession:

Faith-Building Confession:

Dear Heavenly Father, Your Word says to ask, and it will be given me. I have asked You to reveal to me the amount in money that You have bequeathed to me, through Jesus Christ. I believe in my spirit, by faith, that I have received my answer from You! It is clear to my understanding and I am abundantly joyous for such an awesome blessing of wealth and riches! I promise to be faithful and leave an inheritance to my children's children, to support your storehouse (my local church) and to share with the poor and needy. I confess this under the authority of and in the mighty Name of Jesus Christ of Nazareth! SO BE IT! (Matthew 7:7-8)

<u>Step 3</u>

Write or type this self-talk faith-building confession on an index card 3 X 5 inches or larger. And write the date on the card that you began reading it aloud. Then continue reading this card aloud until God reveals to your understanding your answer. God has made the provision for your covenant inheritance and He will reveal to you the amount of your inheritance. Just be patient, and in faith continue to make your daily deposits of faith-building confessions.

David said, "*Evening, and morning, and at noon, will I pray and cry aloud; and he shall hear my voice*" (Psalm 55:17).

Pastor David Yonggi Cho, the pastor of the largest church in the world (with 750,000 members and growing) said in his book *Prayer That Brings Revival*, that "One of the biggest problems people have in prolonging their prayer lives is that they are not willing to repeat praying for the same thing daily. They think that praying over something once is enough." Yet, daily, God gave Israel manna in the wilderness. Yesterday's manna did not last over twenty-four hours.

So, also, we need daily communication with our savior. We also eat, sleep, and breathe every day. The meal we had yesterday will not satisfy today's need. The breath we took last second will have to be repeated over and over again, or else we will die. Jesus said, *"Give us this day our daily bread."* He did not say that we should get bread so that we won't need to eat again!

This same truth applies to your faith-building confessions. The spiritual law that governs faith states, *"So then faith cometh by hearing and hearing by the Word of God"* (Romans 10:17). It does not say that faith cometh by having heard it once, No! It's a continuous process of feeding your (mind and) heart on God's Word and His promises.

The procedure outlined in Step 3 is the optimal method; it's the most effective because it employs the use of three of the five senses: touching the card which is a point of contact that helps to build faith, reading the faith-building confession involves eyesight, and it also involves the major of the five senses, hearing. This combination of senses operating together is very, very powerful and effective in helping to make your way prosperous in every area of life. It is the way God designed His system to work.

The confession cards are easy to carry, so if I am waiting for my wife at the store, or my daughter at school, I'm reading my confessions. Whenever I know that I'm going to have some idle time, I take my confession cards and read them.

Faith-Building Confession On Audio Tape

Because of our fast-paced schedules and in an effort to make the best use of time, I was led to develop another means of hearing my faith-building confessions. This procedure is outlined in the next step.

Step 4

Record your faith-building confessions on a cassette tape over and over again. I play my faith-building confession tape in the morning while getting dressed and ready for the day. When I drive my car, I take my confession tape with me and insert it in my car's tape player. When I do my three-or-four-times-a-week walk, I'm listening to my faith-building confession tape. Wow! What a spiritual high you get when exercising your physical body and at the same time feeding faith food to your (mind and) heart.

Prayer of Thanksgiving

When God answers your petition prayer and tells you how much your covenant inheritance is, the first thing to do is to reverently offer up a prayer of thanksgiving to your Heavenly Father for answering your prayer.

Step 5

Next, the Holy Spirit said to take one of my blank personal checks and make a copy of if (long-wise) in color and increase the size to 8 1/2 X 11. (Beware that some copy stores may not want to reproduce a check, but there must be one that will or maybe you already own a color copier.) Some may be able to use their computer to scan the check, and make a color copy.

After making an enlarged color copy of the check, write out the check to yourself using a fine tip black marker pen, write the date, your name, your signature and the dollar amount of your inheritance. And on the line where you spell out the dollar amount, use a fine tip green marker pen. And on the memo line write, "my inheritance - it's mine."

The actual size of your enlarged check top to bottom should measure 4 1/2 to 5 inches, and left to right 10 to 10 1/2 inches. When the check is centered on the 8 1/2 X 11 copy paper, you should have 1½ to 2 inches of white space above and below the check. (A sample check is shown in Appendix E.)

I encourage you to read the remaining instructions in this Step 5 before you make entries above or below your check. The following instructions should be tried on a separate 8 1/2 X 11 sheet of paper first to insure that your faith-building confessions will fit.

On the white space above your check, type or neatly write or print this **Super (faith-building) confession:**

This is my covenant inheritance of $XXX million/billion (write in whatever your amount is). It is loosed on earth and it is loosed in heaven. I believe in my spirit, by faith, that I have received my covenant inheritance of $XXX million/billion. I am smiling because I can feel the joy of being richly blessed by God to be a blessing to others, plus all my needs and desires are met! I confess this under the authority, and in the mighty Name of Jesus Christ of Nazareth! SO BE IT! (Matthew 16:19; Mark 11:23)

Set your goal to read this **Super (faith-building) confession** at least eight to ten times daily. After you read this confession **aloud**, touch your check, then close your eyes and feel the emotion of joy! See yourself leaving an inheritance of house and riches to your children. See yourself leaving an inheritance to your children's children. See and feel the emotions of writing out an anonymous check to someone you know who is poor or needy. See and feel the emotions of giving your church a paid-in-full life insurance policy in your name with the church as the beneficiary. See yourself writing a check to your local church to pay your tithes on your covenant inheritance. In other words, use imagination and visualization which help to build strong faith.

The Power Of Imagination And Visualization

The Lord used imagination and visualization to build Abraham's faith. In the book of Genesis, we see how the power of imagination and visualization caused Abram (Abraham) to believe and obey God. The Bible says...

> *Then the Lord said to him, "No, your servant will not be your heir, for you will have a son of your own to inherit everything I am giving you." Then the Lord brought Abram outside*

> *beneath the night sky and told him, "Look up into the heavens and count the stars if you can. Your descendants will be like that - too many to count!" And* ***Abram believed the Lord****, and the Lord declared him righteous because of his faith.* Genesis 15:4-6, NLT

Notice closely that the Lord told Abram to go outside at night and look up into the heavens and count the stars if he could. This was an exercise in imagination and visualization. The Lord used the stars and had Abram imagine and visualize the future to see how many descendants he would have, and this resulted in Abram believing the Lord.

Imaging and visualization are biblically sound and are an effective method in developing strong faith. The Bible says...

> *Since we consider and look not to the things that are seen but to the things that are unseen; for the things that are visible are temporal (brief and fleeting), but the things that are invisible are deathless and everlasting* (2 Corinthians 4:18, Amp.).

The method of using visualization was used by Jacob to produce strong and healthy livestock (Genesis 30:31-43). Moreover, for you to look to the things that are unseen requires you to imagine and visualize the results long before they occur. Now back to your covenant inheritance check.

On the white space below the check, type or neatly write or print the following: **Abbreviated faith-building confession:**

This is my covenant inheritance of $XXX million/billion (write in whatever your amount is). It is mine in the mighty Name of Jesus Christ of Nazareth, and I'm joyful! (Mark 11:23)

Your covenant inheritance check should have your super faith-building confession above the check and the abbreviated faith-building confession below the check. Then take the check to a copy store and have it laminated.

<u>Step 6</u>

Hang your check on your bedroom wall (eye level) next to the door that you use most often, preferably right above the light switch.

Every time you pass your inheritance check, stop and take time to read aloud the super faith-building confession. Touch the check and feel the joy, knowing that the amount shown belongs to you. If you are in a hurry, then take a few seconds and read aloud the abbreviated faith-building confession.

Well, praise the Lord! This is the way the Holy Spirit gave it to me, and I am now released after sharing it with you. Remember this, it's your covenant inheritance of wealth and riches—don't leave it unclaimed, don't look back, and don't dare give up.

In the next section, we will discuss the 8 keys to keeping and increasing your covenant inheritance of wealth and riches.

Self-talk faith-building confessions are 100% guaranteed to come to pass in due season when you remain steadfast.

CHAPTER 10

8 KEYS TO KEEPING AND INCREASING YOUR COVENANT INHERITANCE OF WEALTH AND RICHES

KEY #1 Make your desire for wealth and riches to be for the purpose of supporting God's storehouse (the local church) and ministries that seek to save the lost, to share cheerfully with the poor and needy, and to establish an inheritance for your children and your children's children.

The Bible tells us to consider our character, consider our ways, consider how things are going with us now (Haggai 1:5). Are your desires for wealth and riches for the purpose of storing it up and hoarding it for yourself? Is it your desire to squander it on lavish or riotous living the same way the prodigal son did? (Luke 15:13). Or is it your desire to use your (weekly, bi-weekly, monthly) income and covenant inheritance of wealth and riches to pay your tithes and offerings, to share bountifully with the poor and needy and to leave an inheritance to your children and your children's children?

The apostle Paul writes the following beneficial instructions for all believers.

> *Tell those who are rich in this world not to be proud and not to trust in their money, which will soon be gone. But their trust should be in the living God, who richly gives us all we need for our enjoyment.*
> *Tell them to use their money to do good. They should be rich in good works and should give generously to those in need, always being ready to share with others whatever God has given them. By doing this, they will be storing up their treasure as a good foundation for the future so that they may take hold of real life.*
> 1Timothy 6:17-19, NLT

Notice closely that the apostle Paul didn't say to tell those who are rich in this world that they are ungodly, and that they will not see the Kingdom of Heaven. No! He said to tell them:

1. Not to be proud.
2. Not to put trust in money.

3. Trust in the living God.
4. Be rich in good works and give generously to those in need.
5. Be ready to share with others whatever God has given them.

The overriding revelation that has resonated throughout the pages of this book is that it is God Who gives you power to become rich. Not only does He give you the power to get wealth and riches, but it belongs to Him in the first place.

Believers Are Earth-Realm Distributing Managers

The Bible says, *"For the earth is the Lord's and everything in it."* (1 Corinthians 10:26). *"For all the animals of the forest are mine, and I own the cattle on a thousand hills, every bird of the mountains and all the animals of the field belong to me"* (Psalm 50:10,11). *"The silver is mine, and the gold is mine, says the Lord Almighty"* (Haggai 2:8). *"The earth is the Lord's, and everything in it. The world and all its people belong to Him"* (Psalm 24:1).

First, you must clearly establish in your (heart and) spirit that the wealth and riches that God empowers you to get, do not belong to you. They are entrusted to you to carry out the work that Jesus left behind; that is to seek and save the lost, which requires mega dollars to effectively accomplish today.

Believers are Jesus Christ's officially appointed distributing managers here on earth. Their mission is to help support the work of the ministry (monetarily), seeking to save the lost, and always being ready to share with those in need whatever God has given them.

Purpose Of The Wealth And Riches

God's purpose for giving believers the power to get wealth and riches and then entrusting them to distribute it for Him in this earth realm are twofold:

1. To fulfill the covenant He made with their ancestors to bless believers with abundant increase of favors (wealth and riches) and make their name famous and distinguished.
   Genesis 12:2-3, Amp.
2. So that believers will be a blessing (dispensing good) to others.
   Genesis 12:2, Amp.

Note 1: The leftovers from your covenant inheritance of wealth and riches will be more than enough to make you abundantly rich and wealthy.

Note 2: Your name becomes famous and distinguished when you are obedient to God's Word and distribute the wealth and riches He gives you according to His will. It is not meant for you to store up or hoard or squander on yourself.

Illustration Of An Earth-Realm Managing Distributor

Can you imagine for a moment that a wealthy man in your city had appointed you manager of one of his stop-hunger food bank centers. One of your responsibilities is to seek out people within your city who need food and then distribute it to them. The owner spends most of his time in a foreign country where he is establishing other stop-hunger food bank centers. Therefore, at the beginning of each year he writes a check for an enormous amount of money to cover the cost of operating the center, which also includes your wages. Included in the check is a sizeable amount to be held in escrow until the end of the year. This becomes yours if you perform your duties as a distributing manager according to the will of your boss.

The money held in escrow is your reward or bonus for a job well done. Your boss told you when he appointed you to the job that your character and the kind of love shown to others will determine whether you keep the job, and whether or not you get the sizeable bonus each year.

The conditions cited in this earthly illustration are very much the same as those that apply to believers who receive their (supernatural) covenant inheritance of wealth and riches. In other words, your character, your ways, and your obedience to God's Word will determine how long you get to keep the wealth and riches and whether or not you receive increase or decrease.

I have one question for you. In the earthly illustration cited, who owned the stop-hunger food bank center? The check? The food purchased? And the money in escrow? The rich owner or the managing distributor?

Well, quite obviously, everything belonged to the rich owner and not the manager of the stop-hunger food bank center. The same holds true with what God gives you. It belongs to Him. You are entrusted to be Jesus Christ of Nazareth's distributing manager in this earth realm. You are entrusted to be a distributor and not a hoarder of God's money. You are His appointed representative here on earth.

The Almighty Lord tells us to consider our ways, consider our character, when things are not going well (Haggai 1:5). The bottom line is – are your desires for wealth and riches to benefit self or to benefit God's Kingdom?

If you are living from paycheck to paycheck, pension check to pension check, or social security check to social security check, then consider your ways.

If your wages disappear as though you were putting them in pockets filled with holes, consider your ways.

If your covenant inheritance of wealth and riches is rapidly disappearing, consider your ways.

Are you a good distributing manager? Are you paying your tithes and giving offerings consistently? Are you sharing with the poor and needy? Have you set aside an inheritance for your children and your children's children? Are you obedient to God's Word? Consider your ways and make the changes in your attitude, your character, and your actions that will be pleasing to God. Then you will enjoy your covenant inheritance of wealth, riches, and increases. Praise the Lord!

The best rule to follow is: God first, others second, and me last!

Knowing that the fleshly side of individuals fights to make selfishness dominate in their (minds and) hearts and lives, then the next two questions are paramount:

1. Do you desire wealth and riches for your own selfish gains?
2. Do you desire wealth and riches for the purpose of distributing it to God's Kingdom and to the poor and needy?

Your answers to these questions must be firmly resolved in your (mind and) heart; especially the answer to question number two. It must be in the affirmative if you expect true fellowship with your Heavenly Father.

Don't Fall Victim To The Greatest Temptations

Although many people become millionaires and successful without acknowledging God, the Bible is clear that it is God who gives His people the power to get wealth (Deuteronomy 8:18). Through much of history, the church has tended to equate poverty with spirituality. This is because Jesus said those who have wealth will find the pursuit of God much more difficult, although He never condemned wealth. As well, Paul warned against the love of money, calling it the *"root of all evil,"* and said that *"those who desire to be rich fall into temptation and a snare"* (1Timothy 6:9-10).

Nevertheless, God does not forbid His people to make money and has often caused His people to gain great wealth. But with this wealth comes great responsibility and significant temptations, the greatest of which is to forget that it is God Who gives us the power to get wealth.

First, your covenant inheritance of wealth and riches must be used to support the work of the ministry to seek and save the lost. Secondly, it should be used to share cheerfully with the poor and needy. Thirdly, it should be used to leave an inheritance of house and riches to your children and to your children's children.

The Bible has many warnings to believers whose desire for wealth and riches is for their own (me, myself, and I) selfishness and greed.

The apostle Paul writes the following to Timothy, and it is written also to you and me.

> *But those who crave to be rich fall into temptation and a snare and into many foolish (useless, godless) and hurtful desires that plunge men into ruin and destruction and miserable perishing.* ***For the love of money is a root of all evils****; it is through this craving that some have been led astray and have wandered from the faith and pierced themselves through with many acute (mental) pangs (*1Timothy 6:9-10, Amp.).

Notice closely that the apostle Paul said that it is through the "craving for money" that some believers (some, not all) have been led astray and have wandered from the faith.

I seriously submit to you that you should avoid the "love of money" and its pitfalls. Instead, channel your craving toward strong desires to support God's storehouse (the local church) and the work of the ministry, which is to seek and to save the lost. Develop a cheerful spirit (bias) towards sharing with the poor and needy. Be relentless in your efforts to leave an inheritance of house and riches to your children and to your children's children. Doing these things will guarantee that God will open the windows of heaven and continue to pour out abundant blessing so great you won't have enough room to take it in, praise the Lord!

Consider your ways. Is your covenant inheritance of wealth and riches being devoured by unexpected circumstances? If so, chances are great that if your desire for wealth and riches is for your own selfish gain, then you are out of fellowship with your Heavenly Father. As long as you are out of fellowship with Him, you open the door for Satan to strip you clean financially and otherwise.

The Love Of Money Is The Root Of All Evil

This is one of the most misquoted Scriptures in the Bible. Most people misquote the Bible as saying "money is the root of all evil" which the Bible does not say. It actually states that it is the "**love of money**" which is the root of evil. Money is neither good nor bad; it is neutral. However, you need money to have food, clothing, shelter, and to support the ministry. In today's world, you cannot exist without money. There is nothing wrong with God's people having money or becoming wealthy. However, money leads to sin when you worship it instead of God, and let it direct your life.

Add this nourishing faith food to your daily menu of faith-building confessions.

Faith-Building Confession:
I acknowledge that my God has given me power to get wealth and riches for the purpose of fulfilling the covenant He made with my ancestors. Therefore, I know that my God has richly blessed me with abundant wealth and riches, and I am a blessing to His storehouse (my local church), to the poor and needy, and to my children and my children's children. I am abundantly blessed, and all my needs and desires are met. I speak these faith-filled words under the authority and in the majestic Name of Jesus Christ of Nazareth! SO BE IT! (Genesis 12:2, Deuteronomy 8:18, Galatians 3:29, Haggai 2:8, John 14:13-14)

KEY #2 Make your mouth tell the truth always and make your words reliable by doing what you say.

The Bible says to consider your character, consider your ways, consider how things are going with you now (Haggai 1:5). Do you allow your mouth to cause you to sin by telling lies?

Satan, who is the father of lies, has clearly used lies in one form or another to keep believers from true fellowship with God. The definition of the word "lie" is: to speak falsely, to tell a falsehood, to say with your mouth a statement or declaration that is not true, to make statements that are intended to deceive. To help illuminate this word more, let's look at some of its synonyms; canard, falsehood, falsity, fib, misrepresentation, false statement, prevarication, story, tale, fabrication, evasion, subterfuge, and untruth.

Consider your character, consider your ways. How would the Holy Spirit grade you today on being a man or woman of your word? How would He grade you on keeping appointments and promises. What about lying in other ways, such as saying to your children or others "Tell him I'm not home." Would the Holy Spirit give you an F, a C, or an A? Or an A+?

The Bible says that God hates a lying tongue (Proverbs 6:17); He hates lying lips (Proverbs 12:22); and He hates a false witness who speaks lies (Proverbs 6:19).

Lying Is Inspired By Satan

Brothers, sisters and friends, I submit to you that if God hates lies, then you and I should hate lies also. Lying is inspired by the Devil. It is ungodly, and I believe that lying is one of the major causes of believers being held in bondage spiritually, physically, mentally, financially, and otherwise. The main reason for this is because some people do not think before they speak. When words are spoken without thought, effortlessly, then lying in one form or another becomes easier.

Jesus Christ of Nazareth was speaking to a gathering of people about truth and character, and this is what He said...

> *Jesus told them, If God were your Father, you would love me, because I have come to you from God. I am not here on my own, but he sent me. Why can't you understand what I am saying? It is because you are unable to do so! For you are the children of your father the Devil, and you love to do the evil things he does. He was a murderer from the beginning and has always hated the truth.* ***There is no truth in him. When he lies, it is consistent with his character; for he is a liar and the father of lies.*** *So when I tell the truth, you just naturally don't believe me!* (John 8:42-44, NLT)

You are probably aware that in most cases when someone has lied, they will hold fast to the lie, but they almost always end up being trapped by the lie. The Bible says... "*You are snared with the words of your lips, you are caught by the speech of your mouth*" (Proverbs 6:2, Amp.).

When the words from an individual's lips are a lie, you can be certain that sooner or later that individual will be snared (trapped) with those words. We witness this truth all the time in our everyday lives with others, and in the courtrooms across our country.

Whether people tell big lies or little white lies, they are speaking evil words and they are speaking idle (worthless), untrue words that guarantee a fate of condemnation unless they repent and ask God for forgiveness. Jesus Christ of Nazareth gives us some valuable advice concerning evil and idle words. Here is what He has told us...

> *A tree is identified by its fruit. Make a tree good, and its fruit will be good. Make a tree bad, and its fruit will be bad. You brood of snakes! How could evil men like you speak what is good and right? For whatever is in your heart determines what you say.* ***A good person produces good words from a good heart, and an evil person produces evil words from an evil heart.*** *And I tell you this, that you must give an account on judgment day of every idle word you speak.* ***The words you say now reflect your fate then; either you will be justified by them or you will be condemned.***
> Matthew 12:33-37, NLT

Jesus mentions three things that provide stupendous revelation knowledge. The first is revealed in His statement which says, "a good person produces good words from a good heart." Secondly, He said, "an evil person produces evil words from an evil heart." The third thing that He reveals in this Scripture is "for whatever is in your heart determines what you say."

Brothers, sisters, and friends, I submit to you that the resolve for an evil heart, a heart that produces lies, is to perform radical heart surgery by repenting and asking God to forgive you. Then immediately begin to self-talk a faith-building confession of speaking truth and good words that are reliable and pleasing to God.

Examples Of People In The Bible Who Lied

The Bible contains many intriguing and sometime appalling accounts of liars. In the first book of the Bible is an account of Cain lying to God. It is written,

> *Later Cain suggested to his brother, Abel, "Let's go out into the fields." And while they were there, Cain attacked and killed his brother. Afterward, the Lord asked Cain, "Where is your brother? Where is Abel?" "I don't know!" Cain retorted, "Am I supposed to keep track of him wherever he goes?" But the Lord said, "What have you done? Listen, your brother's blood cries out to me from the ground! You are hereby banished from the ground you have defiled with your brother's blood. No longer will it yield abundant crops for you, no matter how hard you work! From now on, you will be a homeless fugitive on the earth, constantly wandering from place to place"* (Genesis 4:8-12, NLT).

Another form of lying is revealed when an uncle tricked his nephew into working for him for fourteen years and then having him marry both the uncle's daughters. This intriguing account unfolds this way,

> *After Jacob had been there about a month, Laban said to him, "You shouldn't work for me without pay just because we are relatives.*
> *How much do you want?"*
> *Now Laban had two daughters: Leah, who was the oldest, and her younger sister, Rachel. Leah had pretty eyes, but Rachel was beautiful in every way, with a lovely face and shapely figure. Since Jacob was in love with Rachel, he told her father, "I'll work for you seven years if you'll give me Rachel, your younger daughter, as my wife."*
> *"Agreed!" Laban replied, "I'd rather give her to you than to someone outside the family." So Jacob spent the next seven years working to pay for Rachel. But his love for her was so strong that it seemed to him but a few days. Finally, the time came for him to marry her. "I have fulfilled my contract," Jacob said to Laban, "Now give me my wife so we can be married."*
> *So Laban invited everyone in the neighborhood to celebrate with Jacob at a wedding feast. That night, when it was dark, Laban*

> *took Leah to Jacob, and he slept with her. And Laban gave Leah a servant, Zilpah, to be her maid.*
> *But when Jacob woke up in the morning – it was Leah! "What sort of trick is this?" Jacob raged at Laban. "I worked seven years for Rachel. What do you mean by this trickery?"*
> *"It's not our custom to marry off a younger daughter ahead of the firstborn," Laban replied. "Wait until the bridal week is over, and you can have Rachel, too – that is, if you promise to work another seven years for me."*
> *So Jacob agreed to work seven more years. A week after Jacob had married Leah, Laban gave him Rachel too. And Laban gave Rachel a servant. Bilhah, to be her maid. So Jacob slept with Rachel, too, and he loved her more than Leah. He then stayed and worked the additional seven years (Genesis 29:15-30, NLT).*

Throughout the Old and New Testament, the Bible reveals many accounts of lying. The New Testament gives an astounding account of two people who falsely reported their income, resulting in their demise. The following is a narrative of this intriguing story:

According to Acts 2:44, the believers in the early church in Jerusalem had all things in common. All the believers were selling their land and possessions and bringing what they earned back to lay at the apostles' feet (Acts 4:34-37). Ananias and Sapphira had sold their land for a certain price, but kept back part of the earnings.

Ananias lied about the sale, but the truth was revealed to Peter through the word of knowledge. Peter asked him, "Why has Satan filled thine heart to lie to the Holy Ghost?" And Ananias fell down dead. Some three hours later, when Peter questioned Ananias' wife Sapphira about the matter, she lied, then fell down dead also (Acts 5:1-10).

Lying To The Holy Spirit Is Very Risky

Deceiving the Holy Spirit brings destruction and death. The Spirit of Truth reveals every lie in our lives. We can lie to everyone, including ourselves, perhaps fooling others while deceiving ourselves. But lying to the Holy Spirit is quite impossible. Never lie to the Spirit of Truth. Ananias and Sapphira lied to the Spirit of Truth and it cost them their lives.

Lying and godliness cannot share the same stage – one must leave. The Bible says that truthful lips shall be established forever, but a lying tongue is (credited) but a moment (Proverbs 12:19). It also says that a (consistently) righteous man hates lying and deceit (Proverbs 13:5).

Big Lie Or Little White Lie

First, I'll say up front that a lie is a lie. There is no such thing as a little white lie, a big fat lie, or a bold-faced lie; they are all lies and God hates lies and so should we. Be forewarned that we are not to hate the liar (the person) but, instead, we are to hate the spirit of lies that oppresses the liar.

The devil has cleverly masqueraded the statement "little white lie" with the word "little," which is an adjective suggesting that the lie is not big, not much, and not important. All of these are deceptions, inspired by the devil to get you to fall into his trap of accepting (so called) lesser lies as okay, when in fact they are not!

You Are Only As Good As Your Word

I must be very candid with you and inform you now that the principles and techniques outlined in this book will not work for you if your word is no good. You can lie to others and then tell another lie to cover up the first lie. As an example, let's say you promised to meet someone at a certain place at a certain time, and you didn't show up and you didn't call or notify the person.

That's the first lie. Then suppose that person confronted you as to why you stood them up, and you tell them a cover-up lie and say that you got tied up in traffic, or that you had a flat tire, etc. This cover-up lie may fly some of the time, but there is a truthful saying that goes like this: You can fool some of the people some of the time, but you can't fool all of the people all the time.

So we can see that one can temporarily get away with lying and covering up to others, but the buck stops at you. You cannot escape when you lie to yourself or the Holy Spirit.

You Can't Fool Your Recreated Human Spirit Or The Holy Spirit

Your (heart and) recreated human spirit (your inner person) and the Holy Spirit know when you lie. The reason why lying is life defeating is because it destroys your faith in your own words. You get to the point where you don't believe the things that you say. You can lie to others but the inner person (the real you), your human spirit, and the Holy Spirit know when you lie. And you can't cover the lie up with them.

Metaphorically, when an untruth is told, it is transmitted to your (mind and) heart memory file and a search command takes place to determine its validity.

An internal search of your spirit and the Holy Spirit takes place to determine a match for truthfulness. When the statement made is a lie, the internal search results in a "no find." In other words, there was no similar statement located, resulting in the statement being a bona fide lie. When this keeps occurring over a period of time, the individual becomes desensitized, and lying becomes an easy thing to do.

Author's Personal Experience With Some Believers Who Lied

Well, brothers, sisters, and friends, there is no easy way to say what I have to say next. It is sad but true, that some of the most blatant lying that I have personally experienced has come from the mouths of believers in one form or another. Their word was just no good; they were not dependable.

The form of lying that I have experienced over the years coming from the mouth of believers has been mainly in their not keeping their word when they say they are going to do something. You would think that you could stake your life on a believer's word. The same as you can stake your life on God's Word, but I have found that some believers' word was just no good. Their word wasn't worth a lead penny. Let's face it, if God's Word was wishy washy and unreliable, I wouldn't put a lead nickel's worth of trust in it, but thanks be to God, He is not a God Who lies!

The Bible says,

> ***God is not a man that he should lie****, He is not a human, that he should change his mind. Has he ever spoken and failed to act? Has he ever promised and not carried it through?*
> Numbers 23:19, NLT

The apostle Paul said this about God,

> *This letter is from Paul, a slave of God and an apostle of Jesus Christ. I have been sent to bring faith to those God has chosen and to teach them to know the truth that shows them how to live godly lives. This truth gives them the confidence of eternal life, which God promised them before the world began –* ***and he cannot lie*** (Titus 1:1-2, NLT).

The apostle Paul, inspired by the Holy Spirit said that God cannot lie. The Bible commands believers to imitate God, to act and speak just like Him. Here is what it says,

> *Therefore be imitators of God (copy Him and follow His example), as well-beloved children (imitate their father).*
> Ephesians 5:1, Amp.

One of God's character traits is that His word is always truthful and He follows through on His promises. Since believers are commanded to imitate God and follow His example in everything we do, then we should take on His character traits, and make our mouth speak truthful words at all times and at all costs.

There was a pastor whom I knew (and I won't mention his name) who would say that he would be at a certain place at a certain time, but almost always he would be late by 30 minutes, one hour or more. And sometimes he didn't show up at all. To make matters worse, sometimes there would bc half a dozen people or more waiting for the pastor, but not even a telephone call or message was received to indicate a reason for the hold up.

I have had this same experience with a few Christian brothers also. This is one form of lying that I have experienced with a few believers; not all, but a few. Their word was just no good. The memories of being stood up, having to wait in vain were discouraging, especially when it was a man of God who is supposed to represent and imitate Jesus Christ of Nazareth. During that time, I worked on the corporate staff of the then Ohio Bell Telephone Company, and when I contrasted my co-workers'and my executive officers' promptness and reliability with that of the pastor and a few of the brethren, it is sad to say but, the secular folks were the most reliable.

If a division manager asked you to attend a meeting at a certain time, you could be sure that he would be there early, all set up with charts, seating arrangements, name tags, and handouts, all done before the meeting started. He would be there early, not late.

I still remember another time I attended a Bible training session and afterward I asked the pastor who taught the class a question, but he didn't have an answer. He sincerely promised me that he would get the answer to my question and that he would get back to me. Well, guess what? It has been six years and counting, and he has not given me an answer, nor has he acknowledged that he exhausted his efforts and couldn't provide an answer.

This is another form of lying in which some believers are easily snared. Their word is no good; you can't depend on what they say; they are not reliable.

Recently, while preparing the manuscript for this book, I experienced at least four different incidents where the words that the believers spoke didn't match their actions. In other words, they didn't follow through on what they said they were going to do. And lo and behold, one of these incidents involved yet another pastor. Could this be one of the reasons why so many people turn away from the faith?

The Bible tells us to consider our ways. Let's consider Jesus'ways. Do you believe that the examples cited of believers' words not corresponding to their actions are the ways of Jesus? I will be the first to raise my hand and shout No!

The Bible says *"the Lord hates those who don't keep their word, but He delights in those who do* (Proverbs 12:22, NLT).

Author's Friend's Word Is Pure As Gold

I have a friend named John, whom I have known for over three decades. Back then, we attended sporting events, concerts, dances, and parties, sometimes with dates and other times just the guys. Always enjoying the worldly pleasure of bachelorhood and the fast life. Down through the years, John's word has always been reliable. He has truly been a good friend and a man of his word. I salute him now for being steadfast in his truthfulness and reliability throughout the years!

If John said that he would meet you at a certain place at a certain time, you were close to 100 percent guaranteed he would be there on time or, in most cases, he would be there early.

I was in John's wedding, and he and his lovely wife Jackie were in my wedding. Throughout the years, John's word has been proven in the fiery furnace to be pure as gold. In more than three decades, I have never known John to lie or not keep his word.

The Bible says *"do not lie to one another, for you have stripped off the old (unregenerated) self with its evil practices"* (Colossians 3:9). Notice closely that the Bible calls lying an evil practice.

Along these same lines, Dr. Ed Dufresne in his book, *Faithfulness, the Road to Divine Promotion*, writes...

> "If you start watching over your words and begin keeping your word to people, then you will know in your heart that you can believe in God's Word. Until you make the quality decision to be a man or woman of your word, you will be a miserable Christian.
>
> "If you have made an appointment with a person, but know you will be late, call and tell him. Don't promise to give money out of emotion. Give at the level of faith where you are, so you won't get under condemnation if you can't keep your word.
>
> "When you agree to do something, make every effort to see it come to pass. God has put His integrity on the line. Now how about you?"

I exhort you to add the following character-building faith food to your daily menu of faith-building confessions.

Faith-Building Confession:

> My Bible tells me to imitate my God, and it says that my God is a God who cannot lie. Therefore, I purpose in my heart and

spirit that I will never allow my mouth to speak a lie. And I make my actions line up with what I say. I'm reliable and dependable. I speak the truth at all times, and nothing but the truth! I confess this with my mouth under the authority and in the wonderful Name of Jesus Christ of Nazareth! SO BE IT. (Ephesians 4:29-5:1; Titus 1:2; John 14:13,14)

Faith-Building Confession:

I will let no foul or polluting language, nor evil word, nor unwholesome or worthless talk (ever) come out of my mouth again. I make my mouth tell the truth always, because my word is me, and I make my word good always. I'm reliable and dependable. I vow to use only such speech as is good and beneficial to the spiritual progress of others and myself. I speak these faith-building words aloud under the authority and in the mighty Name of Jesus Christ of Nazareth! SO BE IT! (John 14:13,14; Ephesians 4:29-5:1; Titus 1:2)

KEY #3 In all things forgive and forget.

The Bible says to consider your ways, consider how things are going with you now (Haggai 1:5). Are the mountains in your life because you are carrying a grudge or holding unforgiveness in your heart toward someone?

Jesus Christ of Nazareth provides us with an enlightening Scripture on this subject.

> *If you forgive those who sin against you, your heavenly Father will forgive you.* ***But if you refuse to forgive others, your Father will not forgive your sins*** (Matthew 6:14-15, NLT).

Brothers, sisters, and friends, Jesus makes it perfectly clear that if you have a spirit of unforgiveness in your heart toward another, your Heavenly Father will not forgive your sins.

I submit to you that what this means is that as long as you harbor unforgiveness in your heart, you are out of fellowship with your Heavenly Father. When you are out of fellowship with your Heavenly Father, you are live bait for Satan's attacks on your health, your wealth and riches, and anything else that you have.

It Is A Command From Jesus That You Forgive Others

Jesus Christ spoke these words to His disciples and His words are meant for us today.

> *Listen to me, you can pray for anything and if you believe, you will have it. But when you are praying, **first forgive** anyone you are holding a grudge against, so that your Father in heaven will forgive your sins, too* (Mark 11:24-26, NLT).

God's Word means exactly what it says. God forgives us our sins as we forgive others who have sinned against us. To hold unforgiveness in our hearts toward others is to block the flow of God's forgiveness to us. To help avoid this deadly trap, we should include the forgiveness of others into our prayer life as a daily discipline, never allowing an offense to fester and grow.

In His teachings, Jesus was very concerned with showing how to build and maintain right relationships with God and man. Forgiveness from God to us and between ourselves and others is essential if these relationships are to flourish. If we have an argument or a disagreement with someone, we must practice instant reconciliation, and understand that conflicts cause much greater damage to relationships when left unresolved (Matthew 5:24, Luke 12:57-58). When we find ourselves angry at someone, it is good to remember the verse, "*Be angry, and do not sin*" (Ephesians 4:26). Know that Jesus equates anger with murder. When angry, we must be very careful how we speak to others lest hateful words bring us into God's judgment (Matthew 5:21-22).

Finally, walking in an attitude of forgiveness toward others means that we do not judge them. We need to correct our own faults and solve our own problems before attempting to correct faults or problems in others. We must let any judgmental attitude in ourselves signal the need to examine ourselves for things that bother us about others (Matthew 7:1-5; Luke 6:37-38, 41-42).

Revealing Example Of An Unforgiving Servant

Note: The Amplified Bible refers to the servant as an attendant.

> *Then Peter came up to Him and said, Lord how many times may my brother sin against me and I forgive him and let it go? (As many as) up to seven times? Jesus answered him, I tell you, not up to seven times, but seventy times seven! (Genesis 4:24)*
> *Therefore, the kingdom of heaven is like a human king who wished to settle accounts with his attendants.*
> *When he began the accounting, one was brought to him who owed him 10,000 talents (probably about $10,000,000).*
> *And because he could not pay, his master ordered him to be sold, with his wife and his children and everything that he possessed, and payment to be made.*

> *So the attendant fell on his knees, begging him. Have patience with me and I will pay you everything.*
> *And his master's heart was moved with compassion, and he released him and forgave him (canceling) the debt.*
> *But that same attendant, as he went out, found one of his fellow attendants who owed him a hundred denari (about twenty dollars); and he caught him by the throat and said, pay what you owe!*
> *So his fellow attendant fell down and begged him earnestly, give me time, and I will pay you all!*
> *But he was unwilling, and he went out and had him put in prison till he should pay the debt.*
> *When his fellow attendants saw what had happened, they were greatly distressed, and they went and told everything that had taken place to their master.*
> *Then his master called him and said to him, you contemptible and wicked attendant! I forgave you and cancelled all that (great) debt of yours because you begged me to.*
> *And should you not have had pity and mercy on your fellow attendant, as I had pity and mercy on you?*
> *And in wrath his master turned him over to the torturers (the jailers), till he should pay all that he owed.*
> *So also my heavenly Father will deal with every one of you if you do not freely forgive your brother from your heart his offenses.*
> *Matthew 18:21-35, Amp.*

It is so easy for us to forget how gracious God has been in forgiving us when we are called upon to forgive others. This parable warns against such smallness of soul. Here, Jesus showed how unforgiveness can bring a person into bondage. (Note: The jailed fellow servant is still in prison at the end of the story.) Every Kingdom person is advised to extend a forgiving heart toward all other persons.

Believers Must Extend Unlimited Forgiveness

The lesson that we learn from Jesus' teaching about forgiveness is that you must extend unlimited forgiveness to others. Hence, to do otherwise, you put yourself out of fellowship with our Heavenly Father and His protection. You are then open prey for Satan to move in swiftly and devour your health, your wealth, riches, your family, and anything else that belongs to you (the same as he did with Job; (Job 1:13-22, 2:1-8).

Unforgiveness Is Like A Cancer

A cancer is a malignant tumor that tends to spread. It generally spreads slowly and, if allowed to continue, it can contaminate the whole body and lead to expiration.

Unforgiveness is similar to a cancer in the way it progresses. If it is allowed to continue, it can spread and lead to physical and spiritual expiration. The way this happens is that, under the direction of Satan unforgiveness starts out as a small matter, it then gets bumped up to dislike and hatred, and then its contamination can escalate to violence and even murder, all of which God hates.

Unforgiveness Weakens The Body System

The Bible says,

> *Be not wise in your own eyes; reverently fear and worship the Lord and turn (entirely) away from evil. It shall be health to your nerves and sinews and marrow and moistening to your bones.* Proverbs 3:7-8, Amp.

Now, let's take a minute or two and dissect this Scripture. Using my flip-flop method of looking at Scripture, it would read this way.

If you be wise in your own eyes, and show no (reverent) fear of the Lord, and you refuse to repent and turn away from unforgiveness; then your ways shall bring destruction to your nerves and sinew systems. And you will suffer a lack of marrow and moisture to your bones.

I submit to you that the lack of marrow and moisture to your bones implies that the bones are dry, and dry bones imply death.

The apostle Paul wrote these instructions to God's holy people at Ephesus who were faithful followers of Christ Jesus, and these instructions are also meant for us today.

> *Get rid of all bitterness, rage, anger, harsh words, and slander, as well as all types of malicious behavior.* ***Instead, be kind to each other, tenderhearted, forgiving one another, just as God through Christ has forgiven you*** (Ephesians 4:31-32, NLT).

Brothers, sisters, and friends, the matter of forgiving others is not an option but, rather, it is a matter of obedience which is commanded by our Lord and Savior Jesus Christ of Nazareth.

The Bible admonishes you to consider your ways if you are living from paycheck to paycheck! Consider your ways if your covenant inheritance of wealth and riches which God so graciously gave you is now rapidly disappearing!

If these things are happening to you, chances are great that your ways of unforgiveness have caused you to be out of fellowship with your Heavenly Father. Consider your ways; are you a forgiving person? How would the Holy Spirit grade you on forgiveness? Would you get an F, or a

C, or an A or an A+?

To remain free from the spirit of unforgiveness, repent and ask God to forgive you; then I exhort you to immediately begin saying a faith-building confession for a spirit of forgiveness. Add this nutritional faith food to your daily menu of faith-building confessions:

Faith-Building Confession:

> My Lord and Savior, Jesus Christ of Nazareth, forgive me of all my sins. I'm thankful! Now, I forgive all those who sin against me, my family, or my church family. I can forgive, I do forgive as I do everything with the help of Christ Who gives me the strength I need. And therefore, I'm free from any unforgiveness! I confess this under the authority and in the majestic Name of Jesus Christ of Nazareth! SO BE IT! (Colossians 3:13; Philippians 4:13; John 14:13-14; Matthew 6:14-15 NLT)

KEY #4 Love your neighbor and your fellowman as yourself.

The Bible says to consider your ways; consider how things are going with you now (Haggai 1:5). Are there storms in your life because you are carrying dislike, bitterness, prejudice, or hatred in your heart for another fellow human being?

The Most Important Commandment For Believers

Jesus Christ of Nazareth commands believers to love your neighbor as yourself. In the first book of the New Testament, Jesus reveals this commandment.

> *But when the Pharisees heard that he had silenced the Sadducees with his reply, they thought up a fresh question of their own to ask him. One of them, an expert in religious law, tried to trap him with this question: "Teacher, which is the most important commandment in the law of Moses?"*
>
> *Jesus replied, "You must love the Lord your God with all your heart, all your soul, and all your mind. This is the first and greatest commandment. A second is equally important: Love your neighbor as yourself. All the other commandments and all the demands of the prophets are based on these two commandments"* (Matthew 22:34-40, NLT).

The opposite of love is dislike, prejudice, bitterness, and hatred toward another human being. These evil character traits are generally the result of a person being controlled by their old sinful nature, which loves to do evil. This is just the opposite of what the Holy Spirit wants.

Believers who carry dislike, prejudice, bitterness, or hatred in their heart for another are instantly out of fellowship with God the Father; hence the individual is left exposed to Satan's attacks to kill, steal, and destroy.

We must avoid at all cost the old sinful nature and its pitfalls. By doing so, we place ourselves in a favorable position not only to maintain our covenant inheritance of wealth and riches, but to also see it increase.

Commandments To Do Good Deeds Are Beneficial For Everyone

The Bible says,

> *Remind your people to submit to the government and its officers. They should be obedient, always ready to do what is good. They must not speak evil of anyone, and they must avoid quarreling. Instead, they should be gentle and show true humility to everyone. These things I have told you are all true. I want you to insist on them so that everyone who trusts in God will be careful to do good deeds all the time. These things are good and beneficial for everyone* (Titus 3:1-2, 8, NLT).

Consider Your Ways! Do You Really Love And Pray For Your Enemies?

Jesus said in the book of Matthew,

> *You have heard that the law of Moses says, "love your neighbor, and hate your enemy. But I say,* ***love your enemies. Pray for those who persecute you!*** *In that way, you will be acting as true children of your Father in heaven. For he gives his sunlight to both the evil and the good, and he sends rain on the just and on the unjust, too. If you love only those who love you, what good is that? Even corrupt tax collectors do that much. If you are kind only to your friends, how are you different from anyone else? Even pagans do that. But you are to be perfect, even as your Father in heaven is perfect"* (Matthew 5:43-48, NLT).

How To Have Christ-Like Love For Your Enemies And Others

Jesus taught us to have Christ-like love for others. When the love of God is poured out in our hearts, we don't look for opportunities to get even; we often show goodness to those who don't deserve it. The love of God causes us not to be stingy and cheap in our spirits, but abounding with love for others.

It takes a mighty big person to love his/her enemies. In fact, it takes the big person of Jesus living in an individual for that to really happen. The commandment to love is easier to embrace when we have not been offended by someone else. The commandment takes on new meaning once we have been spoken evil of, cheated, or rejected. It is here that we learn to walk with God or go on stubbornly in our bitterness.

There is a dimension of God's love that can be experienced in no other way than through forgiving those who have become enemies. God is not asking anything of us that He Himself has not already done. When we consider that all men have offended God, becoming His enemy, and that God has loved us anyway and has forgiven us, it is easier to understand why God tells us to forgive.

Steps To Forgiveness

The first step in forgiveness is to recognize your resentment against an enemy. You must understand who the enemy is and what he has done to hurt you. Then you must consciously say, I forgive that person for the following wrongs against me. Then repent of your feelings against your enemy and ask God to forgive you.

After that, begin to pray actively for your enemy's good. Jesus told us to pray for our enemies and love them. **When you pray for yourenemies, asking God to meet their needs and manifest Himself to them, you are overcoming evil with good**. Instead of fighting negative thoughts in your mind, you are filling your mind with positive thoughts of God's love for that person. When God answers your prayer, the person prayed for will be blessed and he will experience redemption – the ultimate form of forgiveness. So, if you ask God to bless someone who has wronged you, the result may well be a repentant sinner and a new brother or sister in the Lord.

The Bible Calls Love The Royal Command

This letter is written by James, who identifies himself as a slave of God and of the Lord Jesus Christ. It is written to Jewish Christians scattered among the nations and it is written to you and me today. The following is an excerpt from James' letter.

> *My dear brothers and sisters, how can you claim that you have faith in our glorious Lord Jesus Christ if you favor some people more than others?*
>
> ***Yes, indeed, it is good when you truly obey our Lord's royal command found in the Scripture: "Love your neighbor as yourself."***
>
> *So whenever you speak, or whatever you do, remember that you will be judged by the law of love, the law that set you free. For there will be no mercy for you if you have not been merciful to others. But if you have been merciful, then God's*

mercy toward you will win out over his judgment against you.
James 2:1, 8, 12, 13, NLT

How Does The World Know That You Are A Christian?

Jesus Christ of Nazareth said,

> *I give you a new commandment: that you should love one another. Just as I have loved you, so you too should love one another.* ***By this shall all (men) know that you are My disciples, if you love one another*** *(if you keep on showing love among yourselves). John 13:34-35, Amp.*

Notice closely that Jesus said that it is by your love for one another that men will know that you are His disciple (His believer). My flip-flop of this Scripture would read...if you do not love and show love one to another (regardless of race, creed, color, or station in life), then the world will not see the Christ-kind of love on display. Men will not know that you are one of Jesus' disciples. Why? Because you failed to show any love one to another.

God So Loved The World

Jesus Christ of Nazareth revealed these famous words in the book of John,

> ***For God so loved the world*** *that he gave his only son, so that everyone who believes in him will not perish but have eternal life.*
> *God did not send his Son into the world to condemn it, but to save it* (John 3:16-17, NLT).

John 3:16 is perhaps the most quoted verse in the Bible, and it contains the most important truth in the Bible; God loved humankind so much that He sent His Son to die on the cross. Through this sacrifice, God offers His gift of salvation to anyone who will receive it by faith. In order to be forgiven of your sins and live eternally with God, you must believe in Jesus Christ and receive Him into your life.

Definition Of The God Kind And Believers' Kind Of Love

The kind of love that God has for humankind is totally different from any human kind of love. The Greek word "agapao" means unconditional love, love by choice and by an act of the will. This word denotes unconquerable benevolence and undefeatable goodwill. Agape will never seek anything but the highest good for fellow humankind. Agapao (the verb) and agape (the noun) are the words for unconditional love. This love does not need a chemistry, an affinity, or a feeling. Agape is a word that exclusively belongs to the Christian community. It is a love virtually unknown to writers outside the New Testament. The world does not understand this kind of love because it is a totally selfless and spiritual love. Agape is the God kind of love, which is pure and giving, unlike the world's love which is based on feelings. God has this love for you and wants to pour it into your heart.

All Are Lovingly Welcomed

I have known a few believers who were not only heavy fingered, but heavy fisted and downright overbearing in their approach toward non-believers. These self-appointed holier-than-thou believers probably mean well, but they are operating in a lack of knowledge of God's Word.

God did not send Jesus Christ into the world to point the heavy finger of condemnation. Through Jesus Christ, God's loving arms are open wide to all people everywhere, no matter how evil their lives may be. God will welcome them into His Kingdom of light if they repent of their sins and obey the gospel. However, the sad fact is that some people will still choose to reject God and love the darkness.

Love Is The Greatest Thing

The apostle Paul provides the foremost cutting edge, inspired inscription of agape love, and how it should work in the life of all believers – rich, poor or in-between. He writes this to you and me...

> *Love is patient and kind. Love is not jealous or boastful or proud or rude. Love does not demand its own way. Love is not irritable, and it keeps no record of when it has been wronged. It is never glad about injustice but rejoices whenever the truth wins out. Love never gives up, never loses faith, is always hopeful, and endures through every circumstance...*
> *There are three things that will endure – faith, hope, and love – and the greatest of these is love* (1 Corinthians 13:4-7, 13, NLT).

Jesus Christ Of Nazareth Prescribes The Cure For Dislike, Prejudice, Bitterness, And Hatred

We have witnessed unprecedented portions of hate and violence during the latter part of the twentieth century and now all too common are domestic violence, sexual and physical child abuse, date rape, murders, workplace shootings and killings, and school and church shootings and killings. The list goes on with bombings of government and private buildings, terrorist attacks, gang violence, car jackings, and senseless drive by shootings and killings. Open hate crimes against gays, Blacks, Jews, abortionists, and others are all on the increase. And let's not forget the latest form of violence; road rage which involves out of control drivers on our roadways who act out in violence against other drivers.

Prescription For Hate And Violence

The cure for all the dislike, prejudice, bitterness, hatred, and violence is revealed in five words spoken by Jesus Christ of Nazareth and they are, "Love your neighbor as yourself."

Jesus Christ of Nazareth reveals true agape (God kind of love) in His illustration widely known as the Parable of the Good Samaritan.

> *One day an expert in religious law stood up to test Jesus by asking him this question: "Teacher, what must I do to receive eternal life?"*
>
> *Jesus replied, "What does the law of Moses say? How do you read it?"*
>
> *The man answered, "You must love the Lord your God with all your heart, all your soul, all your strength, and all your mind, And, love your neighbor as yourself." "Right!" Jesus told him. "Do this and you will live!" The man wanted to justify his actions, so he asked Jesus, "And who is my neighbor?"*
>
> *Jesus replied with an illustration: "A Jewish man was traveling on a trip from Jerusalem to Jericho, and he was attacked by bandits. They stripped him of his clothes and money, beat him up, and left him half dead beside the road. By chance a Jewish priest came along; but when he saw the man lying there, he crossed to the other side of the road and passed him by. A Temple assistant walked over and looked at him lying there, but he also passed by on the other side. Then a despised Samaritan came along, and when he saw the man, he felt deep pity. Kneeling beside him, the Samaritan soothed his wounds with medicine and bandaged them. Then he put the man on his own donkey and took him to an inn, where he took care of him. The next day he handed the innkeeper two pieces of silver and told him to take care of the man. "If his bill runs higher than that," he said, "I'll pay the difference the next time I am here."*
>
> *"Now which of these three would you say was a neighbor to the man who was attacked by bandits?" Jesus asked. The man replied, "The one; who showed him mercy." Then Jesus said, "Yes, now go and do the same"* (Luke 10:25-37, NLT).

Sincerely consider your ways; are you the priest or the temple assistant in this illustration? Or are you the good Samaritan?

Hatred often stands in the way of fulfilling God's two great commandments – that we love Him and that we love one another (John

13:34-35). Prejudice is frequently one of hatred's powerful assistants. The Bible makes it clear that in Christ, God sees all people alike (Colossians 3:11). To think otherwise is to be deceived. When Jesus ministered to the woman of Samaria, He was showing us that the barriers that exist between peoples – barriers of race, color, social views, economics, gender, and a host of other things people use to separate themselves – can be crossed by God's love. The human race was not originally created to have walls between its members that would prevent men from loving one another. These were introduced by the fall of man directed by Satan and now can be removed only in Christ.

The Bible tells us that we can do everything with the help of Christ Who gives us the strength we need (Philippians 4:13). Jesus Christ will give you the strength you need to have an agape spirit of love for your fellowman.

The Two Great Commandments

Jesus Christ of Nazareth established the two greatest commandments of all, in the book of Matthew this way...

> *Jesus replied, "**You must love the Lord your God with all your heart, all your soul, and all your mind.** This is the first and greatest commandment. A second is equally important: Love your **neighbor as yourself**. All the other commandments and all the demands of the prophets are based on these two commandments."* Matthew 22:37-40, NLT

Brothers, sisters, and friends, now comes the big questions. The Bible clearly tells you to consider your ways. If you are living from paycheck to paycheck, consider your ways. If your weekly, bi-weekly, or monthly income hastens from you, leaving you broke, busted and disgusted, if your wealth and riches are being drained from you by unexpected events or occurrences, consider your ways.

If these things are happening to you, you should do a reality check of yourself right away. The cause for the mountains in your life could be that deep down on the inside you are harboring some form of dislike, prejudice, bitterness, or hatred in your heart for another fellow human being.

The Problem

Know that if you have any dislike, bitterness, prejudice, or hatred in your heart for anyone, you have put yourself out of fellowship with your Heavenly Father. When you are out of fellowship with your Heavenly Father, you are a target (visibly) exposed to Satan's onrush of attacks to defeat you financially, spiritually, physically, mentally, and otherwise.

Consider your ways; do you truly love all fellow human beings as yourself? How would the Holy Spirit grade you on your daily agape love performance towards others? Would you get an F, or a C, or an A, or an A+?

The Cure

The prescription for spirits of dislike, bitterness, prejudice, and hatred is to do what the apostle Paul said to do, and that is to get rid of it. Repent, pray, and ask God to forgive you, and He will forgive you and cleanse you from every wrong.

This prescription also contains the following advice. To remain free from spirits of dislike, bitterness, prejudice, and hatred, I implore you to immediately begin saying a faith-building confession for a spirit of agape love.

Add this essential faith food to your daily faith-building confessions. It will help keep you in fellowship with your Heavenly Father and help you keep and increase your covenant inheritance of wealth and riches.

Faith-Building Confession:

I'm obedient to the words of my Lord and Savior, Jesus Christ of Nazareth. First, I have unwavering (agape) love for my Heavenly Father and for my Savior, Jesus Christ! Secondly, I make myself love my fellow human beings as I do myself. I do this through Christ Jesus Who gives me the strength when I need it. I am a good Samaritan, I am greatly blessed by God, and I seek out others to be a blessing to. I have taken on a spirit of agape love and I walk by faith and in obedience to God's Word in love. I speak this confession under the authority and in the mighty Name of Jesus Christ of Nazareth! SO BE IT! (Matthew 22:37-39; Genesis 12:2,3; 2 Corinthians 5:7; John 14:13,14).

KEY #5 Go out daily to seek and to save the lost.

The Bible says to consider your ways; consider how things are going with you now (Haggai 1:5).

Is the inheritance of wealth and riches, which your Heavenly Father so graciously gave you, rapidly running through your hands as water runs down a drain?

I summon you to consider your ways. Are you a doer of the Word or a hearer only? Do you go out daily to seek and to save the lost?

The Bible tells us to:

> *But be doers of the Word, and not hearers only, deceiving yourselves. For if anyone is a hearer of the Word and not a doer, he is like a man observing his natural face in a mirror.*
> *For he observes himself, goes away, and immediately forgets what kind of man he was. But he who looks into the perfect law*

> *of liberty and continues in it, and is not a forgetful hearer but a doer of the work, this one will be blessed in what he does.*
> James 1:22-25, NKJV

It is one thing to discipline ourselves to read, listen to, and even proclaim the Word of God. It is another thing to act on that Word. However, if we hear the Word and don't practice it, the Word of God tells us that we are deceiving ourselves. It goes on to explain that if we will become doers of the work, rather than forgetful hearers of the Word, we will be blessed in what we do.

This is not a teaching on works. Obviously, we cannot earn our way into heaven, nor can we ever earn any amount of righteousness, since entrance to heaven through the righteousness of Christ can only be received as the free gift that it is. Yet James pointed out here that simply hearing the Word of God does not mean that we believe it. By acting on what we hear, we show that we truly believe. Faith is an action word; those who claim to have faith because they hear and know the Word of God yet do not practice it in their lives, have deceived hearts.

Examine the areas in your own life where you claim to have faith. Do your actions prove that faith, or do they declare your unbelief? If there are areas in your life where your words of faith and your actions don't line up, confess them to God, then make a decision to begin acting on the faith God has given you.

As we practice what we preach and proclaim, our faith will grow, and our words will have a much more life-changing impact on those around us.

Be A Doer—Not A Hearer Only

There are many Christians who gather to hear the Word of God preached, but there is a far smaller number who actually do what the Word of God says. Statistics say that in a nation like America there are 50 million "born again" Christians. Yet you would never know it by looking at the spiritual climate of the nation. What is needed is for God's people to not just hear the Word, but also to do what the Word says to do. This is the mark of a real Christian.

How would the Holy Spirit grade you today based on your being a doer of the Word? Would He give you an F, a C, an A, or an A+?

Do You Strive To Daily Imitate Jesus Christ Of Nazareth?

This is what the Bible commands...

> *Therefore, be imitators of God (copy Him and follow His example), as well beloved children (imitate their Father).*
> Ephesians 5:1

Simply put, godliness is living the way God wants us to. Few books in the Bible speak as clearly and succinctly to this subject as does Ephesians.

Godliness is advised in terms of behavior, motivation, and example. Godly behavior is modeled after God Himself, especially as He has revealed Himself in His fullness in Jesus Christ.

If we desire to live our lives God's way, we should model our lives after Jesus, imitating Him, understanding that Jesus is the perfect example of the love God requires from us. Our conduct is the most effective sermon we will ever preach. Because people watch our lives, it is important to live a life that gives consistent, undeniable evidence of the truth of the gospel. The only way to do that is to be filled continually with the Holy Spirit.

Our lives should overflow with a continual song of praise and thanksgiving if we want to maintain a Spirit-filled flow in our lives. By giving ourselves to constant, faithful prayer, God will change our prayer life to a life of prayer. We will then be living God's way, for that is how Christ lived His life here on this earth – in constant communion with His Father.

We are to imitate God and walk in love and light. Sexual impurity and sexual immorality should not be part of a Christian's life. We are not to live the same lifestyle as unbelievers because the wrath of God comes upon the sons of disobedience. The bottom line is that God is not playing games, and He expects His children to live holy and pure lives by the Spirit's power.

I have another question. Have you considered your ways when it comes to your being obedient to God's Word to imitate Him? How would the Holy Spirit grade you today based on how well you imitate Jesus Christ of Nazareth? Would He give you an F, a C, an A or an A+?

What Was Jesus' Mission?

Jesus Christ reveals what His mission was in the book of Luke. He says... *"For the son of Man came to seek and to save that which was lost."* Luke 19:10, Amp.

Now we know that we should imitate Jesus, and now that we know that His mission (His task, His ministry) here on earth was to seek and to save the lost (save sinners from the penalty of eternal death), we now have a clear understanding of what our daily ministry should be; that is to seek and to save the lost. His plan and purpose become the believer's plan and purpose.

Jesus uses the word "seek" to describe His mission here on earth. This word is a very interesting word. It is a verb, expressing action, meaning to search for, to try to reach or obtain, to look for, to make an effort to do or accomplish something.

Consider your ways; how many times during the last five days did you make a conscientious effort to seek and save the lost? During the last thirty days, how many unsaved or backslidden individuals have you brought to your church? (Backslidden means someone who turned away from God after conversion.)

To Seek And To Save The Lost

Let's say a wealthy man hired you and four other people to hit the streets to seek and to save the lost. For each person that you share the Good News of Jesus Christ with, you will receive $10. For each person that you convert to Jesus Christ, you will be paid $20. For every unsaved or backslidden person that you take to church, you will receive $30, and you will be paid $100 for every person you helped who needed food, clothing, shelter, or medical attention.

Based on your performance during the last five days, how much money would you have earned seeking and saving the lost?

Parable Of The Sheep And The Harvest

In this next narrative, Jesus Christ of Nazareth superbly used an agricultural setting to present an earthly story of flocks of scattered, sheperdless, starved and dying sheep to emphasize a heavenly message and the overwhelming need for harvest gatherers.

Jesus Christ spoke these words to His disciples and He is speaking to all believers today. His words are timely!

> *Jesus traveled through all the cities and villages of that area, teaching in the synagogues and announcing the Good News about the Kingdom. And wherever he went, he healed people of every sort of disease and illness. He felt great pity for the crowds that came, because their problems were so great and they didn't know where to go for help. They were like sheep without a shepherd. He said to his disciples, "**The harvest is so great, but the workers are so few. So pray to the Lord who is in charge of the harvest; ask him to send out more workers for his fields**."*
> Matthew 9:35-38, NLT

Jesus told His disciples that there were many more people who were spiritually ripe to accept Him into their lives than there were laborers to bring them in. Christians need to listen to the Holy Spirit and let God lead them to people who are open to the gospel. There should be no secret-service Christians. We should conduct our lives with wisdom and grace so that people can be won to Jesus Christ. The key is to share our faith in Christ under the leadership of the Holy Spirit and with sensitivity and genuine love.

Work At Bringing Others To Christ

In this next passage of Scripture, the apostle Paul tells us how to go about soul-winning, and he tells us why we should work at bringing others to Christ.

> *And so I solemnly urge you before God and before Christ Jesus – who will someday judge the living and the dead when he appears to set up his Kingdom. Preach the word of God. Be persistent, whether the time is favorable or not. Patiently correct, rebuke, and encourage your people with good teaching.*
> *For a time is coming when people will no longer listen to right teaching. They will follow their own desires and will look for teachers who will tell them whatever they want to hear. They will reject the truth and follow strange myths.*
> *But you should keep a clear mind in every situation. Don't be afraid of suffering for the Lord.* ***Work at bringing others to Christ****. Complete the ministry God has given you.*
> 2 Timothy 4:1-5, NLT

Never be ashamed or embarrassed by the gospel of Jesus Christ. With sensitivity and under the direction of the Holy Spirit, look for opportunities in life to share your faith in Christ. If you ask Him to, God will send people into your life who need to hear the gospel and whom you can lead to Jesus Christ. Part of the Christian life is lovingly sharing your faith with others. There is nothing as exciting as leading somebody else to Jesus Christ.

Believers' Ministry Is To Seek And To Save The Lost

Paul urged Timothy to do the work of an evangelist and to lead others to Jesus Christ. God has given every Christian the ministry of sharing his/her faith with others and leading people to Christ. God wants all His children to fulfill their ministry. Maybe God has not called you into full-time service. But He does have a ministry for every believer. It may be helping your church feed the hungry, putting on an evangelistic outreach, or visiting someone who is sick or elderly. Whatever God gives you to do, fulfill your ministry!

How To Remain In Fellowship With God And Keep Your Inheritance

First, the Bible tells us that we must be doers of the Word, and not hearers only. For if anyone is a hearer of the Word, and not a doer, it is like looking at your face in a mirror, but doing nothing to improve your appearance. You see yourself, walk away, and forget what you look like.

In the book of James, it tells us...

> *But he who looks into the perfect law of liberty and continues in it, and is not a forgetful hearer but a doer of the work, this one will be blessed in what he does* (James 1:25, NKJV).

Another translation says...

> *But if you keep looking steadily into God's perfect law – the law that sets you free – and if you do what it says and don't forget what you heard, then God will bless you for doing it.*
> James 1:25, NLT

The Word of God says that a doer of God's Word shall be blessed in his doing. I submit to you that my flip-flop method of this Scripture would read thusly:

A non-doer of God's Word shall be cut off from God's blessings and out of fellowship with Him. This means that the divine protection over your health, wealth, and riches are also cut off. When you are out of fellowship with God, it puts you in harm's way of Satan, it opens the door for Satan to move in and carry out his plan and purpose which is to kill, steal, and destroy you.

Brothers, sisters, and friends, the Bible clearly tells us to be a doer of God's Word; it tells us to imitate Jesus and to seek and to save the lost.

If your covenant inheritance of wealth and riches is rapidly disappearing right before your eyes due to strange occurrences, then consider your ways. Chances are great that you are out of fellowship with your Heavenly Father because you are a hearer only and not a doer.

Consider your ways, as to going out to seek and to save the lost. How would the Holy Spirit grade you based on your being a doer who seeks to save the lost (spiritually, physically, and financially)? Would you get an F, or a C, or an A, or an A+?

I exhort you to immediately begin reading aloud the following faith-building confession. It will help to keep you on a path that is pleasing to God, the path of a doer and not a hearer only. Add this enriched faith food to your daily menu of faith-building confessions:

Faith-Building Confession:

I purpose in my heart and in my spirit to be a doer of God's Word and not a hearer only. I strive to imitate my Lord and Savior Jesus Christ and His ways. I effortlessly and joyfully go out each day to seek and to save the lost. I know that my God blesses me because I am obedient to His

Word. I confess this under the authority, and in the mighty Name of Jesus Christ of Nazareth! SO BE IT! (James 1:22-25; Ephesians 5:1; Luke 19:10; John 14:13,14)

KEY #6 Pray first for your political leaders and those who have authority over you.

The Bible instructs us to consider our ways; consider how things are going with you now. Are you seeing plummeting decreases in your finances? Are unexpected storms in your life using up your covenant inheritance of wealth and riches? If these things are happening to you, consider your ways. Do you put the president, the governor, the mayor, and the city council persons first on your prayer list? In other words, do you pray and intercede first, for your political leaders and those who are in authority over you, including your employer and your boss?

When you pray, who do you place as number one on your prayer and thanksgiving list? Yourself? Your spouse? Your children? Your family?

If any one of the above areas are number one on your prayer and thanksgiving list, then you are not operating in obedience to God's Word.

Let's go to the Bible and see what the Word of God has to say on this subject.

The Bible says...

> *First of all, then, I admonish and urge that petitions, prayers, intercessions, and thanksgivings be offered on behalf of all men. For kings and all who are in positions of authority or high responsibility, that (outwardly) we may pass a quiet and undisturbed life (and inwardly) a peaceable one in all godliness and reverence and seriousness in every way.*
> 1 Timothy 2:1-2, Amp.

Concerning this Scripture, the Reverend Kenneth E. Hagin wrote the following in one of his inspiring Faith Food books:

"When we follow the directions in God's Word and put first things first, we get results. This is especially true in regard to Scripture. If we follow the directions and put first things first, we can expect to receive from God the things He has provided for us.

"First of all' means first of all.

But also notice that along with supplications, along with prayers, along with intercessions, the Word inserts 'giving of thanks.'

"Lest we misunderstand exactly who these 'all men' are. Kings would include presidents, rulers, and other leaders of nations. All that are in authority would include state, county, city leaders, etc.

"If we as Christians want to please God, who will we place as number one on our prayer and thanksgiving list? Ourselves? Our children? Our grandchildren? Our church? No. If we want to please God, we will have to do exactly as God said to do. We will have to pray and offer thanks for all who are in authority first.

"God did not call us to criticize our political leaders and those who are in authority over us; He called us to pray and intercede for them. There is nothing wrong with Christians becoming active in the political process, trying to change ungodly laws, and bringing a righteous perspective to the political scene. However, the real power of the church is experienced when the church is on its knees. Prayer can change the political landscape. We are responsible to pray, fast, and intercede for the leaders of our nation, so that we may lead a quiet and peaceable life in all godliness and reverence."

Why Does God Tell Us To Pray For Those In Authority First And What Is The Purpose?

The Bible tells us to...

> *Pray this way for kings, and all others who are in authority, so that we can live in peace and quietness, in godliness and dignity. This is good and pleases God our Savior, for he wants everyone to be saved and to understand the truth* (1 Timothy 2:2-4, NLT).

God doesn't tell us to do something just to fill up space in the Bible. He has a purpose in mind. We are to pray for those in authority so that we who are Christians may lead a quiet and peaceable life. God is concerned about us and will work on our behalf, even when those in authority are not Christians.

God's ultimate purpose is that we be able to spread the gospel freely. If we do not live under a stable government, the spreading of the gospel is hindered. Times of political upheaval, war, travel restrictions, and other limitations hinder the spread of the gospel. "*And this gospel of the kingdom shall be preached in all the world for a witness unto all nations; and then shall the end come*" (Matthew 24:14). The devil will try his best to see that this is not accomplished. Therefore, we are exhorted to offer intercessory prayer, supplications, and the giving of thanks for those who lead our nation.

Rev. Kenneth E. Hagin offers in his book, *Faith Food*, the following summary concerning prayers for those in authority over you.

"The Word of God is clear on this subject. I believe many Christians have practiced this Scripture to some extent, but I believe we have somewhat neglected the 'giving of thanks.' God wants us to offer thanksgiving to Him. And we have much to thank God for! But too many Christians are always griping and talking about what is wrong with our nation. The Bible does not tell us as Christians to do that. Instead, as Christians we are exhorted to make supplications, prayers, intercessions and the giving of thanks for our leaders. (It is impossible that our prayers for them would work at the same time we're criticizing them."

Brothers, sisters, and friends, God is a God of order, and the bottom line is that you ought to always pray first for your political leaders and those who have authority over you. We do not have the luxury to pick and choose which one of God's precepts we will follow. Instead, we must strive to walk in obedience to His Word; this is His plan and purpose for us to follow. Simply put, just do what His Word says and be blessed!

My morning and nighttime prayers consist of praying first for our president and his family. I ask God to keep them safe and healthy. I ask Him to give the president wisdom in the governing of affairs of our country and those of other countries. I ask God to lead the president, the governor, the mayor, the council persons, and all others who have authority over God's people, to rule, govern, and oversee, in a fair and just manner, without prejudice due to race, creed, color, sex, age, religion, economic status, or health. I ask God to lead all political leaders and others who have authority over God's people to establish procedures, rules and regulations that are fair, just, and in line with God's Word.

I thank God for setting the political leaders and those in authority in their positions. I thank Him that my country is at peace and not at war, and that I can freely worship and practice my faith at home and at church without attacks of reprisal, persecution, or violence.

Are You In Line For Increase?

Are you obedient to God's Word when it comes to praying for your political leaders and those who have authority over you? How would the Holy Spirit grade you on this precept? Would He give you an F, a C, an A, or an A+?

Those who remain steadfast in obeying God's Word to pray for our leaders will enjoy marvelous fellowship and benefits as a result of being obedient. Their obedience will also place them in a position to see their covenant inheritance of wealth and riches increase abundantly.

I encourage you to add this highly beneficial faith food to your daily menu of faith-building confessions.

Faith-Building Confession:

I purpose in my heart and in my spirit to pray first for my political leaders and those who are in authority over me. I thank you Heavenly Father for those whom you have set in positions of authority over me. I thank you for the spiritual and material blessings of life that you have bestowed upon me and all others. I thank you, Lord, that my country is at peace and not war, and I live a quiet and peaceful life in godliness and dignity. I confess these words aloud under the authority and in the matchless Name of Jesus Christ of Nazareth! SO BE IT! 1 Timothy 2:1-4

KEY #7 First, pay your tithes and share your offering consistently into God's storehouse (the local church). Seek to cheerfully share your time, talent, and God's money to help the poor and needy. Do not neglect to establish an inheritance of house and riches for your children and your children's children.

The Bible instructs us to consider our ways; consider how things are going with you. If your covenant inheritance of wealth and riches is swiftly leaving you due to unanticipated occurrences, consider your ways! In other words, examine yourself.

Could the reason why things are not prospering in your life is because you are not obedient to God's Word and do not consistently pay your tithes and share your offerings? Are your material losses because you lack a cheerful spirit of sharing of your time, talent, and money with the poor and needy? Or is it because you have neglected to set up an inheritance for your children and your children's children?

The Bible has the following profound and encouraging words about a cheerful giver:

> *It is possible to give freely and become more wealthy, but those who are stingy will lose everything. The generous prosper and are satisfied; those who refresh others will themselves be refreshed* (Proverbs 11:24-25, NLT).

Jesus Christ of Nazareth said,

> *If you give, you will receive. Your gift will return to you in full measure, pressed down, shaken together to make room for more, and running over. Whatever measure you use in giving – large or small – it will be used to measure what is given back to you.* Luke 6:38, NLT

As it was stated before, the principle of giving to God is found throughout Scripture. God certainly does not need our money, but He knows that we need to give it as an act of faith and obedience. Self-centeredness and stinginess short circuit the blessings God wants to open up to us. When we fail to give God our tithes (10 percent of what we earn) and offerings (love gifts that acknowledge God's goodness), we rob both Him and ourselves.

Supernatural Sowing And Reaping

God has His own economic system, which is separate from the world's. God blesses those people who give to meet the needs of others, and who are willing to contribute to the ministry. Financial giving is compared to a seed that a farmer uses to plant a crop. People who cheerfully give to the cause of the gospel can expect that God will meet their own needs in abundance. God has the power to supernaturally supply the needs of His people when they are obedient in giving.

The law of supernatural sowing and reaping is revealed in the book of Galatians. The apostle Paul says, *"Do not be deceived, God is not mocked; for whatever a man sows, that he will also reap"* (Galatians 6:7, NKJV).

Purpose Of Giving And Sharing Your Time, Talent, And Money

We have come to learn that the Bible tells us to do certain things first. It tells us to seek first the Kingdom of God and His righteousness, and all these things will be added to you (Matthew 6:33). Then it tells us to first pray for our leaders (kings, presidents, governor, mayor, and council persons) and all others who have authority over us (1 Timothy 2:2). Why does the Bible tell us to pray for them? So that we can live in peace and quietness, in godliness and dignity.

Then the Bible commands us to honor the Lord with our capital and sufficiency (from righteous labors) and with the "first fruits" of all our income (Proverbs 3:9). Notice that God's Word says to honor Him with the first fruits of all your income, not some. It says to honor Him with the first fruits of all your income, and not your leftover fruits. The words "first fruits" imply giving to God before you give to any other, preceding all others. Pay your tithes first as an act of obedience to God's Word. Your mind set and your actions should be fixed on God always being number one on your list of giving.

Fix Your Mind On Benefits, Rewards, And Increase

The Bible does not leave us in the dark, so to speak, but it tells us what will happen when we honor God with the first fruits of all our income. It says...

> *So shall your storage places be filled with plenty, and your vats shall be overflowing with new wine* (Proverbs 3:10).

In modern times, the storage places that are filled with plenty could be your different bank accounts, money market accounts, stocks, bonds, and other investments, which will all be overflowing with increase when you pay God the first fruits of all your income. Praise the Lord!

Purpose Of Tithes And Offering

It is written in the book of Timothy...

> *Elders who do their work well should be paid well, especially those who work hard at both preaching and teaching. For the Scripture says, do not keep an ox from eating as it treads out the grain. And in another place, those who work deserve their pay!*
> 1 Timothy 5:17-18, NLT

The apostle Paul also tells us,

> *Those who are taught the Word of God should help their teachers by paying them* (Galatians 6:6, NLT).

Ministers, preachers, and teachers in the local church should be supported with tithes and offerings. It is the responsibility of the believers who are being spiritually fed by ministers of the gospel to support them financially. A Christian minister who has been faithful in preaching the Word of God should have his needs and the needs of his family well taken care of by the church. It is the spiritual responsibility of Christians to make sure that they are faithful in supporting God's work.

From time to time you may be led by the Holy Spirit to share an offering with other traveling ministries. You should share with those ministries whose focus is on seeking to save the lost.

Purpose Of Sharing With The Poor And Needy

The Bible says... *"If you help the poor, you are lending to the Lord – and He will repay you!"* (Proverbs 19:17, NLT)

The early church believers set the example for modern day believers to follow.

> *All the believers were of one heart and mind, and they felt that what they owned was not their own; they shared everything they had. And the apostles gave powerful witness to the resurrection of the Lord Jesus, and God's great favor was upon them all. There was no poverty among them, because people who owned land or houses sold them and brought the money to the apostles to give to others in need* (Acts 4:32-35, NLT).

We can clearly see that the early church believers took on their responsibility of sharing with those in need. They didn't depend on the federal government, welfare, state or local programs to take care of the poor and needy. The Bible says that the people who owned land or houses sold them and brought the money to the apostles to give to others in need. And it says there was no, I repeat, No poverty among them. Praise the Lord! In other words, God's people were obedient to God's Word and they helped their own.

Blessed To Be A Blessing To Others

Thousands of years ago when God called Abraham, He told him, "I will bless you and make you famous, and I will make you a blessing to others" (Genesis 12:2). God's plan and purpose for the faithful has not changed, it remains the same; you are blessed by God to be a blessing to others.

As an ambassador of God here on earth, the local church and its believers are responsible for meeting the needs of the poor among them. It is not the responsibility of the heathen.

Be Led By The Holy Spirit When Sharing Spiritual And Material Gifts

All too often people of faith neglect the physical needs of other believers and non-believers. They are sometimes heavy on preaching salvation and spiritual matters, but light on meeting physical needs (that require giving money, time and talent) such as food, clothing, shelter, medical or dental care, etc.

If you closely observe the ministry of Jesus Christ of Nazareth here on earth, it reveals that in most cases He met physical human needs first, such as feeding the hungry, healing the sick, and setting the captives free from Satan's bondage.

Remember the Parable of the Good Samaritan? Jesus' illustration of the good Samaritan shows him meeting the physical needs of the Jewish man who had been attacked by bandits. Jesus said...

> *Then a despised Samaritan came along, and when he saw the man, he felt deep pity. Kneeling beside him, the Samaritan soothed his wounds with medicine and bandaged them. Then he put the man on his own donkey and took him to an inn, where he took care of him. The next day he handed the innkeeper two pieces of silver and told him to take care of the man. "If his bill runs higher than that," he said, "I'll pay the difference the next time I am here* (Luke 10:33-35 NLT).

The writer James, inspired by the Holy Spirit wrote the following in his letter to Jewish Christians scattered among the nations. These instructions are meant for you and me also.

> *Pure and lasting religion in the sight of God our Father means that we must care for orphans and widows in their troubles, and refuse to let the world corrupt us* (James 1:27, NLT).

The Word of God forewarns us about not giving to the poor and needy. It says...

> *Whoever gives to the poor will lack nothing. But a curse will come upon those who close their eyes to poverty.* Proverbs 28:27, NLT

The Word of God also tells us that those who give generously to the poor and needy are blessed.

> *Blessed are those who are generous, because they feed the poor.* Proverbs 22:9, NLT

God Loves A Cheerful Giver

The number one reason why believers are cheerful givers is because they are obeying God's commands, and they know that generous giving pleases God, and that God loves and blesses a cheerful giver.

Along these lines, the apostle Paul writes these inspiring words.

> *But this I say, he who sows sparingly will also reap sparingly, and he who sows bountifully will also reap bountifully.*
> *So let each one give as he purposes in his heart, not grudgingly or of necessity; for* ***God loves a cheerful giver.***
> 2 Corinthians 9:6-7, NKJV

One of the principles of New Testament giving is wrapped up in the last part of this Scripture; "God loves a cheerful giver." The Greek word for cheerful is "hilaros" which means willing, good-natured, joyfully ready, and describes a spirit of enjoyment in giving that sweeps away all restraints. The English word "hilarious" is a transliteration. God loves happy, joyous givers. People who have learned the Kingdom principles of giving have been set free from the living from paycheck to paycheck syndrome, and from the "poverty" mind-set that grips the people of the world.

Looking to God as their source, they can give in total confidence, knowing that God will meet their own needs in abundance. The people of God should not give out of legalistic and fearful obedience. Instead, giving should be a joyous act in which we trust God to meet our needs according to His riches in glory.

Purpose Of Establishing An Inheritance For Your Children And Your Children's Children

Believers are the children of God; not His servants, but His children! As children, believers are members of the royal family and should reign as kings and queens in this life (Romans 5:17, Amp.).

The Bible says...

> *Just as the rich rule the poor, so the borrower is servant to the lender* (Proverbs 22:7, NLT).

Brothers, sisters, and friends, I submit to you that the children of God are not destined to be borrowers and servants. Instead, Jesus Christ said that He came that you may have life, and that you may have it more abundantly (John 10:10). I exhort you to step into your role as royalty and develop a spirit of kingship or queenship; a spirit of soaring high above the circumstances; a spirit of being an overcomer; a spirit of being above and not beneath; a spirit of being victorious in this life; a spirit of being the lender and not the borrower.

The law of inheritance that establishes a legacy of house and riches for your children and your children's children, is a foolproof plan that provides for your offspring the financial and material assistance at different stages when it is needed the most. When this plan is implemented by all parties according to God's Word (see Proverbs 13:22, 19:14), it provides the resources for offspring to start life the way God intended it to be, and that is to have life and to have it more abundantly. Praise the Lord!

Consider your ways; consider how things are going with you now! Have unexpected medical bills, legal bills, repair bills and other unusual occurrences been draining your finances? Could it be because your intentions and your desire for wealth and riches are not in line with God's will?

Consider your ways! How would the Holy Spirit grade you today based on your paying tithes and sharing offerings? Would He give you an F, a C, an A, or an A+?

How would He grade you on your sharing of money, time and talent to help the poor and needy? Would He give you an F, a C, an A, or an A+?

How would He grade you on establishing an inheritance for your children and your children's children? Would He give you an F, a C, an A, or an A+?

If you are disobedient in the way you are distributing God's money, chances are great that you are out of fellowship with your Heavenly

Father, and in fellowship with Satan whose aim is to strip you of all the financial blessings that God has given you.

You can climb aboard the heavenly bandwagon that will carry you back into fellowship with your Heavenly Father. Pray now! Repent and ask God for forgiveness.

I urge you to add the following nutritious faith food to your daily menu of Faith-building confessions.

Faith-Building Confession:

I purpose in my heart and in my spirit by faith that I'm a cheerful giver! I cheerfully pay my tithes and share offerings into my home church! I eagerly seek to share God's money, my time, and my talent with the poor and needy! I am obedient in establishing an inheritance for my children and for my children's children. I do these things in obedience to God's Word, knowing that I am abundantly blessed by God with rich rewards in this life. Praise the Lord! I confess this in the mighty Name of Jesus Christ of Nazareth! SO BE IT! (1 Corinthians 9:6-7).

KEY #8 Save at least 10% of the money that God gives you and invest it wisely using prudent and proven financial counselors/planners.

Previously, we discussed seven ways to keep your covenant inheritance of wealth and riches. In this section, we will expound on ways to increase your covenant inheritance of wealth and riches.

First, I'll restate again that it is God's will that His children (believers) be blessed with abundant wealth and riches. A part of God's blessing includes increase in material and financial prosperity. The Bible states, *"My cup overflows with blessings"* (Psalm 23:5), *"And your vats will overflow with the finest wine"* (Proverbs 3:10). In the book of Malachi, we find the words of the Lord which say... *"I will open the windows of heaven for you. I will pour out a blessing so great you won't have enough room to take it in!"* (Malachi 3:10). These Scriptures are referring to abundant increase.

In the New Testament book of 1 Corinthians, the apostle Paul says... *"I planted, Apollos watered, but God gave the increase. So then neither he who plants is anything, nor he who waters, but God who gives the increase!"* (1 Corinthians 3:6-7)

In this passage, the apostle Paul is talking about himself and Apollos who had preached to some carnal-minded Christians. He says... "but God gave the increase." So we see from the Word of God that He not only gives us the wealth and riches, but He also provides the increase in everything.

Obedience To God's Word Results In Increase

The Word of God is the owner's manual for believers. As long as you follow the instructions in the owner's manual, everything will work just fine. But if you try to short cut, or do things differently, you will run into problems. If you do not put the instructions to use, nothing will happen, no benefits, no increase. Next is an illustration that clearly shows how obedience to God's Word results in increase.

Don't Be Like The Good-For-Nothing Servant

Jesus Christ of Nazareth magnificently illustrates in the parable of the Talents and Rewards that when you follow God's instructions and wisely invest a portion of the covenant inheritance of wealth and riches He has given you, then God is pleased and you will receive increase.

Here is what Jesus had to say...

> *Again, the Kingdom of Heaven can be illustrated by the story of a man going into another country, who called together his servants and loaned them money to invest for him while he was gone.*
> *He gave $5,000 to one, $2,000 to another, and $1,000 to the last – dividing it in proportion to their abilities – and then left on his trip. The man who received the $5,000 began immediately to buy and sell with it and soon earned another $5,000. The man with $2,000 went right to work, too, and earned another $2,000.*
> *But the man who received the $1,000 dug a hole in the ground and hid the money for safekeeping.*
> *After a long time their master returned from his trip and called them to him to account for his money. The man to whom he had entrusted the $5,000 brought him $10,000.*
> *His master praised him for good work. You have been faithful in handling this small amount, he told him, so now I will give you many more responsibilities. Begin the joyous tasks I have assigned to you.*
> *Next came the man who had received the $2,000, with the report. Sir, you gave me $2,000 to use, and I have doubled it.*
> *Good work, his master said. You are a good and faithful servant. You have been faithful over this small amount, so now I will give you much more.*
> *Then the man with the $1,000 came and said, Sir, I knew that you were a hard man, and I was afraid you would rob me of what I earned, so I hid your money in the earth and here it is.*
> *But his master replied, Wicked man! Lazy slave! Since you knew I would demand your profit, you should at least have put my money into the bank so I could have some interest. Take the money from this man and give it to the man with the $10,000. For*

the man who uses well what he is given shall be given more, and he shall have abundance. But from the man who is unfaithful, even what little responsibility he has shall be taken from him. And throw the useless servant out into outer darkness; there shall be weeping and gnashing of teeth (Matthew 25:14-30, TLB).

The heavenly or spiritual meaning to this story is overflowing with revelation knowledge that is beneficial for a good understanding of God's financial system. You will find that much of the revelation knowledge revealed in this parable is also woven throughout the pages of this book. This parable contains the major biblical principles needed to fulfill Key #8.

First, let's establish that the wealthy master is the Lord Jesus Christ. The journey into the far country refers to His departure into heaven after His ascension. The servants were, in the first instances, the twelve disciples to whom Jesus addressed the parable and then, in a broader sense, all born-again believers. Below are some spiritual truths that Jesus reveals in this parable.

1. **All the money belongs to God**. The number-one truth revealed is that all the money in the parable belonged to the Lord and was handed over by Him to His servants to be used in trade. Similarly all that we (believers) have materially and financially belongs to our Heavenly Father. This means that all of our weekly, bi-weekly, or monthly income belongs to Him, and the covenant inheritance of wealth and riches which He graciously gives belongs to Him. Believers are to be good stewards over whatever God gives, by distributing and investing it wisely.

2. **You receive in proportion to your faith and personal ability**. The master entrusted different amounts of money to the three servants. The qualifying clause in the distribution of the talents is – to each in proportion to his own personal ability.
   Likewise, the covenant inheritance of wealth and riches that is available to believers is given by God in proportion to each believer's faith and personal ability. We do not receive more from Him than we can understand and use.

3. **Obedience to God's Word and the Holy Spirit is essential**. The purpose of the master entrusting his money to the servants was for them to trade and earn profits. In essence, the master told them, "Here, take this money and go out and make some

profits while I'm away." Notice that the two faithful servants went at once (obedience) and started trading, but the unfaithful, negligent servant went and dug a hole in the ground and hid his master's money (disobedient). The unfaithful servant didn't follow his master's instructions, he was disobedient in not following his master's words.

Instead, he did what his sense-knowledge mind directed and, at that point, he was out of fellowship with his master which resulted in him being cast into outer darkness. The spiritual lesson we learn from this passage is that we must obey the voice of our Lord. The Bible says, *"For the true love of God is this; that we do His commands (keep His ordinances and are mindful of His precepts and teaching). And these orders of His* ***are not*** *irksome (burdensome, oppressive, or grievous)"* (1 John 5:3, Amp.).

4. **<u>Always be prepared to give a good report</u>**. The servants were not told when their master would return. Therefore, two of the servants promptly started trading. They didn't procrastinate, or assume they had plenty of time to trade before their master returned. Instead, the Bible tells us that they went at once and started trading. Their expediency resulted in their being prepared to settle their accounts with the master when he returned.

   The insight that we gain from this passage can be taken from The Boy Scouts of America motto which says "BE PREPARED!" A believer should be prepared to give an account daily or even hourly of their stewardship in obedience to God's Word, because we do not know the day nor the hour when Jesus will return. The Bible says, *"Watch, therefore (give strict attention and be cautious and active), for you know neither the day nor the hour when the Son of Man will come"* Matthew 25:13, Amp.

   It is also written, *"But of that (exact) day and hour no one knows, not even the angels of heaven, nor the Son, but only the Father"* (Matthew 24:36, Amp.).

5. **<u>Always confess and believe for increase</u>**. The servants who were obedient to their master's instructions and produced profits on their master's money received praise and admiration from their master. The master told them that they had been

faithful in handling this small amount, so he would give them many more responsibilities (promotion).

6. **The faithful are rewarded, and the unfaithful are punished**. The master not only took the talent away from the unfaithful, negligent servant, but he also said to throw the good-for-nothing servant into outer darkness. At the same time, the two faithful servants were to celebrate with their master. The message that we grasp from this passage is that God rewards the faithful and allows punishment to be dealt to the unfaithful, disobedient, and negligent.

   Whatever you do, set your goals and your self-talk toward increase. The first two servants were praised and rewarded for their diligence, but when Jesus told this story the ending seemed unfair. He took away from the man who did not invest and gave his money to the most fruitful investor, firmly announcing this law of the Kingdom. To everyone who has, more will be given, but from him who does not have, even what he has will be taken away.

   In other words, if you use what is given to you wisely, you will be given more. If you fail to use what is given to you, you will lose even what you think you have. Whether in physical, intellectual, financial, or relational dealings, whatever is given to you, however small it is, use it. Use it diligently, and use it on an ever-increasing scale. Set goals to increase whatever you do; and make sure that whatever you do it is done to the glory of God. This is a secret of the Kingdom, which guarantees success to any Christian who applies it.

7. **Save At Least 10% Of The Money God Gives You.**
   The word "save" really translates to the word "invest." We don't want to copy the unfaithful servant by putting God's money in a hole in the ground for safe keeping. Instead, we ought to follow the example of the two faithful servants and use the money wisely to conduct a business enterprise or invest in stocks, bonds, mutual funds or whatever venture the Holy Spirit directs you toward.

   I can remember back when I was around seven or eight years old; my brother and I would visit in the summer with our Uncle Strick, Aunt Mattie, and cousin Claude. My uncle would often sit us down and tell us, "Boys, if you make one dollar, save a dime!" Now that I think back, I wish that I would have used his advice from the very beginning. I started earning money, cutting grass with a push mower at nine years old and I have worked ever since. I think about how much more I would have if I had applied Uncle Strick's advice to my earnings.

8. **Seek God First, Then Seek A Prudent And Proven Financial Counselor/Planner.**
Earlier on in this book, we read about an uneducated East Texas millionaire who always went into his big closet to pray before making any investment decision. He said that sometimes he would be in his closet all night long or in and out of it for three days, just praying and reading his Bible – getting quiet so that he could hear what his heart had to say about the matter. The enlightening thing about this is when he said, "In the many years of investing, I've never lost a dime."
My best advice is for you to go into your prayer closet, which could be any quiet space in your home, and seek God first and ask Him for guidance and direction in locating a prudent, proven, and reliable financial planner. After praying, write a faith-building confession thanking God for leading you to be a qualified, prudent, and proven financial planner. Begin reading aloud this confession when you are in and when you are out of your closet. While in your closet you may read your Bible and/or read all of your other faith-building confessions as well, until you hear from God.
You can rest assured that He will answer your prayer and confession; just be patient and let Him do His work on your behalf. I have found that God has imparted much revelation knowledge to me while reading aloud my faith-building confessions. Divine insight, concepts, and ideas just seem to flow when I confess God's Word to my situation.

What Does God's Word Have To Say About Counsel?

Throughout the Bible, the Word of God refers to seeking counsel from the Lord and in some cases it refers to seeking out other mature Christians for information and advice, especially those who have expertise in the matter at hand.

Following are some Scriptures that speak about counseling and counselors:

> *A wise man will hear and increase learning. And a man of understanding will attain wise counsel* (Proverbs 1:5, NKJV).

> *Where there is no counsel, the people fall; But in the multitude of counselors there is safety* (Proverbs 11:14, NKJV).
>
> *The way of a fool is right in his own eyes, but he who heeds counsel is wise* (Proverbs 12:15, NKJV).
>
> *Without counsel, plans go awry, but in the multitude of counselors they are established* (Proverbs 15:22, NKJV).
>
> *Listen to counsel and receive instruction, that you may be wise in your latter days* (Proverbs 19:20, NKJV).

Proverbs warns, "*Without counsel, plans go awry, but in the multitude of counselors they are established.*" It is wise to ask other mature Christian men and women to review your ideas or plans before undertaking something that is important. Why?

First, God can speak to us through other people and they may offer a perspective on the situation that we may not have seen. Also, other people may have done the very same thing we are thinking of doing, and we can benefit by their experience.

How To Obey God's Word

I'm moved to write this because I once made a big blunder in not fully checking out a (recommended) tax preparer; this mistake involved large sums of money.

Thoroughly investigate the performance of companies within the community.

1. When possible, try to seek out a reliable Christian-based financial planner. Never make a final decision on which financial planner to choose until you have thoroughly reviewed all of his or her credentials. If he claims to be a certified financial planner, then ask to see the documents showing his certification. However, don't stop there. Make phone calls to confirm this certification if necessary. If the certification is real, follow up by asking to speak with some of his clients. Ask questions about how successful this person has been with other clients'money.
2. When you have narrowed your selection down to three or four, check with the Better Business Bureau (BBB) and get a report on each financial planner. In addition to the BBB, some communities have consumer affairs departments that can provide feedback on the performance of companies within the community.
3. Set up personal interviews with financial planners. I suggest that you personally interview three or four financial planners before

making a final decision. The person that you are interviewing to be your financial planner may look great and his results may be impressive, but inside you may not feel comfortable with this person. When you don't have peace, you should take it as a sign that you should keep looking.

It is critical that you have a comfortable working relationship with the person who helps you make financial decisions. If you can't talk with that person, or he doesn't seem to understand your goals, find someone who does. Why? Because you will be sharing very intimate details of your life. If you are not comfortable with your planner knowing these details, look out. Chances are great that your spirit and the Holy Spirit are telling you to find someone else.

This process of selecting a wise and reliable financial planner is vital because you always want to choose a financial planner you can trust and who will do a good job for you. Keep in mind also that the money you are managing belongs to God and you must do all within your power to be a good steward over His money. The money you are managing could grow into millions of dollars and even billions, so make sure God is in the process.

4. Whenever possible, try to seek out at least three valid testimonies from individuals who have used the financial planner's services.

At this point, the one remaining choice should line up 100 percent with what the Word of God imparted to you; and if it does, you will instantly have a sense of peace in your spirit which will confirm your final selection.

I have used a Christian-based financial planner, and I was amazed at all the obstacles you have to overcome to be successful financially, such as: lack of direction, debt, and taxes.

If you don't know where you are going, how can you ever get there? Financial management involves identifying goals such as investing, buying a house, building a retirement fund, or providing an estate for your heirs. Then you chart the best course to reach these goals.

A lack of direction, debt, inflation, and taxes are all obstacles that you have to overcome to be financially successful. The financial woes of noted people such as Donald Trump, the hotel/casino and real estate giant; Elton John, the popular singer/entertainer; and MC Hammer, the former rap singer, generally fall into one or more of the following categories – lack of direction, debt, inflation, or taxes.

A sound financial planner can help you overcome the obstacles that impede financial success. If you don't already have one, I encourage you to begin immediately the process of selecting a sound financial planner. Remember the words of John Fitzgerald Kennedy, "The time to fix the roof is when the sun is shining!" Talk to the financial officer at your bank, get all the free consultation available to you and learn as much as possible about financial management.

The internet provides a wide variety of information on investing and financial management, which in some cases can be down loaded or printed from on-line web pages.

The final choice in these financial matters is up to you. You can either be like the faithful servants and please your master or you can be like the unfaithful servant and displease your master. My desire is that these inscriptions have ignited and inspired you to be like the two faithful servants and invest God's money wisely, so that there will be abundant increase!

I can't imagine a person becoming a success who doesn't give this game of life everything he's got.
Walter Cronkite, American broadcast journalist (b.1916)

CHAPTER 11

PART I

SEVEN REASONS WHY SELF-TALK FAITH-BUILDING CONFESSIONS WORK

First of all, let me say that faith-building confessions are a way to possession. It's not the only way, but it is one of God's principal ways set forth in the Bible. Hence, when you find Scriptures that reveal God's Word in your situation and constantly, relentlessly, and reverently confess those words, then you are guaranteed possession in due season.

When you say aloud what God has said in His Word about a certain thing, you are agreeing with God and you are operating in a powerful biblical principle.

To find out why self-talk faith-building confessions work, we must go to the source to get the answers. The Bible is the source and there are seven primary reasons why faith-building confessions work.

Reason 1. Faith-building confessions work because they are based on a powerful biblical principle of "seedtime, and harvest," also referred to as "sowing and reaping." It is God's way for you to sow (word) seeds into the Kingdom of God and reap a harvest.

The Law Of Seedtime, And Harvest

The first chapter of the book of Genesis contains God's words, which established the law of seed, time and harvest.

> *And God said, Let the earth put forth (tender) vegetation; plants yielding seed and fruit trees yielding fruit whose seed is in itself, each according to its kind, upon the earth. And it was so.*
>
> *The earth brought forth vegetation; plants yielding seed according to their own kinds and trees bearing fruit in which was their seed, each according to its kind. And God saw that it was good (suitable, admirable) and He approved it.*
>
> Genesis 1:11-12, Amp.

God's Word reveals some enlightening truths that every believer must grasp and fully understand:

1. In everything there is a seed, and every word you speak is a seed.

2. Each seed yields fruit according to its own kind – if you speak poverty, your yield will be poverty. If you speak prosperity, your yield will be prosperity.

It's the way God designed His system to work. In other words if you are weak, you don't speak a confession (sow a seed) of weakness; it will reproduce after its own kind and yield even more weakness. Instead, the Bible says... *"Let the weak say, I am strong"* (Joel 3:10). A faith-building confession that says "I am strong" will supernaturally reproduce after its own kind and yield great strength and strong faith.

God's System Of Seed, Time, And Harvest Will Not Cease – It's Here To Stay

God talked to Himself about some very interesting and far-reaching things that affect believers today. Let's listen to what He said to Himself and ultimately to you and me.

> *...And Noah built an altar to the Lord and took of every clean (four footed) animal and of every clean foul or bird and offered burnt offerings on the altar. When the Lord smelled the pleasing odor, (a scent of satisfaction to His heart), the Lord said to Himself, I will never again curse the ground because of man, for the imagination (the strong desire) of man's heart is evil and wicked from his youth; neither will I ever again smite and destroy every living thing, as I have done. While the earth remains,* ***seedtime*** *and* ***harvest****, cold and heat, summer and winter, and day and night shall not cease.*
> Genesis 8:20-22, Amp.

There are two other related Scriptures that reinforce God's law of seedtime and harvest, and sowing and reaping. The first one says...

> *But this I say: He who sows sparingly will also reap sparingly, and he who sows bountifully will also reap bountifully.*
> 2 Corinthians 9:6, NKJV

The second one says...

> *Do not be deceived, God is not mocked; for whatever a man sows, that he will also reap* (Galatians 6:7, NKJV).

In this next parable Jesus eloquently unveils this biblical principle.

> *And he said, "So is the kingdom of God, as if a man should cast seed into the ground; and should sleep, and rise night and day, and the seed should spring and grow up, he knoweth not how. For the earth bringeth forth fruit of herself; first the blade, then the*

> *ear, after that the full corn in the ear. But when the fruit is brought forth, immediately he putteth in the sickle, because the harvest is come* (Mark 4:26-29, KJV).

Now let's identify who and what Jesus is talking about in this parable, so we can uncover its spiritual message meant to benefit you and me today.

A. The Kingdom of God is God's Kingdom and His way, His system of doing things within His Kingdom. In contrast to a kingdom (a country) ruled by man, the Kingdom of God represents His rule, His reign, His triumph over all human affairs and His total authority over His universe. However, under God's law of seed, time, and harvest, before any harvest, the seed must be sown by a believing person.

B. The man casting the seed is the sower and is representative of all those "believers" whom God uses in the establishment of His Kingdom within the hearts of men. Believers are God's representatives here on earth and we are the ones who must plant the seeds which produce harvest. Believers plant seeds into the Kingdom of God by using their mouths to speak God's precepts and promises into their lives and into the lives of others.

C. The seed is the Word of God. If you consider the seeds that farmers use, some could be good seeds and some could be bad seeds; or the seeds could be subject to destruction by the elements, birds, and other parasites, but not so with God's Word. When spoken in faith, God's Word will always produce a harvest.

Reason 2. Faith-building confessions work because God's Word is incorruptible seed. The Word of God says of the new birth, *"having been born again, not of corruptible seed but incorruptible, through the Word of God which lives and abides forever"* (1 Peter 1:23, NKJV).

In this Scripture, the apostle Paul unveils a powerful biblical truth concerning God's Word; he says that God's Word is incorruptible. This means that it is incapable of being destroyed; it lives and abides forever.

The ground or the soil that Jesus refers to in the previous parable is a vital part because it represents the human heart. Not the muscular organ that pumps blood throughout the body; the heart that Jesus is speaking of, in a general sense, means the center, the core of one's being, the inner man or the real you. It's the seat or center of thoughts and emotions.

The ground cannot sow, and it cannot reap, but it receives and nurtures the seed, supplying it with all its own nutritional qualities until at last there is a harvest.

Concerning the mystery of growth, Jesus said that the sower, after sowing the seed, sleeps, rises night and day, and "knoweth not how" the seed springs and grows. After he had sown his seed, the man went about his ordinary life. He can do no more now, but watch and wait. He is not guilty of over-anxiety, but patiently waits for the evidence of an imperceptible growth.

Faith Or Proof

It is very strange that when it comes to the things of God, some people take on the same attitude as unbelieving Thomas who said, *"Except I shall see in his hand the print of the nails, and put my finger into the print of the nails and thrust my hand into his side, I will not believe"* (John 20:25).

In natural things, people utilize many modern conveniences each day without full knowledge or proof of what makes them operate. For instance, millions of people travel on commercial airplanes daily around the world, and how many of those millions of people actually know the technical ins and outs of what causes a 747 aircraft to lift? How many know the engineering dynamics that keep the plane in the air?

I would venture to say a very, very few. But not knowing the (unseen) technical workings of the aircraft doesn't stop people from traveling by airplane and taking advantage of the convenience and time savings. When you think about it, most passengers "knoweth not how" the machines and computers keep the plane in the air. They travel on airplanes strictly on the faith of what the airlines promised when buying their ticket.

The internet, which is a rapidly growing phenomenon attracts millions of users each day. Considering the vast number of people who access the internet each day, how many do you think actually know the technical (unseen) workings of the super computer that is the host server providing the internet access? Or how many users actually know how millions of users are linked harmoniously together worldwide?

The truth is that we rely upon the internet for information, communication, and entertainment; and we have faith that it will provide these services, without having bona fide knowledge of its technical features and operation.

In these examples cited, you can clearly see that there are things that we use daily, but we do not have the technical knowledge as to how these things work. How many know how the automatic doors open at your local grocery store?

I would venture to say that most people "knoweth not how." The technical engineering data for an aircraft, the internet, and the automatic door openers fall into this unseen area; in other words, we "knoweth not how" these things work. But we still believe in and have strong faith in these things. We use the services and conveniences they provide, and rightly so.

Believers' faith in the Word of God should be much, much stronger than the faith they put in airlines, the internet, and automatic door openers. All these things can and do fail.

As a passenger, it is not necessary to know how many revolutions per minute the aircraft motor turns. The same holds true with the things of God. For believers to benefit in the things of God, they must develop unwavering faith in the Word of God; not requiring proof, but relying totally on God's Word.

Along those lines, Jesus had a few choice words for unbelieving Thomas; Jesus said to him, "*Thomas, because thou hast seen me, thou hast believed. Blessed are they that have not seen, and yet have believed* (John 20:29).

Now let's resume our discussion about the man who casts seed into the ground, sleeps and rises night and day, and the seed springs and grows up, but he "knoweth not how."

I submit to you that the phrase "he knoweth not how" reveals the fact that the mystery or supernatural working of God is beyond man's understanding. And our understanding of time doesn't fit His timing. The Lord said, "*For my thoughts are not your thoughts, neither are your ways my ways, says the Lord*" (Isaiah 55:8).

Just to show you how man thinks, I have planted seeds and then gotten up early the very next morning and rushed out to the garden to see if there were plants coming up. This clearly shows that my actions were based on my own thoughts and timing and not God's timing.

One thing we can be certain of...when a farmer plants a seed into good ground it begins at once to work toward its designed purpose, namely to bear fruit after its kind. The same holds true when believers plant faith-building confession seeds into the Kingdom of God (into your heart). It begins at once with the power of the Holy Spirit, to supernaturally work toward its designed purpose, to reproduce after its own kind, to spring forth a plant, to bear fruit, to produce a harvest. In other words, when you plant faith-building confession seeds of good health and financial prosperity, constantly, relentlessly, and reverently, you are guaranteed to harvest that which you confessed in due season because God's Word is incorruptible seed!

Reason 3. Faith-building confessions work because they contain the Word of God which is alive and full of supernatural creative power. The

Bible says...

> *For the Word that God speaks is alive and full of power (making it active, operative, energizing, and effective); it is sharper than any two-edged sword, penetrating to the dividing line of the breath of life (soul) and (the immortal) spirit, and of joints and marrow (of the deepest parts of our nature) exposing and sifting and analyzing and judging the very thoughts and purposes of the heart* (Hebrews 4:12, Amp.).

God's Word is very, very powerful, and it is a living force of divine energy which is highly effective at accomplishing God's purposes. People who read the Word of God and allow it to direct their lives soon discover the awesome power of the Living Word. God's Word is not just another book. Every word from the Bible is filled with the same power that resurrected Christ from the dead and created the universe. And that same power is available to believers today! The Word of God is a living and powerful Word, which is able to penetrate the very depths of our hearts and go into the center of our inner person. The Word of God has the power to go beyond our conscious mind to the very core of our spiritual being and to cleanse, convict, and transform us.

Sometimes we think everything is okay, but God's Word has the power to uncover secret attitudes and desires that are not pleasing to God. The Word of God can tear down strongholds of fear, failure, lust, and negativity and then build powerful new habit patterns that produce financial prosperity and victory in every area of life.

Jesus reveals this about His Word. He said... "*heaven and earth will pass away, but my words shall not pass away*" (Matthew 24:35).

David writes this about the Word of God...

> *I will worship toward Your holy temple and praise Your name for Your loving-kindness and for Your truth and faithfulness; for You have exalted above all else Your name and Your word and You have magnified Your word above all Your name.*
> Psalm 138:2, Amp.

> *Your word is a lamp to my feet and a light to my path.*
> Psalm 119:105, Amp.

> *The entrance and unfolding of Your words give light; their unfolding gives understanding (discernment and comprehension) to the simple* (Psalm 119:130, Amp.).

The Lord God Almighty said...

> *So shall My Word be that goes forth out of My mouth; it shall not*

return to Me void (without producing any effect, useless) but it shall accomplish that which I please and purpose. And it shall prosper in the thing for which I sent it.
Isaiah 55:11, Amp.

Jesus Christ of Nazareth said...

It is the Spirit Who gives life (He is the Life-giver); the flesh conveys no benefit whatever (there is no profit in it). The words (truths) that I have been speaking to you are spirit and life.
John 6:63, Amp.

It is written...

For all flesh (mankind) is like grass, and all its glory (honor) like the flower of grass. The grass withers and the flower drops off. But the Word of the Lord (divine instruction, the Gospel) endures forever. And this Word is the good news which was preached to you (1 Peter 1:24-25, Amp.).

If you live in Me (abide vitally united to Me) and My words remain in you and continue to live in your hearts, ask whatever you will, and it shall be done for you (John 15:7, Amp.).

Notice closely in this next Scripture that Jesus tells Peter that via the use of words, believers hold the keys to the kingdom of heaven.

And I also say to you that you are Peter, and on this rock I will build My church, and the gates of Hades shall not prevail against it. And I will give you the keys of the kingdom of heaven; and ***whatever you bind on earth will be bound in heaven, and whatever you loose on earth will be loosed in heaven.*** (Matthew 16:18-19, NKJV).

Jesus tells Peter that the "gates of Hades," or the gates of hell will not be able to overcome His church. This means that hell's gates, which have imprisoned people and put them into bondage, cannot withstand the battering ram of God's church moving against it in Kingdom authority.

Jesus gave His followers the keys of the Kingdom. Through Peter, Jesus passed on to His church His authority or control, to bind or loose things on earth. The power of binding or loosing means the power to stop or release or forbid or permit. We bind Satan and his demon host's activities and we loose divine blessings.

Jesus Christ has given us the keys to the Kingdom, which means that He has given us His Kingdom power to stop evil and release God's power on different situations in life. In a nutshell, because Jesus has given us the keys of the Kingdom, we are not to remain passive in the face of evil. Rather, we are to use the authority of God's Word to break the gates of hell and set ourselves and other people free in the Name of Jesus. It is clear to see that the power to get things done in the Kingdom of heaven is by use of the mouth, speaking words and believing them.

Power Of Words

Brain washing is a well known negative form of repetitive use of words to indoctrinate prisoners of war. It is also used by cult leaders to persuade their followers to remain faithful. And in some cases, it is used by some law enforcers to gain acknowledgment of a fact or the admittance to a crime. Let's read the definition of brain washing.

Brain Washing

> It is intensive forcible indoctrination, usually political or religious, aimed at destroying a person's basic convictions and attitudes and replacing them with an alternative set of fixed beliefs. It is the application of concentrated means of persuasion, such as advertising campaigns or repeated suggestion, in order to develop a specific belief or motivation.

Contrary to brain washing, faith-building confessions are an example of the power of words used rightly to wash the (mind and) heart clean with the Word of God. It changes a person's heart from the sinful nature to a Godly nature, and a steady diet of faith-building confessions will produce victory in every area of the believer's life!

The Blood Of Jesus Christ Is A Powerful Weapon

We understand that the shed blood of Jesus Christ has paid the price for our sin and has thereby set us free; we no longer need to listen to accusations (true and false) that tear us apart inside. We often fail to understand how God has provided victory for us, over Satan, through Jesus' blood. When Satan's demons come against us, we must recognize that the blood of Jesus has satisfied all the charges against us.

This has accomplished three things for us:

1. The blood unites us in fellowship with the Father.
2. The blood gives us power to defeat the forces of darkness.
3. The blood gives us power over our own sinful nature.

The blood has established an unassailable bond with a sovereign God that prevents Satan from separating the embattled Christian from God's eternal and complete resources. We need to continually remind Satan and all of his demons that the blood of Jesus Christ has provided victory over them because there is devil-defeating power in the blood.

The Word Of Your Testimony Is A Powerful Weapon

> It is written...*"And they have defeated him because of the blood of the Lamb and because of their testimony."* Revelation 12:11, NLT

The two primary ways that believers can defeat the powers of darkness is through the blood of the Lamb and the word of their testimonies. One of Satan's key areas of attack is to accuse Christians before the throne room of God by pointing out their sins and failures. However, believers in Jesus Christ have had their sins and failures cleansed by the blood of the Lamb.

I speak the blood in my prayers and in my confessions. I say it this way...I have overcome him by the blood of the Lamb and by the word of my testimony, and my testimony is that I resist you, Satan, and all your evil spirits and you flee from me and my family in the mighty Name of Jesus Christ of Nazareth! SO BE IT! (James 4:7; Revelation 12:11).

Believers who know the reality of this have learned how to overcome Satan. Also, believers' personal testimonies that Jesus Christ is God, destroy the devil's deception over other people because Christians are living proof that God exists and that He is good.

These illuminating Scriptures should erase any doubts that one may have concerning the awesome power of God's Word.

I submit to you that, as you boldly read your faith-building confessions aloud while believing in your heart, the word that goes forth out of your mouth shall not return to you void; but it shall accomplish that which pleases God and His purpose and it shall prosper in the thing for which you sent it. Faith-building confessions work because you mix God's Word into your situation. God's Word is alive; it creates and is full of supernatural power.

The bottom line is..."you shall have whatsoever you saith."

Reason 4. Faith-building confessions work because they activate the divine connection between the "mouth," the "heart," and the "harvest."

First, let's see if we can get a clearer understanding of the biblical meaning of the word "heart." The word "heart" appears in one form or another in 932 verses throughout the King James version of the Bible. This places it high on the list of words used throughout the Bible and demonstrates its importance.

As it was stated before, the word "heart" that is being discussed is not the muscular organ that pumps blood through the body. The word "heart" that this topic is focused on means the center, the core of one's being, the real you. It is the seat or center of thoughts, emotions, desires, knowledge and wisdom. In the parable of the growing seed and harvest, we read that the ground or soil is where seeds are sown in the natural realm. But in the Kingdom of God, man's heart represents the ground or soil where (word) seeds are sown.

In a similar way, metaphorically, I believe that the "heart" which the Bible speaks so much about, is similar to an internal personal computer, but the heart is infinitely far more advanced. In fact, since the (mind and) heart was created first, the computer is really a replication of the human (mind and) heart.

The heart receives, processes, stores, and acts on the input received from the five senses in much the same way that a computer receives its programming. It processes it, stores it, and acts on it. In other words, the quality and the quantity of the input to the heart will directly affect the output in reality. Garbage in, garbage out. The same holds true with the heart, negative, life-defeating, ungodly words result in negative, life-defeating lifestyle.

Deluxe Tour Of The Heart And Its Tenants

I am your tour guide, so first I am asking you to imagine that we just entered a model of a regenerated heart of man. First, we see three rooms; one large bright and busy room similar to a data processing room, and two adjacent see-through rooms that appear peaceful and quiet.

Our first stop in the large room is at the (mind and) heart memory files. We are greeted by a spokesperson who is the manager overseeing the files.

The manager tells us that, at the entrance way to the heart is an on-line internal video/audio camcorder that records all of life's events, speech, thoughts, and acts of behavior. This camcorder also downloads the information it receives to the (mind and) heart memory files. Another function of the on-line video/audio internal camcorder is to move input it receives that requires immediate response, directly to the central processing unit (CPU) which is the "brain" of the heart.

The manager goes on to say that one of the see-through rooms is where the human spirit resides and the adjoining room is where the Holy Spirit resides. There is a direct link from the on-line video/audio camcorder to the human spirit and a direct line to the Holy Spirit. All godly input received by the on-line video/audio camcorder is transmitted immediately to the human spirit and to the Holy Spirit. And it is also downloaded to the (mind and) heart memory files. The manager has to leave for a few minutes, but he will return. Now, the tour guide has something to say...

Before going on, we previously discussed in the preface section of this book the subject of the threefold nature of man, which is spirit, soul, and body. Briefly, man's threefold nature is this: (1) spirit – the part of man which deals with the spiritual realm; (2) soul – the part of man which deals with the mental realm, his reasoning and intellectual powers; (3) body – the part of man which deals with the physical realm. We are concerned in this topic with man's human spirit which is the part of man that contacts God and vice versa.

Man's spirit can be developed, it can be educated and improved just as his mind can be educated and improved. The spirit can be trained and built up. How? Through the daily speaking of your faith-building confessions and the study of God's Word.

Man's spirit should control his other faculties, namely the body and the five senses. The Bible refers to man's human spirit as the inward man. This inward person is the real you on the inside.

The apostle Paul shed some light on this subject when he wrote the following: *"Therefore, we do not lose heart. Even though our outward man is perishing, yet the inward man is renewed day by day."* 2 Corinthians 4:16

The human spirit is also called the hidden man of the heart (1 Peter 3:4). Your spirit is the real you. The body is not the real you; it is merely the home or tent in which your spirit and soul live here on earth. The outward man or the visible man is the one that you salute on the street. The inward man or the hidden man of the heart is the one who gives this outer man either his attractiveness or his repulsiveness.

It is a very remarkable fact that God deals with the inward man instead of the outer man. Spiritual things are unveiled to this hidden man of the heart. The Holy Spirit makes His home with the hidden man (the human spirit). Natural man can develop his spirit until it becomes the force that it was designed to be.

The human spirit should be in control; it should dominate but, unfortunately, many believers are body controlled and sense (five senses) controlled. The human spirit is naturally very religious because it is God-hungry. As the regenerated human spirit is cultured, developed and strengthened with faith-building confessions and God's Word, there is no limits to its possibilities.

We feed our physical bodies wholesome and nutritious food to provide energy, growth, good health, and longevity. A faith-building confession is a spiritually wholesome and nutritional "faith food" to develop and strengthen the human spirit to its intended dominant position.

In fact, faith-building confessions are the premier way to feed and strengthen your human spirit. Believers possess within themselves a force of incalculable power which, when it is managed on the conscious level in a wise manner, gives the believer total mastery over the circumstances, over the five senses, over the body, and a triumphant victory over Satan.

Jesus Christ of Nazareth said...

> *But when the Father sends the Comforter instead of me, and by the Comforter I mean the Holy Spirit, He will teach you much, as well as remind you of everything I myself have told you.* (John 14:26, TLB).

> The apostle John said...*You are of God, little children, and have overcome them, because He who is in you is greater than he who is in the world* (1 John 4:4).

The apostle John tells us that He (the Holy Spirit) Who is in you, is greater than he (Satan and his demon host) who is in the world. This Scripture also establishes where the Holy Spirit resides, and that is on the inside of you.

Back to our tour, the manager has just returned and is now explaining the function of the (mind and) heart memory files. He said to imagine a personal file cabinet that is ten feet tall with ten deep drawers. Each drawer has many files and each file has a folder that is labeled with a specific life event; as an example, one folder is in a file labeled "Negative Life-Defeating Words." Another folder would be in a file labeled "Faith-Building Confessions for Financial Prosperity." Another folder may be in a file labeled "Faith-Building Confessions for Physical Healing."

Similar to a personal file cabinet, when the folder becomes full (overflows), the contents have to be removed to make room for more information. When an overflow occurs in the (mind and) heart memory file, the information is downloaded to the CPU for processing and action. The manager tells us that our next stop on the tour is the CPU.

As we approach this small apparatus called a CPU, we are greeted by the manager responsible for overseeing the CPU. We are told that this CPU is running on a divine regenerated software package. This man had a program conversion from old and defective software to a regenerated issue. The Word of God says...

> *A new heart will I give you and a new spirit will I put within you, and I will take away the stony heart out of your flesh, and give you a heart of flesh. And I will put my Spirit within you and cause you to walk in My statutes, and you shall heed My ordinances and do them* (Ezekiel 36:26-27, Amp.).

We are given a chart comparing the old program characteristics and the new program's characteristics.

Regenerated Software Package
Our New Life in Christ

"sinful nature" (old life)	"regenerated spirit" (new life)
Characteristics	
OLD	NEW
Not responsive to God	Responsive to God
In conflict with the Spirit	In conflict with sin
Ruled by cravings	Ruled by God
Products	
Immorality	love
Impurity	joy
Debauchery	peace
Idolatry and witchcraft	patience
Hatred	kindness
Discord	goodness
Jealousy	faithfulness
Fits of rage	gentleness
Selfish ambition	self-control
Factions	
Envy	
Drunkenness	
Orgies	
Proud	
Lustful	
Full of evil	

The heart's CPU is the center of thoughts, emotions, desires, knowledge, wisdom, action, and creative power. It is the "brain" of the heart. The heart's CPU receives information directly from the internal video/audio camcorder, from the (mind and) heart memory files, from the human spirit and from the Holy Spirit.

The heart's CPU reads and executes its internal program instructions and makes decisions based on data it receives. The heart's CPU is also responsible for storing and moving information from one part of the heart to another. Like a central switching station, it directs the flow of traffic throughout the heart system.

One of the CPU's major tasks is to determine whether overflow data from the (mind and) heart memory files agrees with the human spirit and the Holy Spirit. When there is an agreement, a divine connection is made and the Holy Spirit executes commands to the CPU and its connecting output sources (angels) to fulfill the petition or confession, and promptly makes it tangible in the life of the believer.

When the overflow data received at the heart CPU is ungodly, negative, life-defeating words, then the CPU's software automatically stores it and outputs the negative speech and behavior back to the sender in real time, in real life. This concludes our tour of the heart.

The Divine Connection Between The Mouth, The Heart, And The Harvest

When the mouth and the heart agree over a period of time, it produces a harvest. The Bible places strong emphasis on confessing with the mouth and believing in the heart. The two key words to focus on are "mouth" and "heart."

Some Bible scholars refer to this as the divine connection between the "mouth," the "heart," and the "harvest." The Scriptures clearly show us this divine connection in the book of Romans. In the apostle Paul's letter to the church in Rome, and in a broader sense to believers today, he wrote...

> *That if you confess with your* ***mouth*** *the Lord Jesus and believe in your* ***heart*** *that God has raised Him from the dead, you will be* ***saved*** (Romans 10:9, NKJV).

The action set forth in this Scripture requires a confession with the mouth and believing in the heart that which was confessed. In other words, what comes out of the mouth must be believed in the heart, the two must match to yield a harvest. In the above Scriptures, if you confess with your **mouth** and believe in your **heart**, then comes the **harvest**, which is that you will be **saved**.

Keep in mind that the gift of salvation is free. The only qualification is to confess with the mouth, believe in the heart, and receive the priceless gift of salvation. Unlike petition prayer and faith-building confessions, which may require overflowing faith to witness manifestation, the gift of salvation is instant when the mouth and heart agree.

Another Scripture that discloses the divine connection between the mouth and heart is read thusly:

> *And Jesus answering saith unto them, have faith in God. For verily I say unto you, that whosoever shall* ***say*** *unto this mountain, be thou removed, and be thou cast into the sea, and shall not doubt in his* ***heart****, but shall believe that those things which he* ***saith*** *shall come to pass;* ***he shall have whatsoever he saith.*** Mark 11:23-24, KJV

The total foundation of *Self-Talk And Grow Rich* is based on this Scripture. Notice closely the mouth-heart connection in this Scripture. My paraphrase of this Scripture would sound like this...whosoever will open his/her **mouth** and say to his debts, his marriage problems, or his sickness. "Be removed and be cast into the sea," and does not doubt in his **heart**, but believes that those things he says will be done, **he shall have whatsoever he saith**.

Here we see the awesome benefits of saying with the "mouth" and not doubting in the "heart," but believing that the debts will be removed and cast into the sea, and over time this results in a harvest. **He shall have whatsoever he saith.**

The Following Are Some Very Interesting Scriptures That Reveal The Results Of The Divine Connection Between The Mouth And Heart

> *He who loves purity and the pure in heart and who is gracious in speech – because of the grace of his lips will he have the king for his friend* (Proverbs 22:11, Amp.).

> *The wise in heart are called prudent, understanding, and knowing, and winsome speech increases learning in both speaker and listener* (Proverbs 16:21, Amp.).

> *Receive, I pray you, the law and instruction from His mouth, and lay up His words in your heart* (Job 22:22, Amp.).

> *My words shall express the uprightness of my heart, and my lips shall speak what they know with utter sincerity.*
> Job 33:3, Amp.

My mouth shall speak wisdom; and the meditation of my heart shall be understanding (Psalm 49:3, Amp.).

But the word is very near you, in your mouth and in your mind and in your heart, so that you can do it.
Deuteronomy 30:14, Amp.

For with the heart one believes unto righteousness, and with the mouth confession is made unto salvation.
Romans 10:10, NKJV

To man belong the plans of the heart, but from the Lord comes the reply of the tongue (Proverbs 16:1, NIV).

A wise man's heart guides his mouth, and his lips promote instructions (Proverbs 16:23, NIV).

Disagreement Between The Mouth And Heart Produces Transgression

These people draw near Me with their mouths and honor Me with their lips, but their hearts hold off and are far away from Me.
Matthew 15:8, Amp.

*Their tongue is a murderous arrow; it speaks deceitfully; one speaks peaceably to his neighbor with his mouth, but in his heart he lays snares and waits in ambush for him (*Jeremiah 9:8, Amp.).

To his neighbor each one speaks words without use or worth or truth; with flattering lips and double heart (deceitfully) they speak (Psalm 12:2, Amp.).

You offspring of vipers! How can you speak good things when you are evil (wicked)? For out of the fullness (the overflow, the superabundance) of the heart the mouth speaks.
Matthew 12:34, Amp.

Your Mouth Can Trick Your Heart

The Bible says..."If anyone thinks he is religious, and does not bridle his tongue but deceives his heart, this man's religion is vain" (James 1:26, RSV).

This is a very revealing Scripture. It is saying that if you don't control your tongue, it will deceive (trick or mislead) your heart. This further demonstrates the enormous power of the tongue, and it sends a warning signal to protect your ear gates from negative, unproductive self-talk and speech from others.

Further Evidence About The Divine Connection Between The Mouth, The Heart, And The Harvest

> *My heart is overflowing with beautiful thoughts! I will write a lovely poem to the King, for I am full of words as the speediest writer pouring out his story* (Psalm 45:1, TLB).
>
> Another translation says, *"my **heart** overflows with a beautiful thought! I will recite a lovely poem to the King, for my **tongue** is like the pen of a skillful poet"* (Psalm 45:1, NLT).

In this Scripture, the Psalmist reveals what the tongue does. Notice keenly the heart and tongue connection. We know that a poet does his writing on paper. However, the unanswered question here is, where does the tongue do its writing?

The answer to this question is found in this verse, *"Store my commands in your heart, for they will give you a long and satisfying life. Never let loyalty and kindness get away from you! Wear them like a necklace; write them deep within your heart"* (Proverbs 3:1-3, NLT).

This Scripture reveals that the tongue does its writing on the tablets or deep within the heart. Next, let's look at a living example of the effects of the divine connection between the mouth, the heart, and the harvest.

Why Did God Make Zechariah Speechless?

The Scriptures reveal an indisputable demonstration of the effects of the divine connection between the mouth, the heart, and the harvest. Let's read this very interesting story about Zechariah, who is John the Baptist's father.

> *Zechariah was in the sanctuary when an angel of the Lord appeared, standing to the right of the incense altar. Zechariah was overwhelmed with fear. But the angel said, "Don't be afraid, Zechariah! For God has heard your prayer, and your wife, Elizabeth, will bear you a son! And you are to name him John." ...Zechariah said to the angel, "How can I know this will happen? I am an old man now, and my wife is also well along in years."*
>
> *Then the angel said, "I am Gabriel! I stand in the very presence of God. It was he who sent me to bring you this good news! And now, since you didn't believe what I said, you won't be able to speak until the child is born. For my words will certainly come true at the proper time."*
>
> *Meanwhile, the people were waiting for Zechariah to come out, wondering why he was taking so long. When he finally did come out, **he couldn't speak to them**. Then they realized from his gestures that he must have seen a vision in the Temple sanctuary.*

Luke 1:11-13, 18-22, NLT
Now it was time for Elizabeth's baby to be born, and it was a boy. The word spread quickly to her neighbors and relatives that the Lord had been very kind to her, and everyone rejoiced with her. When the baby was eight days old, all the relatives and friends came for the circumcision ceremony. They wanted to name him Zechariah after his father. But Elizabeth said, "No! His name is John!" "What?" they exclaimed. "There is no one in all your family by that name." So they asked the baby's father communicating to him by making gestures. He motioned for a writing tablet, and to everyone's surprise he wrote, "His name is John!" ***Instantly Zechariah could speak again and he began praising God.*** Luke 1:57-64, NLT

1. I submit to you that the reason God made Zechariah speechless is because the angel Gabriel determined from Zechariah's negative words that he did not believe (in his heart) the words which Gabriel spoke. Instead, Zechariah's heart was overflowing with doubt and sense knowledge evidence. His (mind and) heart memory file was filled with, "I am an old man, and my wife is well advanced in years and we are too old to have a son; plus, how will I know and be sure of what you are telling me?" All of which exhibits doubt and unbelief.
2. Gabriel made Zechariah speechless because God couldn't take a chance on Zechariah hindering God's plan and purpose for Elizabeth to have a son named John. In other words, Zechariah's mouth, his words, could have hindered God's plan and purpose.
3. If Gabriel had not made Zechariah speechless, the abundance (overflow) of negative thoughts and words in Zechariah's heart would cause his mouth to speak the very same negative thoughts and words stored in his heart. Jesus said..."For out of the abundance (overflow) of the heart, his mouth speaks." Luke 6:45, Amp.
4. The mouth and heart connection works with negative words, the same as it works with positive and godly words. Hence, Zechariah's mouth confession would be, "I am an old man and my wife is well advanced in years and we are too old to have a son." This mouth confession now agrees with the thoughts and words stored up in the heart. Remember that Jesus said, "he shall have whatsoever he saith."
5. Gabriel took positive steps to insure that Zechariah's mouth would not say what was in his heart, which was unbelief. He

made his mouth speechless.

6. Keep in mind that Zechariah was bound speechless for quite a long time, so he had lots of time to rethink what the angel of the Lord had told him. Notice closely what happens after nine months and eight days had passed.

In the latter part of this Scripture, it says that someone asked Zechariah what he would name his son. Zechariah motioned for a writing tablet and wrote, "His name is John." Then immediately his "mouth" was opened and his tongue loosed, and he began to speak, blessing and praising and thanking God.

When Zechariah (over time) filled his heart, believing the Word of God which Gabriel spoke to him, he was then operating in the God kind of belief and faith which pleases God. This resulted in Zechariah's tongue being loosed and he was able to speak again.

In summary, this clearly shows that there is a divine connection between the mouth, the heart, and the harvest, and that faith-building confession activates the connection. In this story, the harvest was the birth of John the Baptist, a forerunner of Jesus who preached baptism of repentance in preparation of the coming of Jesus.

In summary, faith-building confessions work because they uniformly manage what the mouth says. It is a means of sowing incorruptible seed in the heart, which is guaranteed to establish a divine connection and will always yield a harvest in due season. The confessing with the mouth and believing with the heart is the way our Heavenly Father designed His system to work. Remember, "you shall have whatsoever you saith!"

Reason 5. Faith-building confessions work because they are in perfect harmony with the spiritual law governing "faith."

The Bible tells us, "*But, without faith it is impossible to please Him, for he who comes to God must believe that He is, and that He is a rewarder of those who diligently seek Him*" (Hebrews 11:6).

How do you get faith? This Scripture reveals three important truths. To please God, one must:

1. have total faith in God,
2. believe that He is their God, and
3. believe that God rewards all who diligently seek Him.

It seems to me that since faith is what is required to please God, then the $64,000 question is "How do you get faith?"

Spiritual Law Governing Faith

This spiritual law says, "*So then faith comes by hearing, and hearing by the Word of God"* (Romans 10:17).

Notice very closely that this Scripture does not say that faith comes by having heard something once. Instead, the apostle Paul, led by the Holy Spirit put two action verbs together "hearing and hearing" in this short but revealing spiritual law.

Let's take a closer look at the word "comes" which is also an action verb. It means to move toward or arrive at something. Some of the synonyms for the word "comes" are grows, adds up, develops and rises. So then, we could say that faith grows by hearing and hearing...or faith adds up by hearing and hearing...or it could be phrased that faith develops by hearing and hearing...or faith rises by hearing and hearing.

Take a closer look at the word "hearing." The suffix "ing" at the end of the word "hear," means the process or power of perceiving sound (words) in the ear gates. This process of perceiving sound (words) doesn't set limits to the number of times something is heard, but it is a process of perceiving sound (words) on an ongoing basis, without limits, until strong faith has been developed. In other words, the more you hear the Word of God over and over, continuously, the more you are developing stronger faith.

One of the key elements involving faith-building confessions is repetition, which conforms in perfect harmony with the spiritual law governing faith. Hence faith-building confessions work when the believer puts them to work building strong faith and pleasing God.

Reason 6. Faith-building confessions work because the Bible says, "you shall have whatsoever you saith."

Jesus Christ of Nazareth spoke the following words, and since He spoke them, I unequivocally believe what He said...

> *For verily I say unto you, that whosoever shall **say** unto this mountain, be thou removed, and be thou cast into the sea; and shall not doubt in his **heart**, but shall **believe** that those things which he **saith** shall come to pass; he shall have whatsoever he **saith*** (Mark 11:23, KJV).

Jesus reveals in this Scripture the foundation on which this book is based, and that is saying it, believing it, and receiving it. He set forth the divine truth concerning the awesome power of simply saying with the mouth, and believing in the heart, which activates the divine connection between the mouth and heart. It works like this...

A. whoever says to this mountain (of poverty, sickness, trials and tribulations) "Be removed and be cast into the Sea,"

B. and does not doubt in his heart, but <u>believes</u> that these things he <u>says</u> will be done,

C. he shall have whatsoever he saith.

Notice closely with your spiritual eyes that Jesus did not say, "He shall have whatsoever he believeth," No! He said, "He shall have whatsoever he saith."

Those things that you say are your words – your faith-building confessions, and those words that you speak give you power over demons, poverty, sickness, disease, and all negative life circumstances. These are life-defeating mountains that can be removed. The ball is in your court; Jesus said to speak to the mountain and demand that it be removed, cast it into the sea, do not doubt in your heart but believe that the things which you say will come to pass; YOU SHALL HAVE WHATSOEVER YOU SAITH!

In addition, pay close attention to the fact that the word "pray" doesn't appear in this Scripture and the word "believe" only appears once, but the word "say" appears three times, which I believe emphasizes the vast importance of speaking words with the mouth.

Another biblical truth is revealed in this Scripture and that is the divine connection between the **mouth**, the **heart**, and the **harvest**. Items A and B involve the mouth and heart connection and agreement, and item C is the harvest. Praise the Lord!

Again, notice closely with your spiritual eyes that Jesus did not say to pray to God about the mountain, nor did He say to meditate or fast about the mountain. No, He said, "whosoever shall **say** (speak) to the mountain..."

If you desire change in your life, Jesus says to speak words to the situations. Jesus is the author and finisher of our faith (Hebrews 12:2). When He said to speak to the mountains, to not doubt in our hearts, and to believe that we will have whatever we say, He was not teaching a superstitious or hocus-pocus ritual. But instead, He was teaching the reality that what we say with our mouths counts mightily when it is united with faith in our hearts.

It is plain to see why faith-building confessions work; they work because Jesus said, **"you shall have whatsoever you saith**."

<u>Reason 7</u>. Faith-building confessions work because they are spoken under the authority and in the mighty Name of Jesus Christ of Nazareth.

Dr. E.W. Kenyon, wrote in his book, "*The Wonderful Name of Jesus"*... "All power is in the Name of the risen man, Christ Jesus Who is seated at the Father's right hand in the heavens. The power is not in fasting or consecration, not in long prayers, but it is the simple Name of Jesus of Nazareth, the Son of God."

The Name Of Jesus Is Above Every Name

The Bible says...

> *This shows that God's Son is far greater than the angels, just as the name God gave him is far greater than their names. For God never said to any angel what he said to Jesus: "You are my Son. Today I have become your Father." And again God said, "I will be his Father, and he will be my Son."*
> Hebrews 1:4-5, NLT

It is written in the book of Philippians...

> *Because of this, God raised him up to the heights of heaven and gave him a name that is above every other name, so that at the name of Jesus every knee will bow, in heaven and on earth and under the earth, and every tongue will confess that Jesus Christ is Lord, to the glory of God the Father.*
> Philippians 2:9-11, NLT

To further illustrate the awesome supernatural power in the Name of Jesus, I will state a mental exercise I often use when conducting seminars, which highlights "authority versus power." Keep in mind that the Chief Executive Officer (CEO) of a company and the Board of Directors have "power" to make drastic changes in the company's operating policy.

The authority to carry out the company's operating policy is delegated authority issued by the CEO and the Board of Directors to its management and work force. With this in mind, I would ask a specific person in my class the following question...

"John, what do you think would happen if you walked up to the busiest six-way intersection in your city and you saw that the traffic was in a chaotic state with near mishaps because the traffic lights were not working. So you decide to walk out to the middle of the intersection in your Levi jeans and Hawaiian shirt to direct traffic. A red sports car traveling at about 40 mph is fast approaching from a busy eastbound street. John, you see this car coming and you raise your hand for the car to stop. Question, what do you think will happen?"

Well, generally there will be a lot of laughter from everyone, and John normally would say that he would probably be hit by the sports car. Some jokingly would say that John would end up a grease spot!

"With this scenario in mind, let's say that John survives and this time he walks over to the trunk of his car and puts on his city policeman's uniform with his sergeant stripes and badge, puts on his white gloves, his policeman's cap and straps on his gun. Now he walks over to the same intersection, the traffic light is not working, the red sports car is fast approaching. John throws up his hand to signal the sports car to stop. "Question, what do you think will happen?"

Well, generally John and most of the class would agree that the red sports car would stop.

At this point, I would explain that in the first scenario, John was not authorized to direct traffic; no city or state official had given him the authority to direct traffic. Therefore, he took on a task that he was improperly dressed to do and not commissioned to do, and he was void of power.

However, the results drastically changed in favor of John in the second scenario. First, he is duly authorized by the city's traffic department to direct traffic. He is wearing the proper uniform and policeman gear. The uniform represents the "power" that is behind John, namely, the mayor's office, police department, city law department, sheriff's department, state highway patrol, and the state national guard to mention a few.

The word "power" means the ability to "act," and all of the agents mentioned above have the power to "act" to aid John in carrying out his duties. Drivers and pedestrians alike recognize the authority that John has, based on his uniform.

In His Name Is Authority And Power

Jesus Christ of Nazareth has given believers the power of attorney to use His Name. In other words, He has given us legal rights to use His Name. Jesus Himself is in His Name, God the Father and God the Holy Spirit are mighty forces of power behind the Name.

The archangel Michael, and Gabriel, along with God's army of angelic beings are all mighty supernatural forces behind the Name of Jesus. Jesus not only authorizes the use of His Name, but He also supplies the power behind His Name.

Jesus gave all believers power of attorney to use His Name. The following is the language of the power of attorney:

> *You can ask for anything in my name, and I will do it, because the work of the Son brings glory to the Father.* ***Yes, ask anything in my name, and I will do it!*** (John 14:13-14, NLT).

> *Ye have not chosen me, but I have chosen you, and ordained you, that ye should go and bring forth fruit, and that your fruit should remain; that* ***whatsoever ye shall ask of the Father in my name, he may give it to you*** (John 15:16, KJV).

> *And when that time comes, you will ask nothing of Me (you will need to ask Me no questions). I assure you, most solemnly I tell you,*

that ***My Father will grant You whatever you ask in My Name*** *(as presenting all that I AM). Up to this time, you have not asked a (single) thing in My Name (as presenting all that I AM); but now ask and keep on asking and you will receive, so that your joy (gladness, delight) may be full and complete* (John 16:23-24, Amp.).

And these attesting signs will accompany ***those who believe; in My name they will drive out demons;*** *they will speak in new languages; They will pick up serpents and (even) if they drink anything deadly, it will not hurt them;* ***they will lay their hands on the sick, and they will get well*** (Mark 16:17-18, Amp.).

First, I want to clarify a misunderstanding among some. When the Scripture states, *"And these attesting signs will accompany those who believe,"* some people among the faithful have mistakenly thought that this meant those who are called to full-time ministry such as ministers, pastors, priests, etc. But the word "believe" used in this Scripture literally means "the believing ones" – every born-again child of God is a believing one; for God is not a respecter of persons.

The Scriptures which we have just read and discussed, unconditionally establish that the Name of Jesus is above every name and that there is unlimited supernatural power in that Name.

Jesus Delegates Authority And Power

Jesus said...

Behold, I have given you ***authority*** *and* ***power*** *to trample upon serpents and scorpions, and (physical and mental strength and ability) over all the power that the enemy (possesses); and nothing shall in any way harm you (Luke 10:19, Amp.).*

And I will give you the keys of the kingdom of heaven, and whatever you bind on earth will be bound in heaven, and whatever you loose on earth will be loosed in heaven.
Matthew 16:19, NKJV

In conclusion, Jesus gave His name to us that we might carry out the will of the Father in this dispensation in which we are living. Whenever we boldly take our privileges and rights in the new covenant, and pray or say faith-building confessions in Jesus' Name, it passes out of our hands and off our shoulders into Jesus' hands and onto His shoulders.

When you use His Name, He shows up on the scene immediately and He then assumes the responsibility of that prayer or your faith-building confession. And we know that He said, "*Father, I thank you that you have heard me. Yes, I know you always hear and listen to me."* John 11:41-42

In other words, we know that the Father always hears Jesus, and when we pray or say our faith-building confessions in Jesus' Name, it is as though Jesus Himself is doing the praying or confessing – He takes our place! Praise the Lord!

Faith-building confessions work because they are spoken under the authority and in the mighty Name of Jesus Christ of Nazareth. His Name is above all names, and in His Name there is supernatural miracle-working power!

All power is in the Name of the risen man Christ Jesus who is seated at the Father's right hand in the heavens. The power is not in fasting or consecration, not in long prayers but it is in the simple Name of Jesus of Nazareth, the Son of God.

Your covenant inheritance of wealth and riches are in your mouth.

Your future lies in your mouth, open it and speak it out.

You possess what you confess

CHAPTER 11

PART II
TESTIMONIALS

The word "testimony" means the evidence given by a witness, generally a solemn affirmation to establish some fact and, commonly among Christians, the statement of one's Christian experience.

The testimonies which I am about to share with you reflect the authenticity, the benefits, and results of self-talk faith-building confessions. The vast number of my personal testimonials and the testimonials of others which I have recorded over the years were a direct result of faith-building confessions, and are far too numerous and extensive to record in this book.

It is my desire that these testimonies that are shared will ignite your (heart and) spirit and will serve to help build your faith in God's Word and His way of doing things.

The ultimate aim is that you will take on the faith-building confessions prescribed in this book and put them into action, so that you too will have a strong testimony to share with others, and that glorifies God.

Author's Testimonials

During the latter part of 1982, things were going well with me (based on my mind-set at that time). I was back on track spiritually; I had a good job; I was in good health; and I had my own home. I was divorced in 1980, but I was spending quality time with my daughter, Juli. So generally speaking, I was at peace with myself except for four unsettled things in my (heart and) spirit: (1) yearning for a Christian mate; (2) desire to totally remodel my home; (3) desire to change my career; and (4) desire to put God's Word about tithing to the test.

Christian Mate Testimony

In October of 1982, I wrote a faith-building confession on an index card that described the mate that I desired. I was really inspired when I read in the Bible where it said, "It is not good that the man should be alone," and "He who finds a wife finds a good thing, and obtains favor from the Lord." I was overflowing with faith in my heart for a mate!!

I was also excited in my (heart and) spirit when the Scriptures revealed to me that my mate may not be in my city, my state, or my country. I read where Abraham sent his head servant to another country to find a wife for his son Isaac, and likewise, Isaac sent his son Jacob to a distant land to marry one of his uncle's daughters.

My faith-building confession started like this:

I believe in my heart and in my spirit, by faith, that I have received the wife that I desire. The reference Scriptures for my faith-building confession were Mark 11:23-24; Genesis 2:18; and Proverbs 18:22.

Relentlessly, three or more times a day I read aloud my faith-building confession card which detailed my mate's height, weight, size, age range, godly character, and abilities such as a good homemaker, neat and clean, with nice hands and feet. My confession also reminded God of what He had said in His word about my finding a mate.

Whenever possible, I would close my eyes and mix visualization with my confession. I would imagine seeing my wife, with the features I desired. I would paint a mental picture of the two of us having dinner by candlelight at a cozy restaurant. I would feel the emotions when friends, relatives, and others spoke highly about my wife.

I would mentally picture her busy, preparing Sunday dinner and my smelling the pleasing spiced aroma of the food, while I was watching the national football play-offs on TV, and I would feel the joy of it all! Each time I would say my confession, I would rewind to those imaginary delightful scenes.

During this time, I met several interesting ladies, but my spirit and the Holy Spirit would plainly let me know that these ladies were not meant for me.

After four years of saying my confessions, I was introduced to a charming lady who lived in Malaysia, which is five miles across the bridge from Singapore. On July 13, 1988, we were married at Johor Bahru, Malaysia. I got exactly what I confessed for. Praise the Lord!

Immediately after our wedding ceremony, I sat down and wrote another faith-building confession of thanksgiving to God, in which I gave God the praise, the glory, and thanks for honoring my desires for a mate and being faithful to His Word. I read this confession of thanksgiving to God aloud until I felt released in my spirit to stop saying it, which was around three months.

I profoundly believe that my obedience in seeking God first and His way of doing things resulted in my **saying** it, my **believing** it, and my **receiving** it!

In fact, I am not bragging, but my wife is very attractive. God matched our personalities perfectly. My wife is so neat and clean that I have to sometimes hide my pajamas and underclothes to keep her from washing them to death. Her custom is, wear it one time and then wash it. She not only keeps the inside of our home sparkling; she can often be seen washing down the front and back porch and walkways.

I write this with a big smile on my face and with laughter in my heart! But there is a lesson to be learned from this. That is, be careful how specific you are with your request to God, because "you shall have whatsoever you saith."

By now, you may be wondering how God handled my confession for nice hands and feet (another big smile!). Well, my wife often receives pleasing compliments about her hands and especially her feet.

I have a lovely seventeen-year-old step-daughter, and my wife and I are blessed with a five-year-old daughter who is the spark plug of the family. I am a witness that God honors His word when you hold fast to your faith-building confessions!

Length of time for this faith-building confession to manifest tangibly was five years and ten months.

Desire To Totally Remodel Home Testimony

I have heard it said that if you want a brand new car, you should first clean out all the junk and old unused stuff from your garage long before you buy the new car. It's called "make ready."

Well, since I was confessing for a wife, I needed to make ready the house. My home was an exceptional, spacious 3 bedroom, 2.5 bath bi-level located in a well-manicured neighborhood. But I felt that some fixing would enhance its appearance inside and out.

So, at the same time I wrote my confession for a wife, I wrote two faith-building confessions covering all the improvements that I wanted done to the house. I estimated the total cost of this remodel to be about $20,000.

One of my faith-building confessions began like this...I believe in my heart and in my spirit by faith that my kitchen has been totally remodeled, the cabinets are unique (woodgrain) and strikingly attractive, and the lighting is perfect. The new air conditioning system feels great! It makes the whole house comfortable and pleasurable.

My other faith-building confession covered the exterior of the house and it included this...I'm receiving nice compliments from neighbors and others about how good my house looks! I used Mark 11:23-24 as the reference Scripture for my confessions.

I read these two confessions dutifully three, four, or sometimes more each day, along with my other twenty faith-building confessions. On October 1, 1986, everything on my make-ready list (and more) was completed. Praise the Lord!

It was utterly amazing how unexpected money started to come after the first two years of confessing for the improvements on my home. As the money came, I gradually had everything on my make-ready list completed. It was mind-boggling how money came from unimaginable sources. A windfall from an old investment that I thought was defunct and had totally forgotten about. An unexpected (huge) refund check including interest from my mortgage bank resulting from a large (escrow) overpayment ten years before. It literally seemed like windows of heaven were propped open for me and financial blessings were overflowing! Smaller checks in the $100 to $500 range would come to me unexpectedly.

One thing that must be made clear is that I used no money from my income for this remodeling, but the money I used came to me **unexpectedly**, and by this you know that it is God's doing, it is supernatural money.

I am a witness that faith-building confessions work when you hold fast to your confessions without wavering. For He Who promised is faithful and He promised that...you shall have whatsoever you saith! Praise the Lord!

Length of time for this faith-building confession to manifest tangibly – four years.

Career Change Testimony

During the first week in October 1982, when I wrote my faith-building confession for a wife, I also had written one for a career change. The technology in the telephone industry was starting to change from electronics to digital applications; this would require a vast amount of retraining for me and possible relocation from Cleveland to Chicago sometime in the future.

At the time, I had twenty years service with my company, but the combination of my age and service was not enough to consider early retirement. Deep down in my spirit, I felt a strong urge to change careers. The many years of driving to and fro while working in downtown Cleveland, during the many blistering, bone chilling, snowy and icy winter months also figured heavily into this prompting.

As before, I needed to find a Scripture that addressed my desire for a career change. Well, I didn't have to look far at all. "Seek first the kingdom of God and His righteousness, and all these things shall be added to you" came to my mind. I qualified for the first part of this Scripture, and the thing that I needed added to me was a new job. So I used Matthew 6:33 as my reference Scripture for this confession.

The confession started like this...I believe in my (heart and) spirit by faith that I now have a new job with a position in sales, sales training and customer service. In my new position, I am performing above average. My job is close to my home and I really enjoy my work.

At that time, staff personnel got an hour and a half for lunch, so I would eat lunch, and then have a lot of time to read eighteen to twenty different faith-building confession cards.

I would also read my faith-building confession cards while waiting for meetings to start. I took my cards to the barber shop and I would read them in a low tone, just loud enough so that I could hear. And whenever I would have some downtime, I would read my confessions. I always made use of any idle time spent in my bathroom by reading my confessions. I reverently and persistently read my faith-building confession cards aloud morning, noon, at night and other times, when possible.

Most of the time when I was at home, I would close my eyes and mix visualization to my confession and I would see myself standing in front of a group, teaching sales and customer service techniques. And after the class was done, I would read the class critique sheets. And I would feel the emotion and joy that resulted from reading all the positive comments made by the attendees.

On October 1, 1987, I signed papers to accept a lump sum buy-out from Ohio Bell Telephone Company. The company changed its policy and relaxed its age-plus-service requirement for retirement. And it offered, for the first time, the option to elect a lump sum buy-out. Praise the Lord! Hence, I was now qualified for full retirement benefit status.

It seems that this change in company policy to offer attractive retirement and buy-out packages came about because of the company's efforts to downsize its centralized computer operations. I have said that an additional reason for the company's change in policy was that Jesus Christ of Nazareth was sitting on the board of directors retirement policy committee, representing me!

Because of unused vacation days and other paid time, my last day at work was November 1, 1987. On November 14, 1987, I accepted a position as sales development manager with a Sears store located eight minutes from my home; praise the Lord!

Length of time it took for this faith-building confession to manifest tangibly – five years, two months.

Tithing Testimony

It was around the first of October 1982, and I had rededicated my life to Jesus Christ about two months earlier. I was now attending a lively Bible-believing, Bible-teaching, spirit-filled church, Christian Fellowship Center (CFC) in Cleveland, Ohio. I had always attended church from an early age; my mother or other family members always made sure that my brother and I attended church school and participated in children's activities at church.

As a teenager and also during my stay in the United States Army Signal Corps, I would almost always attend weekly church or chapel services. When most of the soldiers would be sleeping on Sunday morning after a long night of partying, I would get up and go to chapel services. Although I was living a worldly lifestyle, I would still go to church.

When I finished my tour of military duty, I then began a civilian worldly lifestyle, but I always managed to get up on Sundays and go to church. Over the years, I had heard a lot about tithing, but within my (heart and) spirit I never thought of tithing in a positive sense. Up to this time (October 1982), I had not looked at tithing as an act of obedience to God with overflowing blessings associated with it.

Now, when I look back, I either did not have ears to hear or the messages on tithing had not been presented in a beneficial way. I have since learned from my retail sales experience that customers buy benefits. If they are considering buying a refrigerator, they want to know what the features are, such as water and ice through the door, and how those features benefit them. As an example, the benefits of the ice and water in the door are: ice at your fingertips, cold water always available, filtered and purified water and ice that provide healthy drinking water for the whole family, all of which are very easy, convenient and time saving; plus these are money-saving benefits. You can throw the night light in as an extra benefit.

I do believe that if tithing had been presented to me (over the years) in a similar manner cited with the benefits of the refrigerator, my attitude about tithing would have been totally different.

The ministry at CFC, under the leadership of Bishop Bill McKinney, taught tithing according to the Bible as a positive act and beneficial to believers. During one of Bishop McKinney's teaching sessions on this subject, he read the following Scripture:

> *Will man rob God? Yet you are robbing me. But you say, 'How are we robbing thee?' In your tithes and offerings. You are cursed with a curse, for you are robbing me; the whole nation of you. Bring the full tithes into the storehouse, that there may be food in my house; and thereby* ***put me to the test****, says the Lord of hosts, if I will not open the windows of heaven for you and pour down for you an overflowing blessing. I will rebuke the devourer for you, so that it will not destroy the fruits of your soil; and your vine in the field shall not fail to bear, says the Lord of hosts* (Malachi 3:8-11, RSV).

When I heard the words "put me to the test," it really got my attention, for here was God saying to me, "Let Me prove to you all the things that I will do for you if you tithe."

Well, with my background being in the areas of research, development and training, a major component of my work over the years involved testing and evaluating telecommunication systems and personnel. Therefore, the words "put me to the test" stuck with me. So when I got home, I was eager to see what my parallel Bible said about this Scripture. The Living Bible used the phrase, "Try it! Let me prove it to you!" And the New International Version said, "Test me in this, says the Lord Almighty."

I was inspired to put God's Word on tithing to the test. So in early October 1982, I wrote a faith-building confession stating that I would start at two percent and increase the amount bi-monthly until I reached twelve percent. I started tithing in this manner, and I kept a log of my tithing. I also wrote a faith-building confession for divine return on my tithes and offerings.

I would diligently and reverently read these confessions three or four times daily along with my other confessions. I would close my eyes and mix visualization to my confession on tithing. I would see myself cheerfully writing out my check for tithes first. Also, I would often imagine seeing the postman handing me a letter, then opening it and seeing a six-figure check, and I would feel the excitement and emotions associated with receiving a large check.

After eight months of saying my confessions and paying my tithes, I began to receive unexpected checks in the mail ranging from $50 to $500. Some of the unexpected money came from American Telephone and Telegraph (AT&T) stock splits. Other checks would come from unimaginable sources. I now call this "unexpected" and "unimaginable" money, supernatural money from God.

Side-Bar – Supernatural Money

Supernatural money is far different from any other kind of money. When you think about it, some money comes from labor and it is called wages or earned money. Sometimes money comes from an insurance policy; when the insured dies, the beneficiary collects what is commonly known as insurance policy money. Money sometimes comes when a relative dies and leaves an inheritance, and this is called inherited money. Money sometimes comes from investments in stocks, bonds, mutual funds or business ventures and this money is generally called return on investment money. Money that comes by way of the lottery, slot machines, a contest, a drawing, or other such means would be called chance money.

My definition of "supernatural" money is that it is special money that God supernaturally gives to His children.

First, supernatural money can not be perceived by the mind or senses beforehand. In other words, if you were expecting a check from an insurance claim, this would not be supernatural money because your mind is already aware that the money is coming. I have found that supernatural money always bypasses the mind or senses.

Secondly, supernatural money could be called surprise money because the recipient does not know that it is coming. Hence, I have found that supernatural money always comes as a surprise, unexpectedly.

Thirdly, supernatural money comes from "unimaginable" sources. In other words, if your mind figures out a source by which money should come from beforehand, then that money is not supernatural money. I have found that supernatural money always comes from sources not fathomed by my mind or senses.

An example of how God provides supernatural money can be found in the New Testament:

> *When they arrived in Capernaum, the collectors of the half shekel (the temple tax) went up to Peter and said, Does not your Teacher pay the half shekel?*
> *He answered, Yes. And when he came home, Jesus spoke to him (about it) first, saying, What do you think Simon? From whom do earthly rulers collect duties or tribute – from their own sons or from others not of their own family?*
> *And when Peter said, From other people not of their own family, Jesus said to him. Then the sons are exempt.*
> *However, in order not to give offense and cause them to stumble (that is, to cause them to judge unfavorably and unjustly) go down to the sea and throw in a hook. Take the first fish that comes up, and when you open its mouth you will find there a shekel. Take it and give it to them to pay the temple tax for Me and for yourself (*Matthew 17:24-27, Amp.).

I believe that you will agree that the mouth of a fish is an "unimaginable" place for money. Not only was the money in the fish's mouth, it was the exact amount needed to pay the temple tax for Jesus and Peter.

Floodgates Of Heaven Broke Loose

Five years and five months from the time I purposed in my (mind and) heart to tithe, and five years and five months from the time that I started confessing the reality of being a cheerful giver and confessing for a divine return on my giving, the floodgates of heaven literally broke loose!

On February 19, 1988, I received a check in the mail (an "unexpected" amount) of over a quarter of a million dollars in lump sum buy-out pay from Ohio Bell Telephone Company. Praise the Lord!

I had purchased AT&T stock for over fifteen years under the company's employer/employee matching stock plan. At the time of the AT&T breakup, I converted most of my stocks to Baby Bell Telephone Company's stock. I was led to convert a large portion to Bell South. These Baby Bell companies were up and running strong.

Right after I had received my lump sum buy-out pay, I learned ("unexpectedly") that some of the Baby Bell's stocks that I was holding had split and others were planning to split. Guess which Baby Bell company was the most aggressive in profits and in stock splits? Well, if you guessed Bell South, you got it right! Looking back now, I could have retired on my Bell South investments alone. This company had at least three or four ("unexpected") hefty stock splits which positioned the company as a premiere performer.

All this positioned me as an unshakable believer in God's Word. I put His Word to the test, and He proved His Word to me in reality. Praise the Lord!

I estimate that my net liquid worth during that time period was close to three quarters of a million dollars.

Length of time for this faith-building confession to manifest tangibly was five years and five months.

Debt-Cancellation Testimony

As you can imagine, I paid an enormous amount of money in federal and state taxes in 1988 due to the lump sum buy-out pay from Ohio Bell. However, the State of Ohio Department of Taxation notified my wife and me two years later that we still owed $5,000 plus $3,000 in penalties and interest.

Well, this didn't set very well with my wife, and I wasn't exactly the usual Mr. Cool, calm and collected. We filed an appeal for the tax finding to be reviewed which took almost a year and, at the same time, the clock was running away with penalties and interest. On January 1, 1992, I wrote a faith-building confession that read like this...

I command in the Name of Jesus Christ that the state tax debt be removed from me and be cast into the sea. I believe in my heart by faith that this debt will leave me and be resolved. Therefore, I am debt free. I confess this in the wonderful Name of Jesus Christ of Nazareth! SO BE IT! (Mark 11:23)

Six years went by and we had filed six appeals, but the tax debt still had not been resolved. In fact, the amount now owing was $15,000 which included their penalties and interest. The state offered, from time to time, a ten percent discount off the amount that we were being billed for. But I held fast to my conviction that the state was incorrectly taxing my lump sum payment. All those years, I continued to read my faith-building confession daily.

On November 11, 1998, I received a letter from the Ohio Attorney General's office, undersigned by the State of Ohio Department of Taxation. This letter was a "Release and Satisfaction of Judgment" notice, and this is what it said:

Release and Satisfaction of Judgment

The above tax judgment having been settled, cancelled and/or satisfied, the same is hereby discharged upon payment of the court costs by the defendant to the Clerk of Courts. The Clerk is hereby authorized to enter satisfaction to the said judgment on the records.

State of Ohio
Department of Taxation
Betty D. Montgomery
Attorney General

1998 was truly a year of jubilee for me! I embarked on writing this book, my family and I relocated to San Diego, and to top it off, I witnessed a supernatural debt cancellation, all in one year, praise the Lord!

This release and satisfaction of judgment (over $15,000) was a supernatural debt cancellation. I didn't pay one penny toward the amount that the state was asking, and until this day I have no idea, how, why, when, or who cancelled this ever-increasing debt. What I do know is that this supernatural debt cancellation was inspired by my Heavenly Father, and I believe that He commissioned one of His angelic beings to go to work on my behalf. To God be the Glory!

Length of time for this faith-building confession to manifest tangibly was five years and eleven months.

I now reflect back on God's Word which says, *"So shall my word be that goes forth from my mouth; it shall not return to me void, but it shall accomplish what I please, and it shall prosper in the things for which I sent it"* (Isaiah 55:11).

There are far too many other testimonies to record in this book. There are many other testimonies of my own personal experiences involving faith-building confessions and the healing of my physical body and supernatural results in other areas of my life. Also, there are many testimonies on how my faith-building confessions on behalf of others have produced astounding results.

Some of the additional testimonies will be posted soon on our website, www.confessaholic.com. This website is under construction and will be functioning as soon as possible for your perusal and edification.

Testimonials – Others

I have been a student of Dr. Frederick K.C. Price's dynamic teaching of God's Word since 1981. I first saw him on his "Ever Increasing Faith Ministries" (EIFM) television program. And since then, I have seldom missed viewing or taping his programs. I have attended his EIFM crusades, fellowshipped at his church in Los Angeles, and I have a sizeable collection of his books and tapes.

On one of Dr. Price's recent telecasts, he announced that in 1986 he started confessing that, "Somebody is going to give me a million dollars. And the million dollars will be a personal gift to me and not to the church, but to me personally!"

He also mentioned that around three years later he and his wife, Betty, began confessing for their house to be paid off.

Dr. Price revealed that after confessing for thirteen years that "Somebody is going to give me a million dollars," it finally came to pass. He said that a group whose name must remain anonymous, gave him a check for one million dollars as a personal gift! When I heard that I said, "Praise the Lord!" He stated that he was using a portion of the money to pay off their house, twenty years early!

There are five key reasons why Dr. Price received the one million dollar gift.

1. He held fast to his confession. He didn't give up after one, three, five, eight, or twelve years.
2. He remained in fellowship with God.
3. His confession was guaranteed because the Bible says, "he shall have whatsoever he saith" (Mark 11:23).
4. He is a consistent tither.
5. He held fast to his confession of divine return on his giving.

Low Self-Esteem And Fear Of Flying Testimony

I'm reminded of Joe, who overcame low self-esteem and a fear of traveling in an airplane by reading a set of confession cards that I shared with him back in 1990. Not only did he gain strong self-esteem, he took the next-level job, broke all sales records, won a company-sponsored free trip to Hawaii for he and his wife. They had a wonderful time in Hawaii and a safe return. Joe carries his faith-confession cards all the time and continues to read them daily. He now enjoys flying and he has an abundance of self-esteem.

Length of time for this faith-building confession to manifest tangibly was four years.

Healing Testimony

I remember a senior citizen couple who were members of the same church I attended. The husband, John, asked me if I would pray for his wife, who was grappling with a lingering physical ailment the doctor was not able to cure. My first question to her was, "Do you believe that God can and will heal you?" She said yes, and then I prayed for her along the lines of James 5:14-15.

When I got home, I wrote out three different faith-building confessions and called John. I read them to him and he wrote them down. His wife began reading the confession cards daily. Several months later, I asked her how things were going. Her face lit up and she began to tell me how well she felt and that all the symptoms were gone! Praise the Lord!

Four or five months went by and I called John to chat, and I asked if his wife was still reading the confession cards. He said that she reads them three or four times a day and sometimes more. He also said that he had started reading the faith-building confession cards also.

Length of time for the faith-building confessions to manifest tangibly was two months.

Christian Mate Testimony

I remember a veteran named Robert who attended Bible classes that I conducted at the Breckville, Ohio, Veteran Medical Center. Robert was a recovering addict, who had put his life back on track. When he heard my testimony about how I confessed for and got the wife I desired, he asked me to give him the confessions so he could start saying them. He said that he wanted to start life over again with a Christian wife.

Well, eight months passed and Robert announced at one of our Bible classes that he was engaged to be married to Brenda, another veteran who also attended our Bible sessions. Both of them were being discharged and were flying to her home, so that he could meet her family and set plans for their wedding. They were married two months later, praise the Lord!

Length of time for the faith-building confession to manifest tangibly was ten months.

The Rich And Famous Pilot Their Destiny With Words And Work

A study of the life of the rich and famous, such as Dale Carnegie, Henry Ford, Sam Walton and Bill Gates, reveals one common denominator among them all. That is, they dreamed, thought about, and spoke about things that were unseen.

They used words to pilot their own destiny. Generally, at an early age, they began to speak about big things and they imagined big things.

When reading the life stories of these rich and famous people, one gets the feeling that their lives were on automatic control with missions to carry out what they each spoke with their mouths.

For instance, at the age of thirteen, Bill Gates was saying to his friends, "Don't you think that someday everybody will have one of these things (computer)? And if they did, couldn't you deliver magazines and newspapers and stuff through them? And I wonder if you could make money doing something like this?" Although Bill was only thirteen, he was starting to use positive words mixed with imaginary results, which have shaped and changed the way we communicate and conduct business. He was also speaking to his own destiny.

Dale Carnegie was a boy in high school who came from a poor, struggling family, but he often dreamed and spoke of one day becoming rich and buying his mother a home. We see these patterns among the rich and famous of using words to pilot their destiny.

For the most part, their natures were positive, very optimistic, and they remained focused on the issues and business at hand. In other words, they didn't dab into things outside of their field. They were not double minded.

There are far too many testimonies to record in this book. All of which amplifies how faith-building confessions brought about victory in the areas of physical healing, relationships, new jobs, bills paid, depression, new homes, and financial prosperity.

Some of these additional testimonies will be posted on our web site at http://www.confessaholic.com for your perusal and edification. This web site is under construction and will be active as soon as possible. It will be interactive, therefore you are encouraged to share your testimony on the web site so that others will see God's work in your life (which results in God getting the glory). And with your testimony, you overcome the adversary (the evil one) and you remain victorious in Jesus Christ!

If the Word of God promises you something or says that something is yours, then you have a right to confess that it's yours.

Confession is affirming something you believe, testifying of something you know, and witnessing for a truth you have embraced.

Let the weak say I'm strong!

CHAPTER 11

PART III
HOW TO WRITE YOUR OWN SELF-TALK FAITH-BUILDING CONFESSION

Jesus Christ of Nazareth said, "It is written, man shall not live by bread alone, but by every word that proceeds from the mouth of God" (Luke 4:4).

I believe that you would agree that Jesus is telling us that to give food to our physical bodies is not enough. We also need to feed our (heart and) spirit with God's Word (faith food) in order to build strong faith and maintain a balanced lifestyle.

One of the key ways to feed your (heart and) spirit is by using effective faith-building confessions.

In this section, we will discuss how to write your own self-talk faith-building confession. There are four essential ingredients to writing an effective faith-building confession.

Ingredient 1. Your faith-building confession must be "personal."

Their is the Scripture that says, *"for verily I say unto you, that whosoever shall say unto this mountain, be thou removed, and be thou cast into the sea; and shall not doubt in his heart, but shall believe that those things which he saith shall come to pass; he shall have whatsoever he saith"* (Mark 11:23). This Scripture is talking about speaking a faith-building confession which primarily is an individual situation. Notice the pronouns in this Scripture: you, his, and he, are all pronouns which mean one person.

Let's say it is your desire to have poverty or sickness removed from you. It is you doing the confession; not someone else confessing for you.

An effective faith-building confession must be "personal." It is not someone else agreeing with "you." When you read aloud your faith-building confessions, it is you who must not doubt in "your" heart, but shall believe that those things which "you" said shall come to pass. No one else can do it for you, it is up to you!

Ingredient 2. Your faith-building confession must be positive.

Avoid negative life-defeating words and statements like "I hope...," "I can't...," "I'll try...," "I'd like to...," "I am trying to...," "I can...," "I'd like to change...," "I expect to..."

Instead, build for yourself strong confessions with words like, "I believe that I have...," "It is mine...," "I have it...," "I possess it...," "I own it...," "It belongs to me...," "I will...," "I am...," "I do...," "It is easy for me..."

Believe And Receive

The Bible tells us to believe in the heart. This word "believe" means to accept as true those things which you say will come to pass. And it means that you are believing that those confessions you read aloud will come to pass because you are taking God at His Word.

As an example, when you read your faith-building confession for your covenant inheritance of wealth and riches, it should begin like this...I believe in my heart and spirit, by faith, that I have received my covenant inheritance of...

When you use the word "believe," you are not saying that you physically have your inheritance. Instead, you are saying "I believe I have it!" And when it becomes tangible, then you can say, "Praise the Lord, I have my covenant inheritance of wealth and riches."

In other words, you believe that you have it, based on God's Word. His Word becomes your evidence, and not your present financial situation. God's Word says..."He shall have whatsoever he saith!"

Therefore, when you write your faith-building confession this way, using the word "believe," it erases any element of you lying. You should hold fast to your confession and belief until God supernaturally manifests your covenant inheritance into reality. Then you should shout with joy, "Praise the Lord! I have my covenant inheritance of wealth and riches!"

Some guidelines to use when writing your confessions are...

A. If your confession requires that God move supernaturally on your behalf, then the word "believe" should be used.

B. If your confession involves a change in your character, your beliefs, your habits or behavior, then use words like; "I purpose...," "I acknowledge...," "I am..." Or "from this point on, I will only speak words that are positive and beneficial to me or to others."

The Bible clearly establishes the use of positive confessions in the Old Testament. It is written, *"Let the weak say I am strong"* (Joel 3:10).

We can easily see that there would be no value for a person who has weak faith to say a confession that affirms weakness. If you want a harvest of strong faith, you must plant seeds of strong faith. Another way of saying this is that our faith-building confessions should be written in a positive manner to provide the solution, the answer, or the results, and not to state the problem or present circumstances.

A faith-building confession for strong faith could start like this...I believe in my heart and spirit, by faith, that I am growing stronger in faith day by day. I am reading my faith-building confessions three or four times each day, and I can see myself speaking and exhibiting stronger faith in God and in His Word! I eagerly look forward to reading my confessions!

Ingredient 3. Your faith-building confession must be "present-tense."

Faith is always now! Present-tense. If it is not expressed in the present tense, it is not faith. It is not a faith-building confession to say I am hoping that I get a raise in pay, soon.

Instead, your confession should state...I believe in my (heart and) spirit by faith, that I have received a generous increase in my pay...

Always state your faith-building confession in the present tense using, "I am...," "It is...," "I have...," "I believe...," "It belongs to me...," It is mine...," etc.

An effective faith-building confession must always be stated in the present tense. And it must be a good confession resulting in gladness and joy.

Ingredient 4. Your faith-building confession must be according to God's will.

In other words, your confession must have some biblical reference; it must absolutely line up with the Word of God (1 John 5:14). You must find a Scripture that agrees with what you are confessing for and then include it when writing your faith-building confession.

For instance, if I needed to replace my home air conditioner system and the estimated cost is $3,000, I would locate the following Scripture which says, *"And my God shall supply all your needs according to His riches in Glory by Christ Jesus"* (Philippians 4:19).

Question. Is my need covered by this Scripture? My answer is yes, it qualifies. My family and I need a whole house air conditioning system that operates properly and produces a comfortable and healthy climate within our home, especially during the hot summer months.

My faith-building confession would read like this...It is written that my God shall supply "all" my needs according to His riches in glory by Christ Jesus. Therefore, I believe in my heart and in my spirit by faith that I have received the $3,000 that I need to install a new air conditioning system in my home, praise the Lord!

An Effective Faith-Building Confession Must Include The Following Elements

Your faith-building confession must be read "aloud, persistently, and reverently."

The harvest that results from persistently and reverently reading aloud your faith-building confessions is not based on man's timing. But it is all done supernaturally, and this part is on God's timing. The Bible instructs believers to hold fast to their confession without wavering, for He Who promised is faithful. We are also encouraged not to grow weary while doing good, for in due season we shall reap if we do not lose heart. It could be said another way and that is, when God is involved delay does not mean denial.

So, you must read your faith-building confession aloud at least three or four times each day persistently until the manifestation and tangibility take place. It is not a matter of whether or not it will take place, it is simply a matter of when. The word "reverently" means to show honor and devotion to something or someone.

I take care of my faith-building cards the same as I do my Bibles. When I read my faith-building confessions, it is done in the same setting as when I read my Bible, quiet and peaceful. The same holds true when I am away from home. I read my faith-building confessions in a reverent manner. In essence, I treat my faith-building confessions the same as I do my prayers, because I am saying the confession under the authority and in the Name of Jesus Christ of Nazareth!

Steps To Writing An Effective Faith-Building Confession

At the beginning of this book, under the section titled "Author's Notes," you were asked to conduct a self-analysis of your life – spiritually, financially, mentally, physically, domestically, and socially. And also to write down those areas where you need to improve.

You will be asked to use the results of your self-analysis exercise shortly. Also, you were asked to complete a "Personal Self-Talk Inventory Worksheet." Please have this worksheet available, as you will use the results to write your faith-building confession.

<u>Step 1</u>

I recommend that you write your faith-building confession on a sheet of paper or type it on computer and, once you have edited and refined it, then transfer it to a 3 X 5 or 4 X 6 index card. I also recommend putting your faith-building confessions on audio cassette tape so that you can listen to it in the morning when you are preparing for the day, or in your car when driving, or while walking or doing other exercises. It can also be transferred to compact disc (CD).

Your faith-building confession should contain all four of the essential ingredients previously discussed. It must be personal, positive, present tense, and it must agree with God's Word. It should also be spoken aloud, persistently, and reverently.

It is imperative that your faith-building confession is written with focus on the result, the answer, the solution, the goal which you desire to achieve, and not the problem or the circumstances.

<u>Step 2</u>

Use action words. Words that create movement like, "I easily...," "I quickly...," "I slowly...," etc. And use words that create feeling such as..."I warmly...," "I lovingly...," "I joyously...," "I eagerly...," etc. The more emotion, the faster the change will take place. And by all means make sure that your confession is written with clear definition, accuracy; citing exact income, exact amount in things, in sizes, in money, etc.

In other words, if you desire a new car, your faith-building confession should not read like this...I believe that I have the money I need to buy the car that I want. Instead, your confession should read...I believe in my heart and in my spirit, by faith, that I have received the $28,000 to buy the car that I need and desire.

The focus here is to be specific when it comes to dollar amounts. Somewhat like when the waiter asks you, "What will you have?" You don't say, "Bring me some food"; if you did, he would probably say, "Can you be a little more specific?"

<u>Step 3</u>

Do not set time limits. The time for your harvest is God's part and He does things supernaturally in His own time. Remember your part is to confess, believe, and receive. God's part you cannot do, and your part He will not do.

Setting time limits for confessions to manifest is a deadly trap, because man's timing and God's timing are totally different. We see so-called believers setting doomsday dates for Jesus' return (man's timing) and when the date passes without Jesus returning, they go to other extremes such as suicide and genocide.

I encourage you to do your part and let God supernaturally provide your harvest in His timing. It may not be when you want it, but I guarantee that it will be right on time!

<u>Step 4</u>

Visualize the results desired. After reading your confession, imagine the results, the desired change, as having already taken place. Make your words paint a picture. Use words that describe color, size, looks, and pleasurable things.

As an example...I believe in my heart and in my spirit by faith that I now own a beautiful white, four bedroom home! It is fully paid for and fully insured! It is ultra-modern with a breath-taking view of the bay and its pretty blue waters!

<u>Step 5</u>

Now take a look at your self-analysis sheet and, for the sake of this exercise, let's say you selected "spiritually" as an area that you desire to improve.

I am going to share with you my own personal faith-building confession for spiritual growth.

Dear Heavenly Father, I purpose in my heart and in my spirit that in 1999, my faith will grow stronger. I am determined that my knowledge of Your Word will grow. I enjoy studying your Word and reading my confessions at least three times a day. Therefore, my faith is stronger and I am growing and developing spiritually day by day. I confess this under the authority and in the mighty Name of Jesus Christ of Nazareth! SO BE IT.

Reference Scripture: 2 Timothy 2:15

Notice that this faith-building confession contains four of the essential ingredients needed to write an effective confession.

Personal – I purpose in my heart.

Positive – My faith is stronger.

Present tense - I enjoy reading my confessions at least three times a day.

According to God's Will – I enjoy studying your Word...I am growing and developing spiritually day by day.

Always include the date you start saying your faith-building confessions on the card. And always speak your confessions in the Name of Jesus Christ of Nazareth, and show the Scripture reference on the card.

When your faith-building confession manifests tangibly, then write the date on the card that it becomes tangible or fulfilled.

Then you should write a faith-building confession of thanksgiving to God for fulfilling your confession. This confession should be said persistently until you feel a release in your spirit to stop confessing it.

Next, practice writing a faith-building confession for those areas which you identified on your self-analysis sheet as needing improvement.

Personal Self-Talk Inventory Worksheet

Now, look at your Personal Self-Talk Inventory Worksheet which probably has quite a few negative, life-defeating statements on it.

1. Your goal is to stop using negative, life-defeating words.
2. Find a Scripture that gives instructions on negative, idle, worthless, life-defeating words.
3. Review the method prescribed in Chapter 3 on how to shut off your uncontrollable, negative self-talk. (Stop using negative words.)
4. Practice writing a faith-building confession using the four essential ingredients and the five steps to writing an effective faith-building confession.

Sound Advice

Try to keep the number of words in each faith-building confession to a minimum. Make each word count. If a confession has too many words, you may want to break it up and make two confessions.

I suggest that you start out reading (aloud) around fifteen or less confessions daily, and then gradually add more. It should be a joy to read your confessions and not a burden.

Example of three confessions about sickness:

<u>The Word of God</u>

The Word of God declares, *"By His stripes, ye were healed."*

<u>The Pain</u>

There is the confession of pain in the body, and that pain declares that the body it is not healed. The pain is severe and the sick person can hear nothing but pain.

<u>The Sick One</u>

The sick one declares (confesses), "By His stripes, I believe I am healed," which places his confession alongside of the Word of God.

Your confession must absolutely agree with the Word of God, and when confessed in the Name of Jesus, you are to hold fast to your confession. Beware that it is easy to destroy the effect of your faith-building confession by speaking negative, life-defeating words.

Essential Fact

Faith-building confessions should be spoken with the mouth, out loud, at least in conversational tones. However, when I am in a public place such as the barber shop, I will read my confessions at a lower tone, just loud enough for my ear gates to hear and to not disturb others.

Monthly Confessaholic Contest

We eat food because it provides the essential nutrients that the body needs for growth, development, and energy. The same holds true for faith-building confessions. They provide the essential nutrients that the (heart and) spirit need for growth, development, and a dominate position in the life of a believer. Faith-building confessions are faith food to feed your human spirit.

I have come to the point where I crave and thoroughly enjoy reading my faith-building confessions. I crave them with greater passion than food!

The Psalmist has this to say about the Word of God...*"How sweet are thy words to my taste, sweeter than honey to my mouth"* Psalm 119:103. Jeremiah, the prophet, wrote *"When your words came, I ate them; they were my joy and my heart's delight, for I bear your name, O Lord God Almighty"* (Jeremiah 15:16).

In 1996, I started a Confessaholic Contest between my wife and myself. Whoever said the most faith-building confessions each month got five dollars, which added some excitement and competition. Well, the five dollars has now increased to sixty dollars per month.

In 1999, my wife and I read aloud about 37,200 confessions which averages to around fifty-one confessions for her per day, and fifty-one for me. And it took less than one hour per day for each of us to complete our fifty-one confessions. I would read five or ten in the morning, another fifteen or twenty throughout the day, and the remainder in the evening. She generally read hers in the evening.

Currently, my wife has twenty-three faith-building confessions that she says on an average of three times each day, and I have thirty-eight that I am saying. By the way, my wife was the Confessaholic Contest winner most of the time in 1999.

We have seen some astounding results, big and small; spiritually, financially, physically, and materially in our family as a direct result of holding fast to our faith-building confessions.

You Have A Stump Lot In You

For everyone who has read this book up to this point, I applaud you now in advance, for becoming a persistent confessaholic!

I exhort you to take control of the helm of your mouth and become the pilot of your destiny! Know that you have a stump lot in you!

A father was dying. He had two sons. The boys had always felt that the father had gold hidden away somewhere. He had never been a strong, healthy man so his farm was not properly developed. Back of the house there were ten acres of stump land. When he

was dying, he said, "The stump lot." Again and again he said, "The stump lot."

As soon as the funeral was over the boys said, "The gold is out in the stump lot." How feverishly they worked. They tore up every inch of it. But they found no gold. Then the older one said, "We have the land in good condition, let's put in corn." In the autumn they found, in the ripened corn, the gold.

You have a stump lot in you. Dig it up, clean it up, and you will find the gold in it.

I call upon you to get rid of the negative, life-defeating words that are unproductive and satanically inspired. Develop a passion for building strong faith in God and in His living Word! Start planting incorruptible faith-building confession seeds in your stump lot and know that in due season, your harvest, your covenant inheritance of wealth and riches shall come to pass!

Because Jesus Christ of Nazareth said..."You shall have whatsoever you saith!"

CONCLUSION

Jesus Christ of Nazareth said to the people who believed in Him..."*You are truly my disciples if you keep obeying my teaching. And you will know the truth, and the truth will set you free*" (John 8:31-32).

Self-Talk And Grow Rich's purpose is to reveal biblical truths that will set you free from financial bondage of living from pay check to pay check. It provides the principles and techniques which will increase your faith and move you to a life of royalty status with abundance in wealth and riches and the good health to enjoy them.

Throughout the pages of this book, the focus has been to inform you that born-again believers already have a heavenly bank account which contains their covenant inheritance of wealth and riches. If you follow the principles and techniques prescribed in this book, you will strengthen your faith; and strong faith is required to make withdrawals from your heavenly bank account. Hence, believers should live above life's circumstances as an overcomer, victorious and prosperous in every area of life; because we are blessed, to be a blessing to the Kingdom of God and to others. All of our needs and desires should be met.

Frederick K.C. Price, Ph.D., had this to say in his book titled *The Way, The Walk, And The Warfare Of The Believer*,

"I can imagine how embarrassed Jesus must be when He sees His blood-bought, blood-washed, redeemed people resorting to rummage sales, barbecue dinners, and bake sales in order to raise money to finance the work of the Kingdom, while the cattle on a thousand hills belong to Him, the hills on which the cattle graze belong to Him, and the grass that the cattle eat on those hills belongs to Him. Jesus is there in a city with streets made of gold; and yet, His people are down here begging. What an embarrassment that must be to Him!"

In Chapter One of *Self-Talk And Grow Rich*, there are six key reasons given why God wants you to be rich! And one of the reasons is so that you will be willing and obedient to pay your tithes and share offerings to help support the work of the Kingdom. Tithes and offerings are God's prescribed method for supporting the work of His storehouse, the local church.

I have not found any place in the Bible that mentions rummage sales, barbecue dinners, bake sales or bingo games as a means to raise money to finance the work of the Kingdom.

Chapter One and Chapter Eleven reveal the supernatural blessings and benefits that result from being a faithful tither and a cheerful giver of offerings.

Dr. Leroy Thompson, Sr., had this to say in his book titled, *Money Cometh! To the Body of Christ,*

"Financial prosperity is the divine right of every Christian. In fact, it's more than a divine right. It's a divine obligation! God wants to prosper you, not only to bless you and your family, but also to fund the work of the gospel throughout the world.

"God doesn't want you to have financial pressure. He wants you to have financial power. What's the difference between financial pressure and financial power? Financial pressure means you're in debt, in distress, and you're discouraged. Financial power means you're free from debt. You've got a savings account, and you're looking for somebody to bless!"

Beyond any reasonable doubt, *Self-Talk And Grow Rich* clearly establishes, by using biblical Scriptures in Chapter One and throughout the pages of this book, that our God is a God of prosperity and not a God of poverty. Jesus said, *"Keep obeying My teaching, and you will know the truth, and the truth will set you free!"* This certainly includes freedom from financial pressure and lack.

The faith-building confessions prescribed throughout this book are scripturally based, and if you apply them as prescribed, you will reap a harvest in due season if you do not give up. You will have financial power! It's a spiritual law..."you shall have whatsoever you saith!"

Rev. Ray Gene Wilson had this to say in his book titled, *What You Don't Know Can Hurt You,*

"The first and most important thing we have to do to begin walking in the abundance that God intended for us to walk in is to change the words that come out of our mouths. Yes, that's right. Biblical prosperity begins in your mouth. Healing begins, not in your body, but in your mouth with the words that you say."

Rev. Wilson's statement echoes a truth that is the foundation for *Self-Talk And Grow Rich*; namely, that there is supernatural power in the words that we speak, and we shall have whatsoever we saith, be it negative or positive. It's the way God has designed His system to work.

Rev. Kenneth Copeland had this to say in his booklet titled, *How To Discipline Your Flesh,*

"Your tongue is the rudder of your life. It determines your course, and no matter how hard you try to stop it, it is eventually going to start repeating those thoughts you've been entertaining in your mind."

Self-Talk And Grow Rich devotes a goodly amount of instructional inscriptions on how to change negative, life-defeating words to positive (controlled or managed) self-talk and speech. This vital subject is covered in Chapters Three and Four.

The Bible tells us that, *"Where there is no vision, the people perish."* Proverbs 29:18.

Self-Talk And Grow Rich is a forerunner in its revolutionary approach to managed self-talk, using God's Word and the Name of Jesus applied to a particular situation to bring about results. It's believing that what you confess is already done in the spirit realm. It's visualizing the results, the solution, or the manifestation long before it occurs. In other words, it is confessing and believing in things unseen as though they were seen. It is a godly principle to call those things which be not as though they were. Romans 4:17

The faith-building confessions prescribed in this book are powerful vision setters, and a guaranteed way to achieve your destiny and accomplish your dreams. Most of God's promises set forth in *Self-Talk And Grow Rich* are conditional, which simply means you have a responsibility to do something first, and if you do your part, then God will supernaturally do His part.

Throughout the pages of *Self-Talk And Grow Rich*, this is amplified...to benefit from the things of God we must know God's Word, speak God's Word, believe God's Word, and do His Word. These responsibilities are on the believer. In other words, the ball is in the believer's court to act.

Self-Talk And Grow Rich relentlessly emphasizes the power of words. God used words to create the universe. Jesus used words to raise the dead and He overcame Satan by speaking words.

God's Word is the believer's sword to be used daily on the battlefield of life against Satan and evil forces. Like Jesus, you too can be a winner on the battlefield of life. Set your goals to become a persistent faith-building confessaholic!

As the sun set on the twentieth century, there was much talk by President Bill Clinton, emphasizing the need to bridge the so-called "digital divide" between the nation's affluent and the needful. This divide is between the "haves" who can afford the computers, software, hardware, and internet connections, and the "have nots" who cannot afford it.

The administration proposed $2 billion in tax incentives and $380 million in funding over the next 10 years, for programs aimed at alleviating access concerns. Some of these programs will provide low-cost telephone and internet access to rural and impoverished areas. High-tech businesses have pledged millions of dollars in products, services, and training in response to his call.

These all-out initiatives on the part of the administration and the business sector to close the gap between the haves and the have nots is an effort to extend internet access to schools, rural communities, and low-income neighborhoods. I applaud their efforts.

Self-Talk And Grow Rich sounds an alarm and amplifies a call to believers to close the "wealth divide." This vast divide is between the nation's "non-believing wealthy" and the vast numbers of "believers who are broke, impoverished, or living from pay check to pay check."

The initiatives and the action required to bridge this wealth divide are outlined in this book in a clear, concise, and easy-to-follow format with supporting biblical principles and techniques.

The Bible tells us that, *"Men prepare a meal for enjoyment and wine makes life merry, but* ***money answers everything****"* (Ecclesiastes 10:19).

It takes money to put food on the table for you and your family to eat. It takes money to buy a house for shelter for you and your family. It takes money to buy a safe and reliable automobile for transportation, and it costs money to pay for the required automobile insurance coverage needed to operate your vehicle. It costs money for your family's health and life insurance coverage. It costs money to send children to elementary and high school, and it costs big money to send your children to a private school or college.

It costs mega bucks to seek and to save the lost, and it costs money to operate and maintain God's storehouse (the local church).

Well, I could go on, but I believe that you can see why the Bible says that money answers everything. It takes money and plenty of it, to live an abundant and prosperous life and to financially support the work of the Kingdom. Remember, it is the believer's responsibility to support the work of God's Kingdom. It is not the responsibility of the heathen.

For those who have carefully read aloud and studied the pages of *Self-Talk And Grow Rich*, you have just stepped into the supernatural faith gymnasium. Now begin to exercise your faith-building confessions, which will build strong faith and cause your covenant inheritance of wealth and riches to overtake you. Set your goals to be a financial blessing to the Kingdom of God, to the poor and needy, and to leave an inheritance to your children and your children's children.

Before closing, I must share these vital biblical precepts. Whenever possible, strive to give anonymously (Matthew 6:1-4).

Do hold fast to your confession without wavering, for He is faithful that promised. Jesus Christ of Nazareth promised that you shall have whatsoever you saith!

Finally, it is written, *"Blessed is he who reads aloud the words of the prophecy, and blessed are those who hear, and who keep what is written therein; for the time is near"* (Revelation 1:3).

May God's grace be with you!

CHAPTER 12

SELF-TALK FAITH-BUILDING CONFESSIONS TO GAIN FINANCIAL PROSPERITY

To help gain financial prosperity, read one or more of these faith-building confessions aloud at least three times a day; before meals, at bedtime, and upon awakening in the morning, and throughout the day when possible. Use visualization with each faith-building confession to create a picture-perfect image of the end result you desire, then feel the glad emotions of achieving your goal.

1. I speak God's Word. It NEVER returns to Him void. It ALWAYS accomplishes what He pleases. He desires that I prosper and be in health even as my soul prospers. My soul is prospering. Therefore, I am prospering financially and I'm in good health! Hallelujah! I confess this with my mouth under the authority and in the wonderful Name of Jesus Christ of Nazareth! SO BE IT! (Isaiah 55:11; 3 John 2; John 14: 13,14)

2. With what measure I mete, it is measured unto me; I sow bountifully, therefore I reap bountifully. I give cheerfully, and My God generously provides all my needs. I believe that I always have everything I need and plenty left over to share with others. I confess this aloud under the authority and in the mighty Name of Jesus Christ of Nazareth! SO BE IT! 2 Corinthians 9:6-8; John 14:13,14

3. I call those things that be not as though they were. Therefore, there is no lack in my life financially, for my God supplies all of my needs according to His riches in glory by Christ Jesus. I confess this aloud under the authority and in the mighty Name of Jesus Christ of Nazareth! SO BE IT! Philippians 4:19; John 14:13,14

4. My Lord is my shepherd and I DO NOT WANT because Jesus was made poor that I, through His poverty might be rich (financially). For He came that I might have life and have it

more abundantly. I confess this with my mouth under the authority and in the wonderful Name of Jesus Christ of Nazareth! SO BE IT! (Psalm 23:1; 2 Corinthians 8:9; John 10:10; John 14:13, 14).

5. And I, having received the gift of righteousness do reign as a king/queen in this life by Jesus Christ. I'm a member of the royal family. I'm abundantly blessed to be a blessing to others. I confess this with my mouth under the authority and in the wonderful Name of Jesus Christ of Nazareth! SO BE IT! (Romans 5:17; 1 Peter 2:9; John 14:13,14)

6. My Lord has pleasure in the prosperity of His servant, and Abraham's blessings are mine. I'm blessed with wealth and riches and good health. Praise the Lord! I confess this aloud under the authority and in the mighty Name of Jesus Christ of Nazareth! SO BE IT! (Psalm 35:27; Galatians 3:14; John 14:13, 14)

7. Christ Jesus of Nazareth has redeemed me from the curse of the law; for poverty He has given me wealth. I'm smiling because I'm joyous! I believe in my heart and in my spirit by faith, that I'm richly blessed to be a blessing to others. I confess this under authority and in the mighty Name of Jesus Christ of Nazareth! SO BE IT! (Galatians 3:13; John 14:13,14; Galatians 4:5)

8. I delight myself in the Lord and He gives me the desires of my heart. My desire is to be a consistent blessing to God's storehouse (my local church) and to the poor and needy. I confess this aloud under the authority and in the mighty Name of Jesus Christ of Nazareth! SO BE IT! (John 14:13,14; Mark 11:24; Psalm 37:4)

9. I have given (bountifully) and it is given unto me good measure, pressed down, shaken together, running over, shall men give unto my bosom. I confess this with my mouth under the authority and in the wonderful Name of Jesus Christ of Nazareth! SO BE IT! (Luke 6:38; John 14:13,14)

FAITH-BUILDING CONFESSIONS FOR DIVINE HEALTH

To help achieve good health and healing, read one or more of these faith-building confessions aloud at least three times a day; before meals, at bedtime and upon awakening in the morning, and throughout the day when possible. Use visualization with each faith-building confession to create a picture-perfect image of the end result you desire, then feel the glad emotions of achieving your goal.

1. I pay close attention to God's Word; I listen to what He says. I keep reading and confessing His Word and I keep it in the midst of my heart because His Words are life and health to my body. I confess this aloud under the authority and in the mighty Name of Jesus Christ of Nazareth! SO BE IT! Proverbs 4:20-22; John 14:13,14

2. I serve the Lord my God and He blesses my bread and my water; He takes sickness away from the midst of me. There is nothing barren in my land and the number of my days He will fulfill. I confess this with my mouth under the authority and in the wonderful Name of Jesus Christ of Nazareth! SO BE IT! (Exodus 23:25,26; John 14:13,14)

3. No harm comes near me, no evil befalls me and no plague or calamity comes near my dwelling. My Lord gives His angels charge over me to keep me in all my ways. I'm protected! I confess this with my mouth under the authority and in the majestic Name of Jesus Christ of Nazareth! SO BE IT! Psalm 91:10,11; John 14:13,14

4. I speak God's Word. It never returns to Him void. It always accomplishes what He pleases. He desires that I prosper and be in good health even as my soul prospers. My soul is prospering. Therefore, I am prospering financially and I'm in good health. Praise the Lord! I confess this aloud under the authority and in the mighty Name of Jesus Christ of Nazareth! SO BE IT! (Isaiah 55:11; 3 John 2; John 14:13,14)

5. I have the nature of God in me. I cannot be conquered. I give no place to sickness or disease. I cannot be whipped. No matter what the appearances may be, I am a victor. I am an overcomer. I am bound to come out on top, because "greater is He that is in me than he that is in the world." I confess this with my mouth under the authority and in the wonderful Name of Jesus Christ of Nazareth! SO BE IT!
   Romans 8:37; I John 4:4; John 14:13,14

6. For your part, Lord, may Your kindness, Your love, Your faithfulness, and Your protection from sickness and disease constantly preserve me. I confess this with my mouth under the authority and in the majestic Name of Jesus Christ of Nazareth! SO BE IT! (Psalm 40:11; John 14:13,14)

7. Dear Heavenly Father, I resist the devil in every form that he uses to come against me, and he flees from me. I require my mind, soul and body to be strong and healthy and I enforce it with Your Word. I reject sickness and disease, for my body is the temple of God and I enforce life in this body. I do get great pleasure in serving my Lord and He gives me the desires of my heart. My desire is to be a strong, healthy soldier in my God's army. I believe that I walk in divine health. I believe in my spirit, by faith, that I am set free, delivered, and healed in the mighty Name of Jesus Christ of Nazareth. SO BE IT!
   1 Corinthians 6:19; Romans 6:11; 2 Corinthians 5:21; John 4:4; Revelation 12:11; Psalm 37:4; John 14:13,14

8. No evil shall befall me or my household, for the Word of God says, "Lo, I am with you always; to the close of the age!" My Lord never leaves me, nor forsakes me. I believe that I walk in divine health. Praise the Lord! I confess this aloud under the authority and in the mighty Name of Jesus Christ of Nazareth! SO BE IT! (Matthew 28:20; John 14:13,14)

FAITH-BUILDING CONFESSIONS FOR DIVINE HEALING

1. I am righteous and my Lord delivers me out of all afflictions. I confess this aloud under the authority and in the mighty Name of Jesus Christ of Nazareth! SO BE IT!
   Psalm 34:19; John 14:13,14

2. I know in my spirit, by faith, that Jesus bore all my sickness and all my disease in His body for me! Therefore, by Jesus' stripes and the wounds in His body, I am healed and made whole, praise the Lord! I speak this confession for divine healing under the authority and in the mighty Name of Jesus Christ of Nazareth. SO BE IT!
   Matthew 8:17; I Peter 2:24; John 14:13,14
3. It is written, these signs shall follow them that believe. They shall lay hands on the sick, and they shall recover. I laid hands on myself and I believe in my heart and spirit, by faith, that I have recovered. I confess this with my mouth under the authority and in the majestic Name of Jesus Christ of Nazareth! SO BE IT! (Mark 16:17,18; John 14:13,14)

4. My Lord provides a backup plan for my divine healing. It is written, "Is any sick among you? Let him call for the elders of the church, and let them pray over him, anointing him with oil in the name of the Lord. And the prayer of faith shall save the sick, and the Lord shall raise him up, and if he have committed sins, they shall be forgiven him." Praise the Lord! I confess this with my mouth under the authority and in the wonderful Name of Jesus Christ of Nazareth! SO BE IT! I have been obedient to Your Word. I called upon the elders of my church for prayer, and I believe I am healed.
   James 5:14, 15; John 14:13,14

5. He sent His Word and healed them, and I believe in my heart and spirit by faith, that His Word has healed me. Hallelujah! I confess this with my mouth under the authority and in the majestic Name of Jesus Christ of Nazareth! SO BE IT!
   Psalm 107:20; John 14:13,14

6. I bless You, Lord, O my soul. I forget not all Your benefits. You forgive all my iniquities; You heal all my diseases; You redeem my life from all destruction. I believe in my heart by faith, that I am divinely healed. I confess this with my mouth under the authority and in the mighty Name of Jesus Christ of Nazareth! SO BE IT! (Psalm 103:2-4; John 14:13,14)

7. My Bible says "Confess your faults one to another, and pray one for another, that ye may be healed." As I'm led by the Holy Spirit, I do confess my faults to another and I do pray for others and myself for divine healing. I know that healing is mine. I confess this with my mouth under the authority and in the majestic Name of Jesus Christ of Nazareth! SO BE IT! James 5:16; John 14:13,14

8. With His stripes, I am healed. I confess this aloud under the authority and in the mighty Name of Jesus Christ of Nazareth! SO BE IT! (Isaiah 53:5; John 14:13,14)

9. He Himself took my infirmities and bare my sicknesses. Therefore, I believe that I am healed and made whole, praise the Lord! I confess this aloud under the authority and in the mighty Name of Jesus Christ of Nazareth! SO BE IT! Matthew 8:17; John 14:13,14

10. I believe I am healed today! I am filled with the love of God today! I am filled with the joy of the Lord today! I am filled with the peace of God today! I am filled with the wisdom of God today! I am filled with the Holy Spirit today! These are mine TODAY!! I confess this with my mouth, under the authority and in the majestic Name of Jesus Christ of Nazareth! SO BE IT! (John 16:24; John 14:13,14)

11. My God says, "I am the Lord that healeth thee." When my God speaks, I believe it and that settles it! I believe I'm healed. I confess this with my mouth under the authority and in the wonderful Name of Jesus Christ of Nazareth! SO BE IT! (Exodus 15:26; John 14:13,14)

SELF-TALK FAITH-BUILDING CONFESSIONS TO PREVENT AND OVERCOME STRESS

To help overcome stress, read one or more of these faith-building confessions aloud at least three times a day; before meals, at bedtime, and upon awakening in the morning, and throughout the day when possible. Use visualization with each faith-building confession to create a picture-perfect image of the end result you desire, then feel the glad emotions of achieving your goal.

1. I resist stress by making my mind, my heart, my body and mouth stay cool, calm, and free from rage. I possess daily strength and I have abundance of peace because I give all worries and cares to my God, for He cares about what happens to me! I confess this with my mouth, under the authority and in the majestic Name of Jesus Christ of Nazareth! SO BE IT!
   Psalm 29:1; 1 Peter 5:7; John 14:13,14

2. I am fully aware that stress adversely affects my nervous system and my digestive and intestinal system. I am also fully aware that my body is the temple of the Holy Spirit. Therefore, I resist stress by making my mind and body stay relaxed and under control at all times. I let the peace of God rule in my heart, and I refuse to worry about anything! I speak these words under the authority and in the matchless Name of Jesus Christ of Nazareth! SO BE IT!
   1 Corinthians 6:19; Colossians 3:15; John 14:13,14

3. My body is the temple of the Holy Spirit. Therefore, I eat the proper food, because I know that a good diet will give me the strength I need to keep my nervous system and immune system in great shape, and this helps me to overcome stress. I consistently work at maintaining God's temple. I confess this aloud under the authority and in the mighty Name of Jesus Christ of Nazareth! SO BE IT!
   1 Corinthians 6:19; John 14:13,14

4. I am fully aware and I understand this, that in the last days

there will come times of stress. But I stay prepared and I resist stress at every turn, for "I am more than a conqueror through Christ who loves me." I speak these words under the authority and in the matchless Name of Jesus Christ of Nazareth! SO BE IT! (2 Timothy 3:1, RSV; Romans 8:37; John 14:13,14)

5. When pressure and stress bear down on me, I find joy in your command which says, "Greater is He that is within me, than he that is in the world." I constantly acknowledge that the greater One is inside me. The greater One has control of me and He is far greater than the enemy in this world.
   How dominant this makes me. I overcome every adverse circumstance, every problem, and all anxieties, because the greater One lives within me! I confess this aloud under the authority and in the mighty Name of Jesus Christ of Nazareth. SO BE IT! (1 John 4:4; John 14:13,14)

6. I know that stress can cause cancer, high blood pressure, ulcers and pancreatic disease, among others. I, therefore, constantly work at managing my time to avoid rushing, rage, and other stressful situations. Stress is a missile of the evil one, but I am an overcomer; making the very most of time because the days are evil. But I remain stress free through Jesus Christ of Nazareth. I confess this aloud under the authority and in the mighty Name of Jesus Christ of Nazareth! SO BE IT! (Ephesians 5:16; John 14:13,14)

7. I make my recreated human spirit control my mind and body. Therefore, I make my mind and body obey. I resist stress because I enjoy relaxing; and I live a quiet and peaceful life in all godliness and dignity, free of stress! I confess this with my mouth, under the authority and in the majestic Name of Jesus Christ of Nazareth! SO BE IT!!
   1 Timothy 2:2; John 14:13,14

SELF-TALK FAITH-BUILDING CONFESSIONS TO HELP MANAGE SELF-CONTROL OVER ANGER, BITTERNESS, AND EVIL THOUGHTS

To help overcome anger, bitterness, and evil thoughts, read one or more of these faith-building confessions aloud at least three times a day; before meals, at bedtime, and upon awakening in the morning, and throughout the day when possible. Use visualization with each faith-building confession to create a picture-perfect image of the end result you desire, then feel the glad emotions of achieving your goal.

1. I do not grieve the Holy Spirit because I put all bitterness, wrath, anger, evil speaking and malice far from me. I speak these words under the authority and in the matchless Name of Jesus Christ of Nazareth! SO BE IT!
   Ephesians 4:30,31; John 14:13,14

2. Athletes exercise self-control in all things; they do it to receive a perishable wreath, a gold medal or a championship ring. I am a believer and I choose to exercise self-control over anger, anxiety, bitterness, strife and evil thoughts because in doing so I please my Heavenly Father! And I receive great earthly and eternal rewards. I confess this with my mouth under the authority and in the wonderful Name of Jesus Christ of Nazareth! SO BE IT!
   1 Corinthians 9:25; Hebrews 11:6; John 14:13,14

3. I refuse to let anger and bitterness contaminate my (mind and) heart. It is written that knowing God leads to self-control. Self-control leads to patient endurance and patient endurance leads to godliness. I choose to live a life of love and godliness. I confess this aloud under the authority and in the mighty Name of Jesus Christ of Nazareth! SO BE IT!
   2 Peter 1:6,7; John 14:13,14

4. I do all things through Christ Who strengthens me. I love my

enemies. I bless those who curse me. I do good to those who hate me, and I pray for those who spitefully use me and persecute me! I am a doer of the Word. I confess this with my mouth, under the authority and in the majestic Name of Jesus Christ of Nazareth! SO BE IT!
Matthew 5:44; John 14:13,14

5. My Bible says "A person without self-control is as defenseless as a city with broken down walls." I fully understand that anger, bitterness, anxiety, and evil thoughts leave a believer defenseless, and open prey for Satan's attacks. I put anger, bitterness, anxiety and evil thoughts under my feet, and I remain victorious in Jesus Christ! I confess this with my mouth, under the authority and in the wonderful Name of Jesus Christ of Nazareth! SO BE IT!
Proverbs 25:28; John 14:13,14

6. I am obedient to God's Word. I am not anxious about anything. I have put off the old nature, but in everything, by prayer and supplication with thanksgiving, I let my requests be made known to God. I know that the peace of God which surpasses all understanding, guards my mind and heart through Christ Jesus, and I'm free of anxiety. I confess this with my mouth, under the authority and in the majestic Name of Jesus Christ of Nazareth! SO BE IT!
Philippians 4:6-7; John 14:13,14

7. My Bible says, "The spirit that God has given me does not make me timid." Instead, His Spirit fills me with power, love and self-control over hatred, anger, bitterness, evil thoughts and evil actions. I confess this aloud under the authority and in the mighty Name of Jesus Christ of Nazareth! SO BE IT!
2 Timothy 1:7; John 14:13,14

8. I obey God's Word. I let all bitterness, and wrath, and anger, and clamor, and evil speaking be put away from me with all malice. I practice loving my neighbor and my fellowman as I do myself. I confess this aloud under the authority and in the mighty Name of Jesus Christ of Nazareth! SO BE IT!
Ephesians 4:31; Romans 13:9; John 14:13,14

SELF-TALK FAITH-BUILDING CONFESSIONS TO HELP OVERCOME FEAR

To help overcome fear, read one or more of these faith-building confessions aloud at least three times a day; before meals, at bedtime and upon awakening in the morning, and throughout the day when possible. Use visualization with each faith-building confession to create a picture-perfect image of the end result you desire, then feel the glad emotions of achieving your goal.

1. I boldly proclaim that I am not afraid of anything or anyone. I have strength, power, conviction, and confidence! I like challenges and I meet them head on. For my God has not given me a spirit of fear, but a spirit of power and of love and of a sound mind. I confess this with my mouth under the authority and in the majestic Name of Jesus Christ of Nazareth! SO BE IT! (2 Timothy 1:7; John 14:13,14).

2. My Lord and Savior, Jesus Christ of Nazareth said. "Be of good cheer; it is I, be not afraid." I am of good cheer. I am not afraid. I fear not. That is the message of my Lord and Savior to my heart. I fear not! For greater is He (the Holy Spirit) that is in me, than he (Satan) that is in the world. I confess this aloud under the authority and in the mighty Name of Jesus Christ of Nazareth! SO BE IT!
   Matthew 14:27; 1 John 4:4; John 14:13,14

3. I fear not, because Jesus Christ of Nazareth has given me power to tread upon serpents and scorpions and over all the power of the enemy; and nothing shall by any means hurt me. I confess this with my mouth under the authority and in the wonderful Name of Jesus Christ of Nazareth! SO BE IT!
   Luke 10:19; John 14:13,14

4. I speak peace to my life, for it is written, "Being justified by faith, we have peace with God through our Lord Jesus Christ." I'm fearless, therefore I live a peaceful and quiet life! I confess this aloud under the authority and in the mighty Name

of Jesus Christ of Nazareth! SO BE IT!
Romans 5:1; John 14:13,14

5. Fear of height, fear of darkness, fear of traveling in airplanes, and all other fears, I resist you in the Name of the Lord Jesus Christ. In His mighty Name, I resist you. I refuse to fear; I refuse to be afraid. I speak these words under the authority and in the matchless Name of Jesus Christ of Nazareth! SO BE IT! (2 Timothy 1:7; John 14:13,14)

6. Whenever I travel, I boldly say, "let us pass over to the other side," and I will have what I say. I confess this aloud under the authority and in the mighty Name of Jesus Christ of Nazareth! SO BE IT!
   Mark 4:36; Mark 11:23; John 14:13,14

7. I declare openly that I am never afraid. I do not know fear. I have a spirit of power. I have a spirit of love. I have a sound mind. I confess this aloud under the authority and in the mighty Name of Jesus Christ of Nazareth! SO BE IT!
   2 Timothy 1:7; John 14:13,14

8. It is written that no evil will befall me, neither shall any plague come nigh my dwelling. For my Lord has given His angels charge over me and they keep me in all my ways, and in my pathway is life and there is no death. I confess this with my mouth under the authority and in the majestic Name of Jesus Christ of Nazareth! SO BE IT!
   Psalm 91:10,11; Proverbs 12:28; John 14:13,14

9. I am not afraid of the terrors of darkness (abductions, rapes, robberies, break-ins, evils that happen at night). I am not afraid of arrows that fly by day (riots, attacks, accidents, wars, or whatever). For my Lord orders His angels to protect me wherever I go. I confess this with my mouth under the authority and in the majestic Name of Jesus Christ of Nazareth! SO BE IT! (Psalm 91:5,11; John 14:13,14)

SELF-TALK FAITH-BUILDING CONFESSIONS TO IMPROVE SELF-ESTEEM

To help improve self-esteem, read one or more of these faith-building confessions aloud at least three times a day; before meals, at bedtime, and upon awakening in the morning, and throughout the day when possible. Use visualization with each faith-building confession to create a picture-perfect image of the end result you desire, then feel the glad emotions of achieving your goal!

1. I am a new creature in Christ Jesus, and my Lord will perfect that which concerneth me. Therefore I resist the spirit of low self-esteem and I command it to go in the Name of Jesus. I'm somebody, I'm a child of God. I am developing high self-esteem. I confess this with my mouth under the authority and in the wonderful Name of Jesus Christ of Nazareth! SO BE IT! (Psalm 138:8; John 14:13,14)

2. My Lord has not given me a spirit of fear or low self-esteem but a spirit of power, a spirit of love, and a spirit of sound mind. I am overpowering in achieving abundant victory in every area of my life. I am more than a conqueror through Him Who loves me. I confess this aloud under the authority and in the mighty Name of Jesus Christ of Nazareth! SO BE IT! (John 14:13,14)

3. I boldly proclaim with my mouth that I have set my love upon God; therefore, no matter what the test or trial, I know that El Shaddai is with me to deliver me. And He's more than enough! I speak these words under authority and in the matchless Name of Jesus Christ of Nazareth! SO BE IT! Psalm 91:14,15; John 14:13,14

4. I boldly state that I guide my own destiny and I am accountable for the results of my decisions and actions. I reinforce my successes and correct errors. In all things I am more than a conqueror through Him who loves me. I am not afraid of any circumstances. I am not afraid of any disease. I

am not afraid of any condition. I face life fearlessly, a conqueror! I am a conqueror! In fact, I am more than a conqueror! I confess this aloud under the authority and in the mighty Name of Jesus Christ of Nazareth! SO BE IT!
Romans 8:37; John 14:13,14

5. I am a VIP, a very important person; I am a child of the King. I am a new creation in Christ. I am His workmanship created in Christ Jesus. Therefore I have the mind of Christ and the wisdom of God is formed within me. I confess this with my mouth under the authority and in the wonderful Name of Jesus Christ of Nazareth! SO BE IT.
2 Corinthians 5:17; Ephesians 2:10; 1 Corinthians 2:16; John 14:13,14

6. I am somebody special. I like and respect myself. I know I am a worthy, capable, and valuable person. I live a godly life. I am born again. I live for God. I walk in fellowship with my Lord. This is profitable for me here on earth in the life that now is, and also in the life which is to come. I speak these words under the authority and in the matchless Name of Jesus Christ of Nazareth! SO BE IT!
1 Timothy 4:8; John 14:13,14

7. I openly pronounce that I am a believer. I am not a doubter. I have faith. I am an overcomer. No obstacle to the blessings of God can stand in my way. I overcome all obstacles by faith in God's Word. I confess this aloud under the authority and in the mighty Name of Jesus Christ of Nazareth! SO BE IT!
Mark 5:24,25,27; John 14:13,14

8. My words boldly declare that I am optimistic about life and I look forward to and enjoy new challenges to my awareness. Christ Jesus satisfied the claims of justice against me. He paid the penalty of sin for me. He stripped the hosts of darkness of their authority for me. Satan, therefore, has no dominion over me. I confess this with my mouth under the authority and in the wonderful Name of Jesus Christ of Nazareth! SO BE IT!
Colossians 2:15; John 14:13,14

SELF-TALK FAITH-BUILDING CONFESSIONS TO HELP LOSE WEIGHT AND MAINTAIN WEIGHT CONTROL

To help lose weight and maintain weight control, read one or more of these faith-building confessions aloud at least three times a day; before meals, at bedtime, and upon awakening in the morning, and throughout the day when possible. Use visualization with each faith-building confession to create a picture-perfect image of the end results you desire. Then feel the glad emotions of achieving your goal!

1. I am aware that the crude test for excessive body fat is, "If I can pinch more than an inch at my waistline, I am probably out of shape weight-wise and health-wise." To get into shape, I am now drinking at least two glasses of water or natural apple juice before each meal. I am eating less and I am exercising more. I do these things through Jesus Christ who strengthens me. I confess this under the authority and in the mighty Name of Jesus Christ of Nazareth! SO BE IT! Philippians 4:13; John 14:13,14

2. I am aware that the Bible sternly admonishes, "If you are a big eater, put a knife to your throat. My body is the temple of God, and I purpose in my heart and in my spirit by faith that I am closely managing the quantity and quality of food that goes into my body. I do these things through Jesus Christ who strengthens me. I confess this under the authority and in the mighty Name of Jesus Christ of Nazareth! SO BE IT! Philippians 4:13; Proverbs 23:2; John 14:13,14

3. I purpose in my (mind and) heart to maintain my weight at a healthy level. I am fully aware that the Word of God promotes good health. There are many references in the Bible that say health to the body, health to the flesh, and health to the bones. I know that my body is the temple of the Holy Spirit. I purpose in my mind and heart not to defile the temple of my Lord with gluttony, which is overeating. I see myself fit, trim, and healthy! I confess this with my mouth under the authority and in the

wonderful Name of Jesus Christ of Nazareth! SO BE IT! Proverbs 3:8; 3 John 2; 1 Corinthians 6:19; John 14:13,14

4. I vow to control my weight by keeping my body under subjection to my God's Word. I am maintaining a healthy and appropriate weight level. I praise you, Heavenly Father, because I am fearfully and wonderfully made. I will not be known as a battle-of-the-bulge Christian. I have set goals to eat only proper portions of healthy food and I exercise regularly and fast at least three times a month. I see myself fit, trim, and healthy and ready for warfare. I confess this with my mouth under the authority and by the blood of my Lord and Savior, Jesus Christ of Nazareth! SO BE IT! Psalm 139:14; 3 John 2; John 14:13,14

5. I know that excessive weight can cause a myriad of health problems, such as heart disease, cancer, strokes, and diabetes. I am fully aware that you never get a second chance to make a first impression. I aim to present my body (fit, trim, and healthy) as a living sacrifice, holy and pleasing to God. I do all things through Christ Who strengthens me. I confess this with my mouth under the authority and by the blood of my Lord and Savior, Jesus Christ of Nazareth! SO BE IT! Philippians 4:13; John 14:13,14

6. A recruit in the United States Armed Forces boot camp undergoes an attitude adjustment, fitness, and diet program in preparation for warfare. I am a soldier in God's army. I can do all things through Christ Who strengthens me. I make my body physically fit by exercising regularly. I limit the amount of saturated and hydrogenated fats that go into my body. I maintain a proper diet, and I fast at least three days a month. I believe that my energy is double. I see myself trim, healthy, and ready for warfare! I confess this with my mouth under the authority and by the blood of my Lord and Savior, Jesus Christ of Nazareth! SO BE IT! (Philippians 4:13; John 14:13,14)

SELF-TALK FAITH-BUILDING CONFESSIONS FOR A PROPER MATE

To help find a proper mate, read one or more of these faith-building confessions aloud at least three times a day; before meals, at bedtime, and upon awakening in the morning, and throughout the day when possible. Use visualization with each faith-building confession to create a picture-perfect image of the end results you desire. Then feel the glad emotions of achieving your goal!

1. Heavenly Father, Your Word says "Seek first the Kingdom of God and His righteousness, and all these things shall be added to you." I am seeking You, and I desire to have a mate added to me. I believe in my heart and spirit by faith, that I now have the mate of my choice that you have selected. I am thankful and joyous! I confess this with my mouth under the authority and in the wonderful Name of Jesus Christ of Nazareth! SO BE IT! (Matthew 6:33; Mark 11:23; John 14:13,14)

2. Lord God, You said in Your Word that, "It is not good that man should be alone" so I trust in You to supply me with a help-mate. I thank You, Lord, because You bring upon me all the good You have promised me. I thank You for my mate! I confess this with my mouth under the authority and in the wonderful Name of Jesus Christ of Nazareth! SO BE IT! Genesis 2:18; Jeremiah 32:42; John 14:13,14

3. Heavenly Father, I desire a help-mate who is between ____ to ____ years old, ____ feet ____ inches tall, weight between ____ to ____ pounds. A mate who enjoys ____________, ____________, ___________, and ___________. I lean not to my own understanding, but I trust in You one hundred percent to supply me with a help-mate. I believe that I have received my mate, I am thankful and joyous! I confess this with my mouth under the authority and in the wonderful Name of Jesus Christ of Nazareth! SO BE IT! Mark 11:23,24; Proverbs 3:5; John 14:13,14

4. Lord God, You perfect that which concerns me for I delight myself in You and You give me the desires of my heart, including my godly mate. I believe in my heart and spirit that I now have my mate who possesses the godly characteristics that I desire. I am thankful and overflowing with joy! I confess this with my mouth under the authority and in the majestic Name of Jesus Christ of Nazareth! SO BE IT!
   Psalm 138:8; Psalm 37:4; John 14:13,14

5. Heavenly Father, Your Word says, a man who finds a wife finds a good thing and receives Your favor. I believe in my heart and spirit that You have provided me with the godly mate that I desire, and I thank You, Lord! I confess this with my mouth under the authority and in the wonderful Name of Jesus Christ of Nazareth! SO BE IT!
   Proverbs 18:22; John 14:13,14

6. Heavenly Father, it is written that, "Every man should have his own wife and every woman should have her own husband." According to Your Word, Lord, so be it unto me. I believe in my heart and spirit by faith, that I now have a Christian mate who is strong in faith. I am thankful and overwhelmed with joy! I confess this aloud under the authority and in the mighty Name of Jesus Christ of Nazareth! SO BE IT!
   1 Corinthians 7:2; Luke 1:38; John 14:13,14

7. Heavenly Father, I read in Your Word that I will not fail nor lack a mate. I am fully persuaded that You perform that which You have promised me. I believe that I now have the godly mate that I desire, and I thank you. I am joyful! I confess this aloud under the authority and in the mighty Name of Jesus Christ of Nazareth! SO BE IT!
   Isaiah 34:16; Romans 4:21; John 14:13,14

8. I vow that I will leave my mother and father, and be joined with my mate, the two of us shall be as one. I will love my mate as much as I love myself. I confess this aloud under the authority and in the mighty Name of Jesus Christ of Nazareth! SO BE IT! (Ephesians 5:28; John 14:13,14)

9. I thank You, Father, that my husband will love me as Christ loved the church and gave Himself for it. I can see him showing His love for me in many different and wonderful ways! I confess this with my mouth under the authority and in the wonderful Name of Jesus Christ of Nazareth! SO BE IT! Ephesians 5:25; John 14:13,14

The faith-building confessions prescribed throughout this book call those things that be not as though they were. They renew your mind and heart and cause faith to come. They also call those things (words) that are promised by God, to become a reality (tangible) in your life.

Be positive, hold on to your faith-building confessions, for in due season you shall reap if you do not give up and lose heart. You shall have whatsoever you saith! God is on your side!

APPENDIX A

SALVATION PRAYER

The Most Important Question Of Your Life: What Will Happen To You When You Die?

If you are unsure of the answer to this question, or if you are afraid you will not spend eternity in heaven, there is Good News for you. *"God so loved the world, that he gave his only begotten Son, that WHOSOEVER believeth in him should not perish, but have EVERLASTING LIFE"* (John 3:16).

Because God loves and values you so much, He made a way for you to be saved. He sent His Son, Jesus Christ, to die so mankind could be redeemed from sin. The Bible says concerning salvation: *"Except a man be BORN AGAIN, he cannot see the kingdom of God"* (John 3:3).

Salvation does not come by joining a church, following a certain religion, doing good deeds, or living a good, moral life. The Bible says there is only one way to receive salvation. You must be born again by accepting Jesus Christ as your Savior.

Settle the most important question of your life! Pray the following prayer and receive Jesus as your Savior:

Dear Heavenly Father,

I come to You in the Name of Jesus.

You said in Your Word, *" If thou shalt confess with thy mouth the Lord Jesus, and shalt believe in thine heart that God hath raised him from the dead, THOU SHALT BE SAVED"* (Romans 10:9).

I believe in my heart that Jesus Christ is the Son of God.

I believe that He was raised from the dead for my justification.

Your Word says, *"...with the HEART man believeth unto righteousness, and with the MOUTH confession is made unto salvation"* (Romans 10:10).

I do believe with my heart and I confess with my mouth now, Jesus as my Lord.

Therefore I am saved!

Thank You, Lord!

If you have prayed this prayer sincerely from your heart, then the Bible says you are now saved! To grow in your new Christian life, it is important to study the Bible and to pray every day to your Heavenly Father. It is also vital that you become addicted to self-talk faith-building confessions which build strong faith and please God. You also need to belong to a good, Bible-based church where you are taught the Word of God.

Welcome to the family of God!

APPENDIX B

SELF-TALK FAITH-BUILDING CONFESSIONS FOR DIVINE RETURN ON YOUR GIVING

1. I am obedient to God with tithes and offerings according to Malachi 3, and I believe that God is opening the windows of heaven unto me, and pouring out an overflowing blessing that there will not be room enough for me to receive. I am praising Him for opening heaven's windows of abundant blessing that make me rich and add no sorrow. I confess this with my mouth in the mighty Name of Jesus Christ of Nazareth! SO BE IT!
   Malachi 3:8-11; Luke 6:38; John 14:13,14

2. I know God has promised, in response to my loving obedience in giving, that He will rebuke the devourer for my sake. The devil is the devourer who would devour my finances, the harmony of my home, my health, my peace of mind. I praise the Lord that He is rebuking the devourer for my sake! I hold fast to this confession without wavering, in the mighty Name of Jesus Christ of Nazareth! SO BE IT!
   Malachi 3:8-11; Luke 6:38; John 14:13,14

3. I give cheerfully, and my gift is given back to me in full and overflowing measure, pressed down, shaken together, to make room for more abundant blessings. I hold fast to this confession without wavering in the wonderful Name of Jesus Christ of Nazareth! SO BE IT!
   Luke 6:38; John 14:13,14

4. I am like the farmer who plants a seed and expects a harvest. I cheerfully pay tithes, share offerings, and give my time and talent to the work of the Kingdom, and I am believing for a full and overflowing return on my giving. I hold fast to this confession without wavering in the mighty Name of Jesus Christ of Nazareth! SO BE IT!
   Luke 6:38; John 14:13,14

5. I do honor my Lord with the first fruits of all my income. I know in my heart and in my spirit by faith that it shall be given back to me, good measure, pressed down, and shaken together, and running over shall men continue to give unto me. I hold fast to this confession without wavering in the mighty Name of Jesus Christ of Nazareth! SO BE IT.
Proverbs 3:9; Luke 6:38; John 14:13,14

6. Jesus, You are my Lord and High Priest. I have brought the first fruits of my income to You that you may worship the Lord my God with it! I believe in my heart and spirit that I have received a divine return on my giving, good measure, pressed down, and shaken together and running over shall men give unto me. I hold fast to this confession without wavering in the mighty Name of Jesus Christ of Nazareth! SO BE IT!
Hebrews 4:14; John 14:13,14

APPENDIX C

PERSONAL SELF-TALK INVENTORY WORKSHEET

Words Used By Self

Record the statements or similar statements you have used in the past.

1. ______________________________
2. ______________________________
3. ______________________________
4. ______________________________
5. ______________________________
6. ______________________________
7. ______________________________

Words Used By Others

Record the statements or similar statements that you have heard others use in the past.

1. ______________________________
2. ______________________________
3. ______________________________
4. ______________________________
5. ______________________________
6. ______________________________
7. ______________________________

Note: Copying of this worksheet is permitted.

APPENDIX D

HISTORY OF THE MOTTO "IN GOD WE TRUST"

The motto "IN GOD WE TRUST" was placed on United States coins largely because of the increased religious sentiment existing during the Civil War. Secretary of the Treasury Salmon P. Chase received many appeals from devout persons throughout the country, urging that the United States recognize the Deity on United States coins. From Treasury Department records, it appears that the first such appeal came in a letter dated November 13, 1861. It was written to Secretary Chase by Rev. M.R. Watkinson, Minister of the Gospel from Ridleyville, Pennsylvania, and read:

Dear Sir: You are about to submit your annual report to the Congress respecting the affairs of the national finances. One fact touching our currency has hitherto been seriously overlooked. I mean the recognition of the Almighty God in some form on our coins.

You are probably a Christian. What if our Republic were not shattered beyond reconstruction? Would not the antiquaries of succeeding centuries rightly reason from our past that we were a heathen nation? What I purpose is that instead of the goddess of liberty we shall have next inside the 13 stars a ring inscribed with the words PERPETUAL UNION; within the ring the allseeing eye, crowned with a halo; beneath this eye the American flag, bearing in its field stars equal to the number of the States united; in the folds of the bars the words GOD, LIBERTY, LAW.

This would make a beautiful coin, to which no possible citizen could object. This would relieve us from the ignominy of heathenism. This would place us openly under the Divine Protection we have personally claimed. From my hearth I have felt our national shame in disowning God as not the least of our present national disasters. To you first I address a subject that must be agitated.

As a result, Secretary Chase instructed James Pollock, Director of the Mint at Philadelphia, to prepare a motto, in a letter dated November 20, 1861:

"Dear Sir: No nation can be strong except in the strength of God, or safe except in His defense. The trust of our people in God should be declared on our national coins. You will cause a device to be prepared without unnecessary delay with a motto expressing in the fewest and tersest words possible this national recognition."

It was found that the Act of Congress dated January 18, 1837, prescribed the mottoes and devices that should be placed upon the coins of the United States. This meant that the mint could make no changes without the enactment of additional legislation by the Congress. In December 1863, the Director of the Mint submitted designs for a new one-cent coin, two-cent coin, and three-cent coin to Secretary Chase for approval. He proposed that upon the designs either OUR COUNTRY; OUR GOD or GOD, OUR TRUST should appear as a motto on the coins.

In a letter to the Mint Director on December 9, 1863, Secretary Chase stated: "I approve your mottoes, only suggesting that on that with the Washington obverse the motto should begin with the word OUR, so as to read OUR GOD AND OUR COUNTRY. And on that with the shield, it should be changed so as to read; IN GOD WE TRUST."

The Congress passed the Act of April 22, 1864. This legislation changed the composition of the one-cent coin and authorized the minting of the two-cent coin. The Mint Director was directed to develop the designs for these coins for final approval of the Secretary. **IN GOD WE TRUST first appeared on the 1864** two-cent coin. Another Act of Congress passed on March 3, 1865. It allowed the Mint Director, was the Secretary's approval, to place the motto on all gold and silver coins that "shall admit the inscription thereon." Under the Act, the motto was placed on the gold double-eagle coin, the gold eagle coin, and the gold half-eagle coin. It was also placed on the silver dollar coin, the half-dollar coin, and the quarter-dollar coin, and on the nickel five-cent coin beginning in 1866. Later, Congress passed the Coinage Act of February 12, 1873. It also said that the Secretary "may cause the motto IN GOD WE TRUST to be inscribed on such coins as shall admit of such motto."

The use of "IN GOD WE TRUST" has not been uninterrupted. The motto disappeared from the five-cent coin in 1883, and did not reappear until production of the Jefferson nickel began in 1938. Since 1938, all United States coins bear the inscription. Later, the motto was found missing from the new design of the double-eagle gold coin and the eagle gold coin shortly after they appeared in 1907. In response to a general demand, Congress ordered it restored, and the Act of May 18, 1908, made it mandatory on all coins upon which it had previously appeared. "IN GOD WE TRUST" was not mandatory on the one-cent coin and five-cent coin. It could be placed on them by the Secretary or the Mint Director with the Secretary's approval.

This motto has been in continuous use on the one-cent coin since 1909, and on the ten-cent coin since 1916. It also has appeared on all gold coins and silver dollar coins, half-dollar coins, and quarter-dollar coins struck since July 1, 1908.

A law passed by the 84th Congress (P.L.84-140) and approved by the President on July 30, 1956, the President approved a Joint Resolution of the 84th Congress, declaring "IN GOD WE TRUST" the national motto of the United States. **"IN GOD WE TRUST" was first used on paper money in 1957, when it appeared on the one-dollar silver certificate. The first paper currency bearing the motto entered circulation on October 1, 1957.** (Source: The United States Department of the Treasury, brought to you by the Office of Public Correspondence.)

Several years ago, the appearance of "IN GOD WE TRUST" on our money was challenged in the federal courts. The challenge was rejected by the lower federal courts, and the Supreme Court of the United States declined to review the case.

SUPER (FAITH-BUILDING) CONFESSION:

This is my covenant inheritance of $XXX million/billion (write in whatever your amount is). It is loosed on earth and it is loosed in heaven. I believe in my spirit, by faith, that I have received my covenant inheritance of $XXX million/billion. I am smiling because I can feel the joy of being richly blessed by God to be a blessing to others, plus all my needs and desires are met. I confess this under the authority, and in the mighty Name of Jesus Christ of Nazareth! SO BE IT! (Matthew 16:19; Mark 11:23)

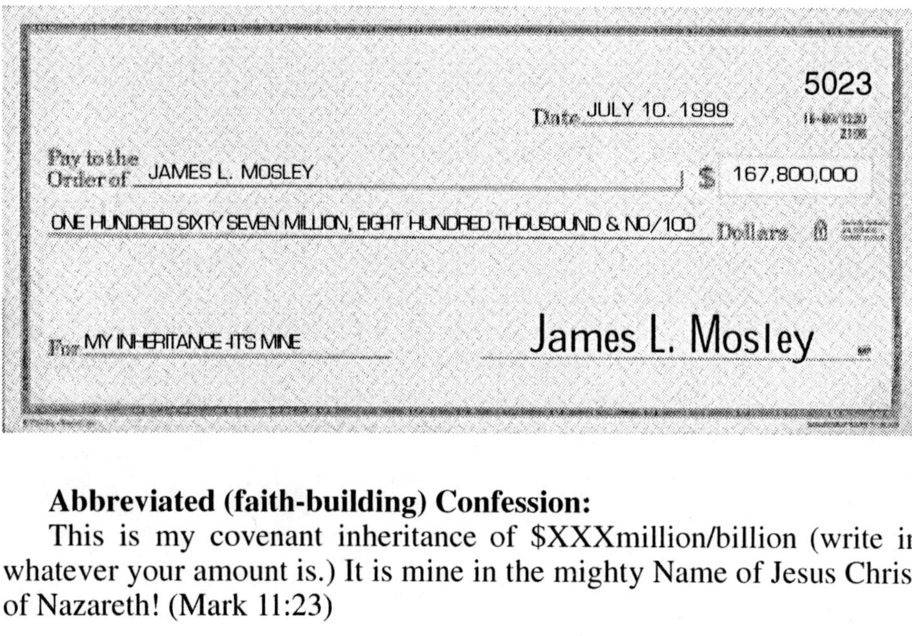
5023
Date JULY 10. 1999
Pay to the Order of JAMES L. MOSLEY $ 167,800,000
ONE HUNDRED SIXTY SEVEN MILLION, EIGHT HUNDRED THOUSOUND & NO/100 Dollars
For MY INHERITANCE -IT'S MINE
James L. Mosley

Abbreviated (faith-building) Confession:

This is my covenant inheritance of $XXXmillion/billion (write in whatever your amount is.) It is mine in the mighty Name of Jesus Christ of Nazareth! (Mark 11:23)

RESOURCES

Ash, Mary Kay, "Mary Kay" (Harper Collins Publishers, Inc., 1994).

Avanzini, Pastor John, "The Avanzini Report" (His Image Ministries, 1999).

Burke, Pastor Dennis, "Breaking Financial Barriers" (published by Dennis Burke Publications, 1997).

Capps, Rev. Charles, "Faith And Confession: How To Activate Them In Your Life" (published by Harrison House, Inc., 1987).

Cho, Pastor David Yonggi, R. Whitney Manzano, "Prayer That Brings Revival" (published by Creation House, Strang Communications Company, 1998).

Copeland, Rev. Kenneth, "How To Discipline Your Flesh" (Kenneth Copeland Publications, 1998).

Dossey, Larry, M.D., "Healing Words" (Harper Collins Publishers, 1993).

Dufresne, Dr. Ed, "Faithfulness, The Road To Divine Promotion" (published by Ed Dufresne Ministries, 1994).

Flores, Bettina R., and Jennifer Basye Sander, "The Millionairess Across The Street" (Dearborn Publishing, Inc., 1999).

Forbes, Steve, Editor-In-Chief, "Forbes Magazine" (publisher, Rich Karlguard, October 11, 1999).

Gilbert, Michael, Publication Director, "The Word Of Faith" (published by Kenneth Hagin Ministries, 1999).

Gossett, Don, and Dr. E.W. Kenyon, "The Power Of Your Words" (Whitaker House, 1981).

Hagin, Rev. Kenneth E., "Faith Food" (published by Kenneth Hagin Ministries, 1978).

Hammond, Frank & Ida Mae, "Pigs In The Parlor: A Practical Guide To Deliverance" (Impact Books, 1973).

Kenyon, Dr. E.W., "The Hidden Man: An Unveiling Of The Subconscious Mind" (Kenyon's Gospel Publishing Society, Inc., 1996).

Kenyon, Dr. E.W., "The Two Kinds Of Faith" (Kenyon's Gospel

Publishing Society, Inc., 1969).

Lockyer, Dr. Herbert, "All The Parables Of The Bible" (Zondervan Publishing House, 1963).

Orman, Suze, "The Courage to Be Rich" (Riverhead Books, A Member Of Penguin Putnam, Inc., 1999).

Peale, Norman Vincent, "Power Of The Plus Factor" (Fleming H. Revell Company, 1987).

Peers, Rev. Tom, "Fit, Function & Flourish" (Albury Press, 1987).

Price, Frederick K.C., Ph.D., "The Way, The Walk, And The Warfare Of The Believer" (Faith One Publishing, 1994).

Stanley, Thomas J., Ph.D., and William D. Danko, Ph.D., "The Millionaire Next Door" (Longstreet Press, 1996).

Thompson, Dr. Leroy, "Money Cometh To The Body Of Christ" (Harrison House, Inc., 1999).

Vine, W.E., M.A., Merrill F. Unger, Th.M., Th.D., Ph.D., William White, Jr., Th.M., Ph.D., "Vines Expository Dictionary Of Biblical Words" (Thomas Nelson Publishers, 1984).

Wilson, Rev. Ray Gene, "What You Don't Know Can Hurt You: Destroying The Deception Surrounding Prosperity" (Published by Harrison House, Inc., 1999).

FAITH-BUILDING PRODUCTS AND MATERIALS

Faith-Building Confessions On Audio Cassette Tapes.

Faith-Building Confessions On Convenient Cards With Handy Carry Case.

Faith-Building Confessions On Compact Disc (CD's).

Categories

- Financial Prosperity
- Divine Health
- Divine Physical Healing
- Prevention of, and Overcoming Stress
- Overcoming Anger, Bitterness and Evil Thoughts
- Overcoming Fear
- Improve Self-Esteem
- Find the Proper Mate
- Employment
- Home Ownership
- Strengthen Faith
- The Unborn
- Help Lose Weight and Maintain Weight Control
- Mental and Emotional Healing
- Healing of Marriage
- Peace in Family
- Deliverance From Addictions
- Buying and Selling Property
- Help in Work or Study
- Divine Return on Giving
- Government Leaders and All Those Who Have Leadership Authority

- Debt Free

Faith-Building Teaching And Study Aids

- "Self-Talk And Grow Rich" Teacher's Faith-Building Study Guide
- "Self-Talk And Grow Rich" Personal Faith-Building Study Guide

Confessaholic Membership Kit

Includes:

- A Lifetime Membership Card to the Confessaholic Club
- A Large "Ask Me, What is a Confessaholic?" Button
- A Gold or Silver-Finish Vehicle License Plate Holder With "I Am A Confessaholic" Engraved
- Periodic E-Mail Updates of The Confessaholic E-Praise Bulletin

Other Confessaholic Products Designed to Create an Opportunity to Witness

- T-shirts
- Caps
- Calendars
- Buttons
- License Plate Holders

For information on how to order faith-building products and materials, visit our web site at www.confessaholic.com or e-mail: testimonies@confessaholic.com. Or write Bountiful Bookstore, 1220 Rosecrans Street, Suite 411, San Diego, CA. 92106-2674.

ABOUT THE AUTHOR

James L. Mosley is an ordained Elder, author, teacher, researcher, and motivational speaker. He is the author of the popular healthcare book, *Snore No More* which was written from a personal viewpoint and broad-based research.

Self-Talk And Grow Rich is another powerful inscription that reveals the author's personal experiences using his revolutionary new application of biblical principles, combined with managed positive speech to achieve prosperity in every area of life (he dubbed the quote, "You get what you say, sooner or later").

He is known to weep. In the summer of 1986, while attending a believer's house ministry gathering, a man of God told him, "You will proclaim God's Word to multitudes like the prophet Jeremiah did. And like the prophet, you will be known as the weeping teacher." This word of knowledge reaffirmed a known fact that the author is easily moved to tears of joy when he witnesses God confirming His Word in the lives of believers.

He was ordained Elder, February 10, 1989 at Christian Fellowship Center Ministries, Cleveland, Ohio, under the leadership of Bishop Bill McKinney. He served as Vice President of "Victory For Veterans," an outreach ministry of Bible studies and enrichment activities for hurting veterans, at Veterans' Medical Centers throughout Northeast Ohio.

His strong research background is a reflection of his fourteen years experience on the corporate staff of Ohio Bell Telephone Company (now renamed Ameritech), where he held a management position on the training, research, and development team.

The author has been featured on NBC's "A Closer Look" telecast, the American Health Network, and other media. James and his wife, Magdeline, and their daughters, Cristel and Abigail, make their home in San Diego, California.

AUTHOR'S VISION

The author envisions the Body of Christ moving to a higher level in providing for the poor and needy. His vision is to see churches across America utilizing their rooms (space) that are unused from Monday through Saturday, to provide basic health, vision and dental care to the poor and needy.

These mini-clinics would provide screening, testing, and basic treatments, along with preventative healthcare and nutritional education.

His vision is that these mini-clinics are manned by professionals; doctors, nurses, dentists, and other caregivers who volunteer their time and talent to help the poor and needy.

He envisions that believers are financially supporting the operation of these mini-clinics without government funding, like Mother Teresa and the Good Samaritan.

Printed in the United States
2336

9 780939 241835